American Realism and American Drama, 1880–1940

Cambridge Studies in American Literature and Culture

Other books in the series:

Robert Zaller: *The Cliffs of Solitude*
Peter Conn: *The Divided Mind*
Patricia Caldwell: *The Puritan Conversion Narrative*
Stephen Fredman: *Poet's Prose*
Charles Altieri: *Self and Sensibility in Contemporary American Poetry*
John McWilliams, Jr.: *Hawthorne, Melville, and the American Character*
Barton St. Armand: *Emily Dickinson and Her Culture*
Elizabeth McKinsey: *Niagara Falls*
Mitchell Breitwieser: *Cotton Mather and Benjamin Franklin*
Albert J. von Frank: *The Sacred Game*
Marjorie Perloff: *The Dance of the Intellect*
Albert Gelpi: *Wallace Stevens*
Ann Kibbey: *The Interpretation of Material Shapes in Puritanism*
Sacvan Bercovitch and Myra Jehlen: *Ideology and Classic American Literature*
Karen Rowe: *Saint and Singer*
Lawrence Buell: *New England Literary Culture*
David Wyatt: *The Fall into Eden*
Paul Giles: *Hart Crane*
Richard Grey: *Writing the South*
Steven Axelrod and Helen Deese: *Robert Lowell*
Jerome Loving: *Emily Dickinson*

American Realism and American Drama, 1880–1940

BRENDA MURPHY

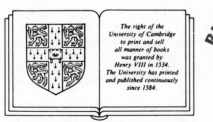

The right of the
University of Cambridge
to print and sell
all manner of books
was granted by
Henry VIII in 1534.
The University has printed
and published continuously
since 1584.

CAMBRIDGE UNIVERSITY PRESS

CAMBRIDGE
LONDON   NEW YORK   NEW ROCHELLE
MELBOURNE   SYDNEY

Published by the Press Syndicate of the University of Cambridge
The Pitt Building, Trumpington Street, Cambridge CB2 1RP
32 East 57th Street, New York, NY 10022, USA
10 Stamford Road, Oakleigh, Melbourne 3166, Australia

First published 1987

Printed in the United States of America

Library of Congress Cataloging-in-Publication Data
Murphy, Brenda.
American realism and American drama, 1880–1940.
(Cambridge studies in American literature and culture)
Bibliography: p.
Includes index.
1. American drama – 20th century – History and
criticism. 2. Realism in literature. 3. American
drama – 19th century – History and criticism. I. Title.
II. Series.
PS338.R42M87   1987   812'.52'0912   86–13694

British Library Cataloguing in Publication Data
Murphy, Brenda
American realism and American drama, 1880–
1940. – (Cambridge studies in American
literature and culture)
1. American drama – History and criticism
2. Realism in literature
I. Title
812'.009'12   PS338.R4

ISBN 0 521 32711 3

To Harry and Will

Contents

Preface

This book is not a history of the drama, nor is it a critical study of realistic plays, nor is it a study of realistic dramatic theory. It is an essay in what Benjamin Hrushovsky calls "historical poetics," that is, the study of the "poetics of literary movements placed in historical periods." This book is a study of literary realism as it evolved in American drama. As such, it is also an attempt to redress the balance between the recognition that scholarly treatments of realism in the American theater have given to European sources and the recognition they have given to American sources. The influence of European dramatists such as Ibsen and Shaw is well known to scholars and is often taken for granted. The influence of American literary realists is generally discounted if it is thought of at all, and part of my purpose in undertaking this study was to reexamine and reevaluate it. It seems to me that one reason scholars deprecate American sources is that they haven't studied them sufficiently. The extent of their relationship to what we think of "real" American drama, the literary drama written after World War I, has never been measured.

Although there are many reasons for this state of affairs, the main one is that a traditional but arbitrary division between literary specialists who study drama and those who study American literature has hindered the study of American drama. The drama specialist sees post–World War I American drama in the context of Ibsen, Shaw, Strindberg, Chekhov, the French symbolists, and the German expressionists because he or she considers the American dramatists before World War I too inferior as artists to have influenced the literary drama of O'Neill and those who followed. The American-literature specialist typically ignores the drama altogether, perhaps paying lip service to the recognized art of O'Neill, Williams, Miller, and Albee, but making no attempt to consider the context of American drama in which it was created. Thus the study of American drama has traditionally been relegated to the pigeonholes of

American Theater History and Anglo-American Drama (Shaw to the present). A close look at the important nineteenth-century literary realists, with the drama reinstated in literary history, led me to suspect that understanding realism as it developed in our drama is intimately connected with understanding the theory of American literary realism as it developed in our critical thought.

In this book I seek to answer two fundamental and related questions. The first is whether there exists a literary definition of dramatic realism upon which criticism of realistic plays can be based. In investigating this question, I found that histories of dramatic literature typically describe realism in terms of the creation of a bourgeois milieu on the stage, the use of "common speech" in the dialogue, and the avoidance of sensational melodramatic effects in the action. It is most often associated with the mundane world of the bourgeoisie in Ibsen and with the talky British and American "high comedy" of the period between 1920 and 1940, which is seen as a mixture of light comedy of manners and witty Shavian discussion of current social mores. Histories of the theater typically discuss realism as a style of stagecraft that aims primarily at reconstructing the real world on the stage and that is associated with the late-nineteenth-century technical wizardry of such producers as Augustin Daly, David Belasco, and Steele Mackaye, who introduced marvelous ways of bringing steam engines and sawmills, restaurants and railroad cars onto the stage and of working wonders with lighting and scenery in order to increase the audience's belief in the actuality of what it saw. Dramatic realism is hardly mentioned in the major books on literary realism and dramatic theory. Erich Auerbach speaks of it briefly in the context of the "bourgeois" aspects of Molière's comedy and Schiller's domestic tragedy. Such writers about American literary realism as Warner Berthoff, Edwin Cady, Harold Kolb, Donald Pizer, and George Becker mention the drama only in passing, for they see American literary realism primarily in the context of fiction. John Gassner makes the most complete attempt to define it, in *Form and Idea in the Modern Theatre;* but his description is couched exclusively in terms of the production – the sense of milieu and the fourth-wall illusion.

A full description of dramatic realism, both literary and theatrical, does exist in the critical writings of the nineteenth-century realists themselves. But unlike Zola's "Naturalism in the Theatre" and Strindberg's Foreword to *Miss Julie,* well-known documents credited with a great deal of influence on turn-of-the-century European drama, the drama criticism of the American literary realists and its influence on the American theater have received little attention. Henry James's drama criticism, collected by Allan Wade into a volume called *The Scenic Art,* is known to scholars of literary realism but has received almost no attention from those whose primary interest is drama. The drama criticism of William Dean Howells, the most voluminous and the most revealing in terms of realist aesthetics, has hardly been noticed as a body. The various articles on realism in the drama by James A. Herne, Brander Matthews, Edward Harrigan, Hamlin Garland, and William Gillette have been similarly neglected.

From this body of critical writing emerges a description of dramatic realism that is peculiarly American because it has primarily an aesthetic orientation, as opposed to the European version proceeding from Zola, which has primarily a sociological orientation. Zola spoke almost exclusively of subject matter: of capturing the social reality of one's time. Although the American realists did speak of the subject matter of realistic drama, typically as the commonplace social reality of a given time and place, they focused chiefly on the *representation* of that subject matter, the creation of an illusion of reality in the text and on the stage by playwright, actors, director, and producer. Their descriptions were exhaustive and specific, for they were concerned with every aspect of the drama, from the playwright's conception of his subject to the final detail in stagecraft and the actor's performance. This book has been written partly to reintroduce their dramatic criticism as a document in realism's evolution and to offer it as a basis for criticizing realistic plays.

The second question I seek to answer is whether the theoretical ideas of these earlier realists influenced the writers of realistic plays who dominated the American theater between the two world wars, playwrights such as Rachel Crothers, Philip Barry, Robert Sherwood, S. N. Behrman, Elmer Rice, and Eugene O'Neill. And if so, how? Examining the nineteenth-century literary realists' plays and criticism convinced me not only that the influence existed but also that its effect created a gradual but clear evolution in every aspect of the drama toward the kind of setting, dialogue, character, thought, and structure that realists like Howells had been calling for during the 1880s and 1890s. Consequently, I attempt four major tasks in this book: first, to describe the dramatic theory the American realists developed; second, to show its immediate impact on the theater in the realists' own drama and that of their theatrical disciples; third, to trace this native realism's slow evolution within American drama between the early 1890s and World War I; and fourth, to describe the resulting innovations in realistic drama that flourished in the American theater between World War I and World War II.

In the course of my investigation, I discovered that there exists for dramatic realism an informing worldview ("theoretic form"), which manifests itself in the patterned action of the play ("technical form"), as Richard Sewall has described the relationship for tragedy. The worldview that produces realistic structure is typically skeptical, ironic, deflating. It rejects both the tragic notion of ultimate transcendence and the comic notion of the ultimate emergence of a new order based on integration and harmony. The realistic play disrupts the traditional patterns of tragedy and comedy precisely in order to express its skepticism. Realism accepts these patterns as part of life but refuses to allow them to account for human experience.

The rhythm of life, these plays constantly suggest, is not a movement toward transcendence or harmony but a continual return to the mundane; not resolution or closure but irresolution and open-ended action; not spectacular, world-rending moments of truth but gradual processes of partial revelation, which may or may not effect some limited change in character or environment. The distinguishing characteristic of realistic dramatic structure is its lack of closure. Realistic dramatic action opens up into the larger and wider rhythms of life that surround and interpenetrate it but can only be hinted at in the space of a realistic play. This action is not "an action" in the conventional Aristotelian sense but a convergence in a particular space and time of the many "actions" of several lives being lived. Realistic theoretic form in drama is precisely the refusal to reduce the complex rhythms of human life to the paradigm of a generically conventionalized "action."

I have tried to chronicle the evolution of this theoretic form along with the evolution of its more material counterpart, the technical form that manifests itself onstage. In approaching this more tangible form, I have, for convenience of analysis, created six categories based loosely on the Aristotelian divisions of plot, character, thought, diction, song, and spectacle, although any student of the drama will recognize that my categories of dialogue, acting, and stagecraft do not correspond to his last three divisions. My discussion of dramatic structure has also been influenced in varying degrees by the writings of Richard Sewall, Susanne Langer, Northrop Frye, and Seymour Chatman. I acknowledge my debts to these theorists with thanks while I take full responsibility for what I do to their ideas.

Acknowledgments

The contributions to this book have been many, and it would be impossible for me to acknowledge all of the debts I have incurred during its composition. Some debts cannot go unrecognized, however. In particular, I would like to thank Don B. Wilmeth and Howard Stein, who first gave me the idea that there was a subject in American realism and American drama; George Monteiro, who read the entire manuscript and offered valuable criticism throughout its composition; Albert Gelpi, whose editorial wisdom helped me shape its final transformation; and Philip Larson, Gail Hemmeter, T. L. Berger, Donald Makosky, Benjamin Hrushovsky, Bruce Weiner, and Kerry Grant, who read various parts of it and gave excellent advice.

I could not have functioned in researching this study without the erudition and help of a number of librarians, particularly Jennifer Knapp, Jon Lindgren, Joan Larsen, and Sharon Pierce at the Owen D. Young Library of St. Lawrence University and Rebecca Sutton at the National Humanities Center. I am also indebted to the staffs and resources of the Wilson Library of the University of North Carolina at Chapel Hill, The Humanities Research Center of the University of Texas at Austin, The New York Public Library, the Chicago Public Library, The Houghton Library of Harvard University, and the John Hay Library of Brown University.

For competent and cheerful typing and retyping of the various versions of the manuscript, I am very much indebted to Barbara McMillan of St. Lawrence and Madeleine Moyer, Jan Paxton, Inneke Hutchins, and Karen Carroll of the National Humanities Center.

For the financial support that allowed me the freedom to do research and writing for a year and two summers, I would like to thank the National Endowment for the Humanities, the American Council of Learned Societies, and St. Lawrence University. Finally, a special form of thanks is due to the National Humanities Center for the special help and support given so graciously by the entire staff during my year of writing and for the advice, help, and moral support of the fellows of the "class of '82," particularly Anna Nardo, John Clark, and Christopher Gill and their equally helpful spouses, Neal Cronin, Lois Clark, and Karen Gill.

I am indebted to the following for permission to quote from published materials: Robert E. Sherwood, from *Idiot's Delight;* copyright 1925, 1936 Robert Emmet Sherwood; copyright renewed 1963, 1964 Madeleine H. Sherwood; reprinted with the permission of Charles Scribner's Sons. Robert E. Sherwood, from *The Road to Rome;* copyright 1926 Robert E. Sherwood; copyright 1927 Charles Scribner's Sons; copyright renewed 1954, 1955 Robert E. Sherwood; reprinted with the permission of Charles Scribner's Sons. Robert E. Sherwood, from *There Shall Be No Night;* copyright 1940 Robert Emmet Sherwood; copyright renewed 1968 Madeleine H. Sherwood; reprinted with the permission of Charles Scribner's Sons. *No Time for Comedy* by S. N. Behrman; first published by Random House; copyright 1939 by S. N. Behrman; copyright © 1967 by S. N. Behrman; reprinted by permission of Brandt & Brandt Literary Agents, Inc. Sidney Kingsley, from *Dead End;* copyright © 1936 by Sidney Kingsley; reprinted with the permission of Random House, Inc. Martin Meisel, *Shaw and the Nineteenth Century Theater;* copyright © 1963, revised ed. 1968 by Princeton University Press. Eugene O'Neill, from *All God's Chillen Got Wings, Desire Under the Elms,* and *Days Without End* in *The Plays of Eugene O'Neill;* copyright © 1923, 1924, 1932; copyright renewed, 1955, 1959 by Carlotta Monterey O'Neill; reprinted with the permission of Random House, Inc. Clifford Odets, from *Awake and Sing!;* copyright © 1933, 1935 by Clifford Odets; copyright © renewed 1962 by Clifford Odets; reprinted by permission of Grove Press, Inc. Eric Bentley, from *The Life of the Drama;* copyright © 1964 by Eric Bentley; reprinted with the permission of Atheneum Publishers. Harold Kolb, from *The Illusion of Life;* copyright © 1969 by Harold Kolb; reprinted with the permission of The University Press of Virginia. Materials from the Elmer Rice Collection, University of Texas, used by permission of Marie Mallot and Norman Zelenko, Trustees of the Rice Literary Trust.

The following journals have allowed me to reprint sections of this study that appeared first, in a somewhat different form, in their pages: *The Eugene O'Neill Newsletter, Modern Language Studies,* and *Studies in American Humor.*

The photograph included as Plate I is reproduced by permission of the Harvard Theatre Collection, Houghton Library, Harvard University. All other photographs are reproduced by permission of the Billy Rose Theatre Collection, The New York Public Library at Lincoln Center, Astor, Lenox and Tilden Foundations.

1

The State of the Art: The American Theatrical Scene in the 1880s

American dramatic realism has consistently been about twenty years behind fictional realism in its development, but when theater historians look back, they generally chart the first impetus toward realism from theatrical and dramatic trends that developed during the late 1870s and early 1880s. During the eighties literary realism took its place as the dominant force in American letters. This was the decade of *A Modern Instance* and *Portrait of a Lady*, *Life on the Mississippi* and *Huckleberry Finn*, *The Rise of Silas Lapham* and *The Bostonians*. It was also the decade that accounted for Edwin Cady's title for the second volume of his William Dean Howells biography, *The Realist at War*. The serialization of Howells's *Modern Instance* and Henry James's *Portrait of a Lady* in 1881 established both authors as major novelists in the realistic mode. Howells's article "Henry James, Jr." in the November 1882 *Century* linked the two writers firmly together in the minds of the public. By 1883, "James-and-Howells" had become the "Siamese Twins of Realism,"[1] and James complained that articles attacking them were "as thick as blackberries."[2] Both writers were well-known and outspoken literary critics, and both were under fire – Howells for having said that realistic fiction was a "finer art"[3] than that of Dickens and Thackeray, and James for having been the object of his praise. Although Howells remained the more aggressive spokesman for realism, James was a finer articulator of its aesthetic principles. Both men are known best for their fiction and their writing about fiction, but both were also prolific, though commercially unsuccessful, playwrights and incisive critics of the theater and drama.

Henry James's drama criticism began with a review from Paris in 1872. Throughout the seventies, eighties, and nineties, it emerged in a steady stream from London, New York, and Boston, as well as Paris, and it was eventually collected by Allan Wade into a volume called *The Scenic Art* (1948). Although Howells's drama criticism has not been published in a body, it is more abundant than James's. Beginning with his long essay on "Recent Italian Comedy" in 1864, Howells's writings on the drama include more than sixty essays and reviews. When he began writing his columns for the Harper magazines in 1886, he included regular reviews of the New York theater season – reviews liberally interspersed with theoretical discussion of the drama from a consciously realistic point of view.

The study of American literary realism's connection with American drama begins naturally with these two writers, who were the chief spokesmen for, as well as practitioners of, realism in both fiction and drama, and it begins naturally during the early eighties, when they were forced to articulate realism's aesthetic principles. To understand what the realistic critics were saying about the plays they saw during the eighties, and about the acting and stagecraft used in mounting the plays, it is important for us, at a century's remove from the theater that lived for them, to consider the context carefully. Their critical standards about everything from the play's structure to the set's furniture were tied to their own experience in the theater. James's standards were particularly complicated by his early exposure to the Théâtre Français and the London theaters, as well as those of Boston and New York.

As a base from which to begin, then, the New York stage during the 1879–80 season has clear advantages. New York is, of course, the central focus for American theater historians, and a wealth of information is available both on its theaters and on the plays produced in them. The year 1879–80 was not only the beginning of that crucial decade for literary realism in America, it was also a season that proved crucial for the introduction of realism in the theater. It was the season when Steele Mackaye's *Hazel Kirke,* recognized by theater historians as a watershed in the development of American dramatic realism, was first produced. It was the season when Mackaye's technically advanced Madison Square Theatre opened and when Augustin Daly began his reign as manager and promoter of realistic ensemble acting at Daly's Theatre. It was the season when James A. Herne (The "American Ibsen") made his first appearances in New York. Finally, the 1879–80 season marks a convenient midpoint between James's first review of a New York season (1875) and Howells's (1886). An overview of the New York theater in this season should yield a good understanding both of what the realist expected and of what he hoped for from the American theater as realism was about to become the artistic standard for American letters.

THE PLAYS

The American theater during the nineteenth century was the nation's major form of popular entertainment. The "legitimate drama" was a minor enterprise among the vast array of popular entertainments available in New York theaters during the 1879–80 season. There were minstrel and vaudeville shows, circuses, burlesques, and "happy parties," which exhibited the specialties of the variety troupes. The peculiarly American genre of the "extravaganza" (a combination of ballet troupe and chorus with a slim plot and as much "stocking" as American prudery would allow) shared the audience with Gilbert and Sullivan and Offenbach. These popular shows were as lavish as they were plentiful. Although they could not be considered in the same light as the legitimate drama of the time, they were enough of a presence in the theater for Howells to write a lengthy article bemoaning "The New Taste in Theatricals" for the *Atlantic*,[4] and he referred to them regularly in his reviews of the more serious drama.

Nearly as evident as these ephemeral popular shows were such perennial adaptations from French, English, and German melodrama as *The Two Orphans, Paul and Virginia, Louis XI, The Hunchback, Richelieu*, and *The Lady of Lyons*. There was a selection of standard comedies, *She Stoops to Conquer, The School for Scandal, London Assurance*, and *Our American Cousin*, as well as Dion Boucicault's "Irish" plays, *The Shaughraun* and *The Colleen Bawn* (and a number of Irish-American imitations). There was also plenty of Shakespeare. Theater-goers in 1879–80 could see the likes of Edwin Booth and Adelaide Neilson in a range of Shakespeare from *Macbeth, Othello, Hamlet*, and *Romeo and Juliet* to *The Merchant of Venice, Cymbeline, The Taming of the Shrew, Twelfth Night*, and *As You Like It*.[5]

Historians and literary critics who are not specifically interested in American drama tend to assume that these foreign imports and adaptations accounted for all the literary drama in nineteenth-century American theater. Like most clichés, this notion has some truth to it. Until the International Copyright Law was passed in 1891, it was always more profitable for a manager to pirate a European play than to buy one from a native dramatist, particularly after 1865, when Congress passed a law giving the American playwright, "along with the sole right to print and publish the said composition, the sole right to act, perform, or represent the same."[6] Thus, between 1865 and 1891, a manager could pirate a European drama but would have to pay for an American one, and because audiences generally were thought to prefer European sophistication and exoticism, the European play was usually the manager's first choice. Consequently, there was little incentive for Americans to write plays. The offerings of the 1879–80 season show, however, that many American playwrights were simply spurred by the copyright situation to act and manage as well as write. Playwrights who were also managers, and actors when need be, during this season included Dion Boucicault, Denman Thompson, Edward Harrigan, Steele Mackaye, Augustin

Daly, and James A. Herne. These managers and others also produced a surprising number of American plays. In all, approximately half the legitimate offerings in the ten most respected New York theaters for 1879–80 were American plays.

The American plays of the period, which reflect both American drama's history and its potential for development, fall naturally into six categories: the one-character vehicle; the play based on American history, legend, or literature; the melodrama; the local-color play; the Western play; and the drama of contemporary life. The first three types had a long history in America before 1880. The last three were somewhat younger and had not yet reached their full development. Each of the six has a direct bearing on the form literary realism was to take in American drama.

The one-character vehicle – the play written for a particular actor's portrayal of a particular character – has been a perennial presence in the American theater since the 1830s. It was then that the famous "Yankee" characters of James H. Hackett and George Handel Hill were created from the Yankee original of the type, Jonathan, in Royall Tyler's *Contrast* (1787). During the 1870s and 1880s, the most famous character role was Joe Jefferson's Rip Van Winkle, which he played for fifty years in a loose and constantly changing adaptation of Washington Irving's story. Other examples in the season were E. A. Sothern's Lord Dundreary, based on the character in Tom Taylor's *Our American Cousin,* Denman Thompson's Joshua Whitcomb, and Neil Burgess's Widow Bedott, all descendants of the "Yankee" character, although Burgess's was a female. None of these plays had any literary pretensions, but for the realist critics, even they presented some signs of hope for realism in the theater. They represented character types that were specifically American, and their popularity was evidence that America wanted to see itself represented on the stage, even at its most eccentric.

The play based on a subject in American history or American literature was also a long-familiar fixture on the American stage. Much of the earliest drama was based on the Revolution, and the Civil War was to figure in some of America's most important nineteenth-century drama. Bronson Howard's *Shenandoah* (1888), William Gillette's *Held by the Enemy* (1886) and *Secret Service* (1895), and James A. Herne's *Reverend Griffith Davenport* (1889) prepared the way for Augustus Thomas's *Copperhead* (1918) and Eugene O'Neill's *Mourning Becomes Electra* (1931). The turn of the century saw a particular vogue of such historical pieces as Clyde Fitch's *Nathan Hale* (1898) and *Barbara Frietchie* (1899), but the 1879–80 season featured only "literary" dramas of this type: *Wolfort's Roost, or A Legend of Sleepy Hollow; Rip Van Winkle;* and America's most produced play, *Uncle Tom's Cabin.* Again, it was the particularly American quality of these pieces that became important to the realists. They represent not only American literature but American life as well.

Melodrama was still the standard fare of the American theatergoer in 1879. With its conventional characters, its oversimplified personifications of good and evil, its contrived plot, its cultivation of the exotic, its sensationalism in staging, and its overall attempt to make the false seem true, the melodrama became the *bête noire* of the realist theater critic. His target was usually the foreign import, but there were plenty of native products as well, and Howells in particular became adept at separating the elements of realism from the old melodramatic conventions in these American plays, to praise the one and excoriate the other. The 1879–80 season saw productions of Boucicault's proven melodrama *The Octoroon* (1859), as well as his new *Rescued, or A Girl's Romance* and Bartley Campbell's *Fairfax* and *The Galley Slave,* none of which had anything to contribute to the development of realism. Steele Mackaye's *Hazel Kirke,* however, was the event of the theatrical season, eventually completing a two-year run of 486 performances. Although *Hazel Kirke* cannot be called anything but melodrama, its lack of a conventional villain, its attempt at natural dialogue, and its treatment of "ordinary" people distinguish it from the typical example of its genre.

Hazel Kirke is perhaps most interesting for the important place theater historians have given it in realism's development, for it offers little that seems realistic today. Its plot is certainly melodramatic. Dunstan Kirke is a miller who has been saved from financial ruin seven years before the events of the play by the local squire, Aaron Rodney. Out of gratitude, both Kirke and his daughter Hazel, then fourteen, agreed to an arrangement whereby Hazel has been educated and prepared to be Aaron's wife. As the play opens, Hazel, now twenty-one, has fallen in love with Arthur Carrington, Lord Travers, whom Kirke has saved from drowning in the millpond and who has now spent six weeks "recuperating" with the Kirkes. Arthur returns Hazel's love but conceals both it and his noble birth out of respect for Hazel's betrothal to Aaron Rodney and his own promise to his mother that he would marry Lady Maude, whose fortune his father has "wrongfully used and lost."[7] Aaron is beginning to suspect Hazel's and Arthur's affection for each other when the pleasantly demented Pittacus Green, who just happens to have saved Arthur's life on a tiger hunt in India a few years previously, arrives at the mill, falls in love with Hazel's cousin Dolly at first sight, and after hearing Hazel's story from her, declares, "I'm tempted to play a new rôle, turn dramatist in real life! We've only to manage a little to make the play what we please. There's the stern father, Dunstan Kirke; the heavy villain, old Rod; the pretty victim, Hazel Kirke; the scheming cousin, that's you [Dolly]; the good-natured idiotic busy-body [Pittacus himself]" (444).

This dialogue reveals Mackaye's ironic attitude toward his melodramatic conventions, but he was a popular playwright who knew well how to "manage a little to make the play what we please."

The events that follow suggest nothing if not sensationalism and contrivance. Kirke misunderstands when his daughter confesses her love for Arthur, and he orders her from the house, thinking his "child avows dishonor." There is a misunderstanding about whether the subsequent marriage in Scotland of Hazel and Arthur is valid, and Hazel runs away in humiliation, having been told by Arthur's mother that it was Arthur who had deceived her about their marriage. Arthur's mother dies on the spot (from the strain) at the end of Act II. Hazel returns to the mill, and, mistakenly thinking that her father refuses to forgive her, tries to drown herself in the millpond. As Act III closes, her father faints because, having been struck blind by grief, he cannot save her. Hazel is saved by a servant boy, who has walked four hundred miles just to be with her, and Arthur, who just happens to be standing on the riverbank at the time. After a letter arrives confirming that the marriage indeed took place in Scotland, that Hazel and Arthur are therefore legally married, and that Arthur's money has all gone to pay his debts to Lady Maude, there remains, in his words, "nothing but my own hands, my own brains, and the endless wealth of my love for [Hazel]" (470). In a final scene, Kirke forgives Hazel; the family is reunited; the union of Pittacus and Dolly, whose humorous courtship has periodically relieved the melodrama, is sealed; and Pittacus declaims an epilogue expressing the moral of the piece:

> You guess the lesson we would fain instill,
> That human heart is more than human will. (471)

The only departure from melodramatic convention in this plot is the often cited absence of a villain.[8] As Pittacus reminds us, Aaron Rodney, Arthur's rival for possession of Hazel, is the natural villain. But Aaron does an unexpected turnabout when he learns from Hazel that she loves Arthur. Hazel asks his forgiveness, ending, "You do not hate me, then?" (450). Aaron's reply combines the self-sacrifice that melodrama usually demands only of women with the conventional tempered wisdom of the elderly man: "Hate ye? Aaron Rodney will never live to see the day he can hate ye. No, lass, I love ye still, God help me; love ye too well to ask anything save your own happiness. I only fear for what your father may do; you know how headstrong he is, and how wildly he rages at things he thinks are wrong" (450). Later, when Hazel believes her marriage to Arthur is a fraud, Aaron offers to make an honest woman of her: "I know all ye'd say, child: your heart has been another's – you could never give me a wife's love. Why, Hazel, dear, I do not ask it. If you will but marry me, it's only as a beloved daughter I will hold ye, a daughter I shall have the right to cherish and to guard" (466). Aaron could not be farther from the personification of motiveless evil that one expects of the rival in a melodrama, but this paragon of selflessness is nevertheless not much more believable than the melodramatic villain. Mackaye has simply substituted the withdrawing-parent figure of comedy for the villain of melodrama.

But even in this he has taken a step forward. He has dared to violate the conventions of melodrama and thus made his play less simpleminded than the typical melodramatic representations of personified goodness versus personified evil. *Hazel Kirke* does not allow the spectator the option of simply hissing the villain. To confront the impediment to the natural union of Hazel and Arthur is to confront not the personified evil of fantasy but the complicated evil of real life. It is not a single evil force in a community of good people that is at fault here but the evil of character that places the human heart at the mercy of the human will, as Pittacus Green would have it, or the evil of social conventions that allow parents to barter away their children in order to meet their pecuniary obligations and then believe they must hold to the bargain because of a perversely inflated ideal of honor. The slight shift in conventions that Mackaye refers to playfully through Pittacus marks a deeper shift in the drama's thematic focus that is a clear harbinger of the realistic movement soon to follow.

Beyond this shift, however, there is not much about the play that could be called realistic by today's standards. Aside from the absence of a villain, the chief element that critics have singled out is the dialogue, which Arthur Hobson Quinn calls "quiet" and "natural"[9] and Garff Wilson, "a fair approximation of colloquial speech."[10] The passages I have quoted should give an idea of Mackaye's moderately successful attempt to reproduce natural speech patterns. But the play also features an impossibly stagy Irish brogue and Scottish burr, many asides to the audience, and extremely artificial set pieces such as Hazel's soliloquy before her attempted suicide: "All is over; I know the worst now, and I know what I must do. I'll go, and there in the water that has brought so much misery to this home, I'll drown my sorrows and my sins. (*Going.*) Good-bye, old home – farewell, sweet memories, fond hopes – farewell, mother, father, life – life – life!" (467). At its core, *Hazel Kirke* is a sensational melodrama with an elaborately contrived and improbable yet conventionally predictable plot; flat characters in conventional roles; a platitudinous moral, which bears little relevance to the plot; stilted, stagy dialogue; and a setting that happens to be in England but could be anywhere if the plot device involving the Scottish border were not an element. To call this play realistic would be absurd after Ibsen and Shaw,

O'Neill and Glaspell, Crothers and Rice, Behrman and Barry. But in the context of *Uncle Tom's Cabin; The Drunkard, or The Fallen Saved;* and *The Octoroon* the epithet has some meaning.

The fourth type of American drama in the 1800s has been called the local-color play, after the similar development in fiction. The local-color play has a conventional plot structure derived from comedy or melodrama but is set in a specifically American locale with American types as characters. One trend, the depiction of urban lowlife, began as early as 1848 with Benjamin A. Baker's *Glance at New York,* which introduced the character Mose the Fireboy, who became the central figure in more than twenty plays about New York street life.[11] Its successors, such as Boucicault's *Poor of New York* (1857) and Augustin Daly's *Under the Gaslight* (1867), combined sensational adventure (a fire scene in the former, a hero tied to railroad tracks in the latter) with the local color of the street scene as a backdrop for its conventional melodramatic action. The type was represented in the 1879–80 season by several plays of the "Mulligan Series" by Edward Harrigan, who, along with Charles Hale Hoyt, represented New York's lowlife during the seventies and eighties. Howells praised Harrigan for creating ethnic types – Irish, German, Italian, and black – that rang true.[12] But his plots were the hackneyed structures of comedy, and if his characters represented some particular ethnic type on the surface, they represented some conventional comic type at bottom. The local color was laid on rather thin over ancient and well-worn dramatic conventions.

Harrigan admitted using "types and never individuals"[13] in creating his pictures of New York lowlife, but he insisted that they were types meticulously studied from life. Richard Moody reports that Harrigan "sat for hours on park benches, observing characters and copying snatches of dialogue"[14] and that he expended an extraordinary amount of energy to secure authentic costumes for his characters.[15] Howells compared his work to that of the Italian playwright Carlo Goldoni, whose roots were in commedia dell'arte, and recognized in it "the spring of a true American comedy, the beginning of things which may be great things."[16] Harrigan was to develop his own theoretical concept of realism a few years later, but a look at the first full-length play of the Mulligan series, *The Mulligan Guard Ball,* shows that he had a long way to go in 1879.

In a sense, it is even more unfair to characterize Harrigan's plays from the printed text alone than those of most other dramatists. Because the Mulligan series resembled a modern television situation comedy, with the same actors in the same parts,[17] a great deal of it depended on characterization, and a great deal of the action came out of rehearsal rather than the script. A sense of the stage business, however, emerges from the stage directions for Scene 7 of *The Mulligan Guard Ball,* which depicts the supper of roast pig after the ball:

> *Rat works on from L. to R. Puter sings a hymn. Sim joins in. Rat crosses and Omnes pelt at it. Business. . . . All sit and pig business on table, Pig gets down and goes off. . . . Set [for a reel] formed again – Enter Caroline Williams – She attacks Puter – Primrose tackles her and a scrimmage ensues – during which enter Lochmuller and six butchers with cleavers. General melee and curtain.*[18]

"In constructing a plot," Harrigan was to write ten years later, "I use one that is simple and natural – just like what happens around us every day."[19] Times change. But what Harrigan referred to, and what Howells praised him for, was his use of real events in the lives of the people about whom he wrote. The play's plot and business were so much malarkey. But the event of the dance or the picnic or the wake was real and recognizable to the audience. Similarly, despite Harrigan's protests, his characters were not so much types as caricatures, but they were new to the stage as well as recognizably American.

In *The Mulligan Guard Ball* the main characters are Dan Mulligan, Harrigan's "typical" pugnacious, impecunious, often inebriated Irishman; his wife, Cordelia, gullible but loving; and their son, Tommy, who wants to marry Katy Lochmuller, the daughter of Gustavus Lochmuller the butcher and his wife, Bridget, originally of County Cork. The supporting cast consists of various ethnic types: Sim Primrose and Brother Palestine Puter of the Ancient Order of Full Moons, "de Colored Secret Society, to Prevent de Irish from Riding on Horse Cars" (553); August Snider, the tailor; Mister Rosenfelt, who is in the garment business; and Mister Garlic, who owns Lyric Hall. The plot is as old and as simple as the Romeo-and-Juliet motif and the comedy of Menander. Mulligan and Lochmuller attempt to block the union of Katy and Tommy on ethnic grounds. Despite a discovery scene in the barbershop while the young people are planning their elopement, which is to take place on the night of the ball, they manage to carry it off anyway, and the after-the-ball supper becomes their wedding reception. Several subplots also punctuate the action, such as the rivalry of the Skidmores (the Full Moons' military association) with the Mulligan Guards and Mulligan's attempts to beat all the merchants out of their bills.

The play does not bear serious literary analysis, but some of its elements suggest future literary developments and nearly justify Howells's designation, the "spring" of American comedy. The dialogue is not careful dialect, nor is it expressive of character, nor is it particularly entertaining humor, but it is colloquial. Nowhere in the serious drama of Harrigan's contemporaries is there a speech with rhythms as natural as

Tommy's complaint about his father: "The bill is all right, Mother, but what I'm kicking about is this. I fetched Katy up here, and he lights that funnel with navy tobacco, and what's the consequence? She sez, 'Tommy, I want to go home,' before I've chinned five minutes" (550). The settings are straight from the everyday life of the people Harrigan depicts: the barbershop, the dance hall, the kitchen, and the parlor. Although the plot is imposed on the daily lives of the characters rather than drawn from them, it is simple and unobtrusive; its events chiefly involve the tangential action, the shaving scenes and brawls; and the conversations of the characters, rather than the story line, provide the unity for the action. In fact, the play is written in seven scenes rather than the traditional three or five acts. This departure from convention led to A. M. Palmer's objection that Harrigan's plays were mere "prolongations of sketches," a charge that both Harrigan and Howells took the time to answer.[20]

The local-color play, as Harrigan developed it, was clearly a transitional mode for the drama in America. On its face, it is a ridiculous farce about impossible characters. But delve a little deeper and there are the beginnings of natural dialogue, recognizable types, and beyond the contrived plot, the reflection of everyday life in action. The two impressions mitigate each other. Harrigan's representation of life, the structured action of the play, is as old and conventional as one could find. It is so hackneyed, in fact, as not to be noticed, and this does not result from poverty of imagination on Harrigan's part. He took the major conventions for granted and worked at creating an illusion of reality from the drama's performance elements, from sets and clothing and diction. That he did so convincingly enough to impress such an adamant realist as Howells is evidence of the power these elements have, but that the play seems exaggerated and hollow today is stronger evidence of their limitations. Edward Harrigan was a convincing local colorist, but he was not a realist.

A second type of local-color play, the rural New England piece, was growing in popularity and would continue to do so throughout the nineteenth century. An offshoot of the Yankee play mentioned earlier, it had a broader scope and more detailed staging. *Joshua Whitcomb*, Denman Thompson's old-fashioned one-character vehicle, was at one end of the spectrum in 1880, and David Belasco and James A. Herne's *Hearts of Oak* was at the other. Belasco had pirated this play from an English melodrama called *The Mariner's Compass*. Then he and Herne set it in a New England fishing village and combined Herne's genius for small realistic touches in characterization with Belasco's genius for realistic staging.[21] The result was a captivating effect of local color that was to become Herne's hallmark, even in his later plays, *Margaret Fleming* (1890) and

Shore Acres (1893), where the realism penetrated much deeper tha
surface. The new notion that local color lies not in a single bit of cl
terization but in the verisimilitude of the entire representation, exte
now to both setting and character, was a major step forward for realism.

The fifth type of native drama in the 1879–80 season might be classed
with the local-color play if it were not such a distinctive aspect of American popular culture. This is the Western play, an offspring of the Indian
play, which had been a part of American drama since Edwin Forrest had
first performed in John Augustus Stone's *Metamora, or, The Last of the
Wampanoags*, in 1829. The Noble Savage held the stage until the Civil
War, but the seventies found the playwrights shifting sides, particularly
after Frank Mayo became a hit in Frank Hitchcock's *Davy Crockett*
(1872). *Davy Crockett* was preceded by *Kit, the Arkansas Traveller* (1870)
and Augustin Daly's *Horizon* (1871), a play that though as frank a melodrama as most Westerns, has been credited with a step toward realism in
"simplicity of language and restraint of passion."[22] Like any form of
local color, the Western consisted of an overlay of the illusion of reality
conveyed by careful staging, costuming, and, later, dialogue upon a
conventional melodramatic or comic structure.

It was a popular form and was attempted with varying results by the
successful Western fiction writers. Although Bret Harte collaborated
with Dion Boucicault on *The Two Men of Sandy Bar* (1876), with Mark
Twain on *Ah Sin* (1877), and with T. Edgar Pemberton on *Sue* (1896), he
never learned how to write a play. Mark Twain did better when his own
adaptation of his novel *The Gilded Age* (1874) became a favorite vehicle
for John T. Raymond as Colonel Sellers.[23] Bret Harte and Mark Twain
were also the victims of many unauthorized adaptations, one of which,
M'Liss, was a hit of the 1879–80 season. The most successful Western
playwrights, however, were Joaquin Miller, whose *The Danites in the
Sierras* (1877) was produced many times,[24] and Bartley Campbell, whose
My Partner, the best-known and most successful of all the Western plays,
was first produced in September 1879 and rivaled *Hazel Kirke* for recognition as *the* major new American play of the 1879–80 season.

My Partner is a straightforward melodrama in structure. Its plot centers
on two miners, Joe Saunders and Ned Singleton, who have been partners
for ten years. As one of the characters puts it, Joe is "the best fellow,"
although Ned "wears the best clothes."[25] Ned has seduced Mary Bran-
don, but Joe loves her purely from afar. In a complicated series of events,
Joe forces Ned to swear he will marry Mary and then splits up the
partnership, saying, "No need to shake hands now. If when ye've made
her your wife – we should ever meet, I'll take the hand ye offer. But I
can't now" (71). Ned is murdered by the villain Scraggs, and Mary goes
off to the mountains to have her baby, who dies immediately. Having

heard that Joe has been accused of Ned's murder, Mary returns; they are married; Joe is exonerated; Scraggs is captured; and Mary and Joe live happily ever after. In Joe's closing words, "The night has been long and dark. But on the heights of happiness, where we are standing now, our love will illuminate our lives forever" (98). To hold the audience's interest, Campbell has included two subplots involving lighter love affairs and the machinations of the comic "Chinaman" Wing Lee.

My Partner shamelessly exploits the conventions of Western local-color stories. Wing Lee is a version of Harte's "Heathen Chinee," a stock character in the Western play since Miller's *Danites* (1877) and Harte and Mark Twain's *Ah Sin* (1877). Major Henry Clay Britt, a version of the Western windbag, is based on Harte's Colonel Starbottle and Mark Twain's Colonel Sellers. The minor characters Sam Bowler and Posie Pentland are types from Harte's mining-camp stories. The major characters, however, must share their Western type quality with their melodramatic type quality. Joe, for example, is capable of the high-flown sentiment and perfect grammar of the line quoted above, but he also says such things as "Well, it's kinder funny, I don't see Mary no whar, nor my partner Ned neither" (56). The "Western" dialogue is an occasional ornament; when a character is to act like a conventional hero or villain, Campbell's dialogue is inappropriately conventional as well. His heroine even begins a speech as a simple Western girl and ends it as a melodramatic victim of seduction: "Why don't he come? My eyes are weary watching, my heart is sore waiting. I've been down to the river's edge! The dark deep waters have a strange fascination for me, as they glide off in the mist and distance to the great ocean. . . . Are there any waters cold enough to cool a feverish fear, deep enough to hide a wretched, sinful woman!" (59).

Although it is neither deep nor consistent, the attempt to suggest the milieu is there in the characters, in occasional touches of dialogue, and in the setting as well. Campbell leaves the details to the technician, but his opening stage directions call for a *"distant view of Mount Shasta"* (49) to overlook the Golden Gate Hotel, and his directions for the interior of Joe and Ned's cabin at the beginning of Act II call for picks and shovels, a map of California, deer antlers on the wall, quartz specimens on the mantel, and a buffalo robe on the floor (63). These touches do for this play what Harrigan's urban and ethnic touches do for his – they evoke a specific milieu. Campbell's recognition of this goal and of some methods for achieving it made him a local colorist, although his adherence to romantic literary conventions show that he was no realist.

The Western was a fad in the drama, as it was in the fiction, of the seventies, but it was not a fad that died easily. At the end of the nineties, it was very much alive in Augustus Thomas's *Arizona* (1899) and Clyde

Fitch's *The Cowboy and the Lady* (1899). But it differed from most local-color drama in the direction of its development. Rather than attempting to achieve verisimilitude in detail and full psychological characterization, the writers of Westerns tended to seek out the romantic aspects of America's Western myth and to dramatize "grand passions" against the background of vast western spaces and primitive social institutions. Unlike the urban and the New England local-color plays, the Western remained melodrama, reaching its full development in the neoromanticism of William Vaughn Moody's *Great Divide* (1906). The melodramatic structure and romantic myth remained intact when the Western was appropriated by the motion-picture industry after *The Great Train Robbery* (1903), and beyond that it has no place in this discussion.

The final type of native drama appearing in the 1879–80 season is the closest to realism of the six, or at least it fulfilled more of the demands made by realistic critics than any of the others. The "drama of contemporary life," the equivalent of the French *drame bourgeois,* might be humorous or serious in tone and, at this stage, comic or melodramatic in structure. These plays pleased the realists insofar as they were attempts to represent, and occasionally comment on, the social conditions, institutions, and problems of American life. A description of these plays must be tentative because in 1879 the type was just beginning its development in America.

Henrik Ibsen's play *A Doll's House,* first produced in 1879, may serve as a touchstone for comparing America's development toward serious realistic drama with that of Europe. William Winter's announcement in the *New York Tribune* after the production of *Ghosts* in 1894 that "the health and good sense of the American audience will never accept the nauseous offal of Mr. Ibsen's dissecting table as either literature or drama"[26] should suggest the readiness of nineteenth-century American theater audiences to grapple with social problems. The serious treatment of the double standard for sexual fidelity in Herne's *Margaret Fleming* (1890) won praise from some daring critics but was never accepted by the public.[27] In short, the American theater was far behind the European in the serious depiction of contemporary life. But American theatergoers were not totally without interest in the subject. In the 1879–80 season, serious though melodramatic attempts were made to treat marriage, jealousy, and divorce in productions of Bronson Howard's *Banker's Daughter* (1878) and two of Augustin Daly's plays, *Divorce* (1871) and *Pique* (1875). These plays were hardly Ibsen, but they opened the way for the subjects Ibsen was beginning to dramatize and the realist critics would soon be demanding. Nor was the representation of contemporary social issues entirely without its tradition in America. One need only remember the enormous impact that the abolitionist plays *Uncle Tom's*

Cabin and *The Octoroon* had on the institution of slavery or that the temperance dramas *The Drunkard, or, The Fallen Saved* (1844) and *Ten Nights in a Barroom* (1858) had on America's attitude toward alcohol to appreciate the social controversy endemic to the American stage. Realism demanded this social content in a new and more credible form.

Bronson Howard, America's "first professional playwright," meaning the first writer to make a living at play writing, revealed his view of the profession in his own account of the evolution of *The Banker's Daughter* from a play first produced in 1873 as *Lilian's Last Love*. His *Autobiography of a Play* (1886) describes his writing and rewriting of the play with the help of A. M. Palmer (the "New York manager") and the "literary attaché of the theatre,"[28] in accordance with what he called the "axioms" of the theater. These axioms provide a unique insight into the serious American playwright's view of his art in the early eighties:

> The love of offspring in woman has shown itself the strongest of all human passions; and it is the most nearly allied to the boundless love of Deity. But the one absolutely universal passion of the race – which underlies all other passions – on which, indeed, the very existence of the race depends – the very fountain of maternal love itself, is the love of the sexes.
>
> It is only when [the dramatist] deals with the love of the sexes that his work is most interesting to that aggregation of human hearts we call the audience.
>
> A play must be, in one way or another, "satisfactory" to the audience. . . . In England and America, the death of a pure woman on the stage is not "satisfactory," except when the play rises to the dignity of tragedy. The death, in an ordinary play, of a woman who is not pure, as in the case of "Frou-Frou," is perfectly satisfactory, for the reason that it is inevitable.
>
> Three hearts cannot beat as one. The world is not large enough, from an artistic point of view, for three good human hearts to continue to exist, if two of them love the third. If one of the two hearts is a bad one, art assigns it to the hell on earth of disappointed love; but if it is good and tender and gentle, art is merciful to it, and puts it out of its misery by death.[29]

One could hardly call writing plays according to these "axioms" a realistic representation of life, and as Howard demonstrates that indeed he did compose *The Banker's Daughter* in accordance with this view, one expects it to be conventional in sentiment, structure, and character. So it is. Its moral, that one should marry for love and not for duty or financial security, is conspicuously stated by the heroic husband, John Strebelow: "Duty! Honor! Who spoke of duty or of honor? I spoke and speak of love; of that love which in a wife is the sole invulnerable armor of a husband's honor; of that love without which honor is valueless, and life a blank; of the love in which honor dwells as unconsciously as flowers bloom and water flows. God help the husband whose honor is guarded by duty alone."[30]

The plot, a combination of convention, coincidence, and "poetic justice," is revealed in the five acts of the well-made play. In Act I, Lawrence Westbrook learns that his banking firm will be forced to declare bankruptcy the following day unless he can produce $30,000. Meanwhile, his daughter Lilian is refusing the marriage proposal of the rakish Count de Carojac and setting up a reconciliation with her fiancé, Harold Routledge, with whom she has had a lovers' quarrel. Westbrook receives a letter from John Strebelow, a wealthy man twenty-one years older than Lilian, who proposes to become her suitor. Westbrook persuades Lilian to accept Strebelow in order to save the bank and thereby rescue him from the consequent "curses of the poor, the wail of the widow, and the tears of the orphan" (95) if it should fail. She agrees on the condition that her father tell Strebelow that he must "accept my hand without the heart I cannot now give him" (96). Knowing that Strebelow would not agree to such a match, Westbrook neglects to tell him of Lilian's condition. The marriage is made, and Strebelow gives Westbrook the $30,000. Act II takes place six years later in Paris. Although the Strebelows have a daughter who occupies her mother's thoughts almost completely, it becomes evident that Lilian still cares for Routledge, who happens to arrive in Paris from Rome. He nearly succeeds in rekindling her passion for him, but she recovers herself in a dramatic scene as Act II closes.

Act III takes place at an American Embassy reception in Paris. The Count appears and incites Routledge to a duel by implying a romantic connection between him and Lilian. Act IV consists of the duel, during which Routledge is fatally wounded and Strebelow and Lilian appear at the opportune moment for Lilian to throw herself beside Routledge crying, "Oh, Harold. My poor Harold! . . . Dying – dying – dying for me, who blighted his heart! Harold! Harold! I've killed him, killed him" (119). Strebelow defends Lilian's honor by killing the Count (offstage), but he is not without his doubts nonetheless. Suspecting that there must, after all, have been something between Harold and Lilian, he discusses the subject with her and learns for the first time that Lilian has never been in love with him. With this knowledge, he decides that they should separate. Act V takes place three years later. Lilian has learned in the course of the separation that she does love Strebelow and has been "courting" him by telling their daughter what to write in her letters to him. Strebelow arrives, and after one final misunderstanding about who wrote the last letter, Lilian confesses her love and the two are reunited.

There is also a comic subplot in which Lilian's friend Florence proves the moral of the piece through *reductio ad absurdam*. She marries a millionaire fifty-two years her senior, inherits his fortune after six years of mothering him through a second childhood, and prepares to marry the man of her choice, a young businessman and caricature of the American tourist, George Washington Phipps. They are sufficiently ridiculous to make her course of action seem less sensible, if infinitely more fun, than Lilian's.

The play departs slightly from the melodramatic formula in that not only the villain Carojac but also the hapless Routledge is dispatched in a duel, but the characters are made to order for the conventional action: Strebelow, the noble and selfless hero; Lilian, the honorable, dutiful, and hopelessly besieged heroine; Carojac, the motiveless villain; and Westbrook, the ineffectual father, undeserving of his daughter's self-sacrificing love. With the possible exception of old Westbrook, who displays natural human weakness in a difficult situation rather than the motiveless villainy of a Count de Carojac, none of the characters is psychologically more complex than the characters in a medieval morality play. Howard, after all, was not trying to depict people; he was trying to depict a moral sentiment, as is clear in his description of the play's revision:

> If . . . we so reconstruct the whole play that the husband and wife may at last come together with true affection, we shall have the moral: Even if a young girl makes the worst of all mistakes, and accepts the hand of one man when her heart belongs to another, fidelity to the duty of a wife on her side, and a manly, generous confidence on the part of her husband, may, in the end, correct even such a mistake. The dignity of this moral saved John Strebelow's life, and Harold Routledge was killed in the duel with the Count de Carojac.[31]

The inflated dialogue, the first characters, the improbable representations of virtue and vice, the dastardly foreign villain, the duel, the complications with the letters, the sentimental climax, and the entire improbable structure of the action all suggest as conventional a melodrama as one is likely to find. But there are two elements in *The Banker's Daughter* that faintly suggest the coming trend of representing contemporary life as one sees it rather than imposing a preconceived formulaic structure on it. First, the play is recognizably American. Westbrook is an American banker. Phipps may be a burlesque of the American businessman and tourist, but the *source* of the burlesque is distinct and recognizable. The sense of the milieu is not by any means central or complete, but it is suggested. Also, although it does so in a sentimental and conventional way, the play discusses current problems in current social institutions. Howard was using his drama to discuss a much debated issue in taking on the Victorian dilemma of duty or honor versus love as a basis for marriage. Although the play's moving force is as far from the artistic impulse of realism as it could be, these less central aspects are precisely what the realists would be concerned with in building a realistic theory of drama.

ACTING STYLES

The acting styles of the eighties are more important to the student of realistic drama than they might appear at first. Theater critics naturally write about what strikes them most immediately in a dramatic representation before they consider the play as a literary text. Because the realist critics were no exception, readers were as likely to learn Henry James's views on Henry Irving and Ellen Terry, Coquelin and Sarah Bernhardt, Charles Coghlan, or Tommaso Salvini as those on Dumas *fils*, Bronson Howard, or Paolo Giacometti. Similarly, Howells was as likely to write about Annie Russell, Joe Jefferson, or Katherine Corcoran Herne as about Bret Harte, Charles Hoyt, or Clyde Fitch. These critics had a great deal to say about acting, what made it good or bad, and, more to the point of this discussion, what made it realistic or unrealistic. Their understanding of the state the art of acting had reached by the eighties in America, and the practical effect the development toward realism would have on it, was fundamental to their understanding of the theater in realistic terms.

The seventies were a period of transition for acting in America, just as they were for the drama. Using the touchstone of the 1879–80 season, we can clearly see two generations of actors on the American stage toward the end of the century performing different types of drama in different styles. The older generation came into its own when America was very much a part of the "star system." Although the actors of that generation would all be recognized now as of a type – histrionic, emotional, and "stagy" – they represent three distinct styles, and their development points the way to what the next generation would attempt to do. The most old-fashioned of the three is the classical style, which Edwin Booth perfected:

> He was a master of the techniques of speech and movement and although he aimed to give the impression of being perfectly natural, his naturalness was the suggestive, idealized behavior which suited the characters of poetic tragedy. The player of the classic school studied his roles penetratingly, fitted them into the overall design of the play, and rehearsed his effects carefully so that in performance, his acting appeared spontaneous and effortless. In every part he played he tried to transform his personality so as to project the illusion of a separate dramatic character, and he sought to feel the emotions of his role without losing control of his body or voice and without wallowing in his emotions.[32]

This classical style had been a change for the better from the romantic "rippling muscle" school of acting practiced by Edwin Forrest and his followers. It reached its height in the sixties and early seventies and was on the wane by the late seventies, eclipsed by newer, less studied and artificial styles.

In the next wave, there grew up a school of "emotionalism," which rejected the studied, calculated acting of classicism in favor of a freer play of emotions and a spontaneity of effects. Garff Wilson describes three characteristics of the school: the attempt actually to experience the character's emotions and surrender oneself to them; the cultivation of a "lush, overt display" of the passions one is feeling; and the neglect of classical technique in elocution, gestures, movement, and business. He notes that the typical performance is marked by "sobs, tears, screams, shudders, heaving, writhing, panting, growling, trembling, and all manner of other physical manifestations."[33] Not surprisingly, the members of this school achieved their greatest success in melodrama. The emotionalism, the cultivation of sensation, and the somewhat hysterical view of life's difficulties that the school fostered were clearly antirealistic, as even its contemporaries recognized. One critic described Matilda Heron as a "high pressure first class Western steamboat, with all her fires up, extra weights on the safety valve, and not less than forty pounds of steam to the square inch," adding, "The effect is fine, but the danger of an explosion is imminent."[34]

The realist critics felt much more comfortable with the third school in the older generation, the character acting of the comedians. These actors, who invested their energy in the complete creation of a single role, often one the actor played for a lifetime, were particularly dear to Howells, who referred to Joe Jefferson's acting as an "art which he has dignified and refined to an ideal delicacy and a beautiful reality never surpassed, to our thinking. We believe those who have seen his Rip Van Winkle have seen the perfection of that art."[35] Jefferson's art was often called "quiet." It was the attention to detail in a unified characterization that made his Rip special and that naturally appealed to the realistic sensibility.

In the next generation, the actors just beginning their careers in 1880, James A. Herne might be seen as a direct descendant of Jefferson's, with a concern for quiet and detail in his portrayals. He was best as the simple country heroes in his own plays *Hearts of Oak, Sag Harbor,* and *Shore Acres.* The chief Shakespearean actors, E. H. Sothern and Richard Mansfield, can be distinguished from those who came before by their much greater range of roles, from contemporary comedy to romantic tragedy. Although Henry James would complain that their very versatility ruined them for Shakespeare, others thought their more natural and psychological style made Shakespeare more accessible than the declamatory style of the classicists did. In any case, they marked a departure from the classical style and helped break down the strict division between serious Shakespearean actors and actors of contemporary drama, suggesting that Shakespeare could be contemporary and that contemporary drama could be serious.

Richard Mansfield was an American version of the most controversial British actor of the period, Henry Irving. Both men shared with some actors who were less serious about their craft, including the famous Daly costars Ada Rehan and John Drew, a peculiarity of the acting in the second half of the nineteenth century, the cult of personality: "the substitution of the performer's personality for the dramatic character, or the portrayal of dramatic characters which fit the performer's personality so exactly that performer and character are practically identical."[36] This form of acting could hardly be called great art, for there was no need to create an illusion of reality when the reality was staring one in the face, but the "naturalness" and "quiet" of the performances appealed to realist critics. These actors were good transition figures, for the projection of personality, even the actor's own, onto a character was one step in the move toward psychological realism in acting. The concept that the character was a "person" rather than a series of attitudes or emotions was important, and one that was to be carried to fruition by such actors in the next generation as Minnie Maddern Fiske and George Arliss. Like the drama of the period, the acting of the seventies and eighties was undergoing a transition. It was clear both that the acting was far from what the realists were to demand from it and that it was slowly developing toward a school that would meet those demands.

STAGECRAFT

A major event in the 1879–80 season was the reopening of the Madison Square Theatre, refurbished and largely redesigned by Steele Mackaye. *Hazel Kirke* certainly became a hit on its own merits – in 1882–83 fourteen road companies toured with it[37] – but many in the opening-night audience had come as much to see Mackaye's theater as his play. That night he was introducing, among other innovations, his new "elevator stage," a two-level set that allowed scene changes to be made in an unprecedented forty seconds. Mackaye's architectural changes, though less exciting than these innovations to his contemporaries, were more important for the realist movement. He removed the forestage and the proscenium doors, moved the orchestra to a recess *above* the stage, and installed seats in what had formerly been the orchestra pit of the theater.[38] The changes made the atmosphere in the 700-seat auditorium much more conducive to the subtle effects required in realistic plays than that in any other New York theater.

Mackaye was ahead of the rest in stagecraft and theater design, but in many ways he was simply continuing a trend toward greater and greater verisimilitude in staging that had been in motion since the 1840s. Charles Kean had had great success with his "historically accurate" productions of Shakespeare's *King John* and *Richard III* during the forties, and Booth and others had followed suit. Beginning in the fifties, managers had constantly tried to outdo one another at producing more and more elaborate rivers and ice floes, scenes of plantation life, and celestial tableaux in their versions of the ubiquitous *Uncle Tom's Cabin*. Also, as Richard Moody has demonstrated, the very romanticism behind the creation of the landscape panoramas and "sublime" natural settings for romantic tragedy had made for greater artistry in re-creating the landscapes, resulting eventually in greater verisimilitude in the overall productions.[39] The romantic sensibility might have favored "exterior scenes of deep woods, bald mountain peaks, rushing cataracts, and mysterious caverns"[40] over the drawing rooms, railroad cars, and restaurants of realism, but it required them in exquisite detail. William Dunlap's *Trip to Niagara* (1828), for example, required twenty-five thousand square feet of moving canvas to depict the trip from New York to the Catskills by way of the Hudson River in eighteen detailed scenes.[41]

As must be obvious by now, there is a crucial distinction to be made between realism in staging for visual effect and staging designed to contribute to the overall effect of realism in a production. In the 1870s, Moody notes, "the average spectator was attracted to the theatre not to appraise the degree of realism in the representation of a locomotive on the stage but to delight in the striking and thrilling melodramatic action in which the locomotive played its part."[42] It would be misleading to equate the quick advance toward technical perfection in stagecraft during the second half of the nineteenth century with the advance of realism as a movement in the theater. The realists certainly made use of the art to reach their goal of a complete illusion of reality once they had defined it, but the great designers and technicians of stagecraft, Mackaye and David Belasco, were temperamentally and artistically romantics, not realists, and for the most part, they aimed to heighten the sensational, the exotic, and the unusual in their productions rather than to create the recognizable illusion of everyday life that the realists were seeking. What's more, they used their talents to create reflexive effects, which were antirealistic because they were meant to call attention to themselves as artistic or technical feats. The development of stagecraft certainly had a life of its own, and consequently, it must be treated as a separate art. Whereas stagecraft was crucial to realism's development in the drama – and it became a powerful medium in the hands of the playwright and director of a play whose aim was realistic – its verisimilitude could and did serve the romantic's ends just as easily as it did the realist's. It is not the technical perfection of the representation but its artistic purpose that must be considered in evaluating the stagecraft of the 1880s.

The efforts of Mackaye and Belasco to make the scenic illusion technically perfect tended toward the production of spectacular effects. Mackaye's greatest accomplishment, the plan for his "Spectatorium" at the Chicago World's Fair in 1893, is an excellent example. He hoped to build a theater "completely equipped for the exhibit of all the latest inventions, machinery, and appliances, connected with electricity in its practical application to Panoramic and Dramatic Art."[43] The building was to be 480 feet long, 380 feet wide, and 270 feet high, accommodating ten thousand spectators. It was to house twenty-five "telescope stages," which would move around on six miles of railroad track. This colossal project was never completed, but a smaller version called the "Scenitorium" was built, and there Mackaye staged *The World Finder,* a romantic pageant that recorded the life of Christopher Columbus.[44] Here he replaced the traditional footlights with an arc of lighting that approximated the light of the sun and moon, a pattern of stars created by electric lighting, and a "real" rainbow simulated with a mist machine and lighting. He also invented the "luxauleator," a curtain of light created by illuminating the proscenium arch with strong electric lights, which made the dimmer stage look black to the audience. His new devices were used to represent such scenes as the "celestial vision which illumined the darkest hour in Columbus' struggle," including Christ, his angels, and a "a number of the world's rejected"; sunrises and sunsets on romantic landscapes; and all the changing effects of the ocean during the voyage. There is no doubt that Steele Mackaye was a genius and that the realistic playwrights to come could not easily have done without him, but he was no realist. He was a romantic playwright who was adept at using realistic effects to heighten his romantic illusions.

David Belasco is not quite so straightforward a case as Mackaye. He was an avowed proponent of realism in staging, yet the plays he produced, including his own, were romantic, melodramatic, or both. During the eighties and nineties, Belasco quickly came to be recognized as a wizard with lights and technical effects, although in 1880 he was still in California, where he had collaborated with Herne on *Chums,* the original version of *Hearts of Oak.* Even then, his penchant for realistic staging was active. His San Francisco production of the play featured "real" rain, a working gristmill, a dinner with real food, and a cat that ran across the stage to a fireplace, stretched itself, and drank milk from a dish, on cue.[45] Belasco was to come into his own, however, only after he took over the management of the Madison Square Theatre from Mackaye in 1882. His feats in New York have become legendary: reconstructing a Child's restaurant right down to the forks and spoons for *The Governor's Lady* (1912); rebuilding an entire room from a real boardinghouse as the set for *The Easiest Way* (1918);[46] and discarding a lighting effect for *The Girl of the Golden West* (1905), upon which he had spent three months and $5,000, because although it was a "very beautiful" sunset, "it was not . . . Californian."[47] He also went to great lengths to secure the "real thing" in costumes, from sending his casts to secondhand shops for their wardrobes and buying clothes off the backs of incredulous tramps and streetwalkers to sending an agent to France after the fabrics for *DuBarry* and having them dyed "to reproduce exactly the dresses and styles of the Court of Louis XV, as shown by portraits painted during that period."[48]

Because he insisted on attention to the smallest details that contributed to the illusion, Belasco's name became synonymous with "finish" in theatrical production. He was particularly known for his patient experiments with lighting, originating the "DuBarry" light and the baby spotlight and using colored silks and gelatin slides to get the effects he wanted. He also had a clear idea of the aesthetic uses of these effects. About his production of *The Darling of the Gods,* he wrote, "Every particle of color used on the stage, every ray of light cast upon its scenes, was carefully calculated to symbolize its moods, interpret its meaning, and direct and strengthen its emotional appeal. I meant that its lighting accompaniment should stand in the same relation to it as music written by a composer to express and elaborate the thought and sentiment of a poem."[49] And it was not only the "large effects" of the melodrama that he sought to achieve. His explanation shows he fully understood how stagecraft could be used to serve the illusion of realism:

> Such effects . . . are, of course, more noticeable to the layman when used in romantic and fantastic plays than in modern dramas, in which the scenes are laid in interiors and among the conventional surroundings of contemporaneous, everyday life. By the broader, more vivid stage pictures the eye is consciously assailed. But there are also thousands of chances for delicate strokes of illumination in a well-managed modern play which neither audience nor critic is likely to notice, yet which work unconsciously upon the feelings and imagination.
>
> To select the right opportunities for their use, to know how to contrive them, and at the same time how to conceal them, is what makes the profession of the stage director so difficult. Not only should he have a comprehensive knowledge of all the arts, he must understand psychology and the physical sciences besides. In the intricate process of producing a play he must be the translator of its moods, and supply the medium by which they are transmitted to audiences.[50]

Reading this, one might well ask, where is Belasco's realism? His remarks show that he was clearly interested in the precise detail, the quiet effect, the overall illusion that the realist sought, but he spent his time constructing "effects" for pageants like *DuBarry* and unabashed melodramas like his own *Madame Butterfly* and Eugene Walter's *Easiest Way*, rather than following the route that his old-time collaborator Herne had taken toward a greater realism in the total representation. If these two had continued working together, perhaps Herne's "Ibsenist" attempts would have been saved in production, and perhaps George Jean Nathan, summarizing Belasco's career in 1917, could not have said, "to applaud the practice of Mr. David Belasco . . . is akin to an admiration for the sort of adult who triumphantly expends painstaking effort and time in putting together the several hundred little pieces of a jig-saw puzzle."[51] To be meaningful, realism in stagecraft must be part of an overall design in representation. When the illusion of reality created by the technical wizards merged with the honest attempt to depict human life as it was lived, in such plays as Edward Sheldon's *Salvation Nell* (1908) and Elmer Rice's *Street Scene* (1929), this was accomplished, but in the seventies and eighties it had hardly been considered.

CONCLUSIONS

It should be evident from this short survey that the American theater was far from realistic in 1880. Its drama was primarily formulaic melodrama or comedy; its acting was stagy and self-conscious; its stagecraft was sensational. It should also be evident, however, that there were hints of a nascent realism in all three areas. The dawning concern for verisimilitude in setting, costume, and dialogue was the harbinger of a deeper concern for the illusion of reality in the thought, character, and structure of the play. The notion of "quiet" and concern for the full representation of a character that the new generation of actors evinced prepared the way for the appropriate representation of realistic plays. The technical wizards had already produced the stagecraft necessary to sustain the illusion of reality in the entire representation, once that aim had been established. The American theater of the eighties had the raw materials for realism. It simply needed realist critics to articulate its principles and determined playwrights and managers to put them into practice. The articulation and realization of realistic principles proved to be slow processes, but they had clear beginnings in the theater of the eighties.

2

Realistic Dramatic Theory

The realists' theories of the drama, founded as they are on the realists' theories of art, should hold no surprises for anyone who knows the aesthetic principles common to the critical writing on fiction by William Dean Howells, Henry James, Hamlin Garland, and other spokesmen for realism. Howells's statement that "the primal purpose of a play is to illustrate life or to reproduce it"[1] echoes the realist's basic pronouncement on the novel. But the writing, production, and apprehension of a play are much more complex aesthetic processes than the writing and reading of fiction. What's more, any theoretical statement about drama is further complicated by the long-established conventions of criticism that have grown up around it since Aristotle, conventions that, we must remember, were more firmly entrenched in the critical mind of the nineteenth century than they have been since the liberating influence of the realists and the experimenters who followed them. How did the "illustration" or "reproduction" of life take place in the drama, and what precise meaning did Howells intend to convey when he used these terms? If we want to understand what the nineteenth-century realists meant by "realistic drama," we need to pursue answers to these fundamental questions.

DEFINING TERMS
The first term of the representational process, the drama's subject, seems at first glance simple and straightforward, if all-encompassing: "life." Of course, there was a hidden agenda in Howells's remark, which is gradually revealed as one delves deeper into his criticism. In 1891 he commented that a "nascent reform of the stage (if it is not too hopeful to call it so) began, we think, when our playwrights turned to real life with a tentative question whether there might not be something there that was worth the attention of the drama."[2] He used similar terms to praise Herne's *Reverend Griffith Davenport* in 1899: "It is an attempt,

24

and a successful attempt, to put upon the stage a carefully studied passage
of life once real, in which only such incidents as express character are
employed, and no mere effects are sought for the sake of effects."[3] While
commending the major British playwrights of the nineties – George
Bernard Shaw, Oscar Wilde, Henry Arthur Jones, and Arthur Wing
Pinero – Howells conveyed a fuller sense of what he meant to imply with
the phrase "real life":

> In the plays . . . there is distinctly a disposition on the part of the author
> to grapple with actualities of several kinds, and especially to wrestle
> with problems, and to struggle with motives. Their scene is always a
> recognizable semblance of the world. . . . I perceive in their work the
> interests and motives that impel people in life. The persons are some-
> thing like, the love is something like, the hate is something like, the vice
> is something like, and the virtue is something like. . . . To the inward
> truth, or measure of truth, there is a pleasing response of outward truth;
> the plays have good form.[4]

This is a fairly neat expression of the way Howells viewed the drama's
essential function. Little troubled by the imprecision of such terms as
"the world" and "truth" (let alone "inward truth" and "outward
truth"), he sought an artistic reflection of reality as he saw it, making the
naive philosophical assumption that reality was an empirically verifiable
entity that could be reproduced through an artistic medium. Other realists made a distinction between the world of human experience and the
world of the stage. Most assumed that the conventions of dramatic representation have evolved a "world" of their own, which the realists were
seeking to displace with their representations of reality. Shaw's description of the difference is telling in its assumption that the two worlds exist
simultaneously, ready to the hand of a playwright who is seeking the
subject for a play:

> We have, then, two sorts of life to deal with: one subjective or stagey,
> the other objective or real. What are the comparative advantages of the
> two for the purposes of the dramatist? Stage life is artificially simple and
> well understood by the masses; but it is very stale; its feeling is conven-
> tional; it is totally unsuggestive of thought because all its conclusions
> are foregone; and it is constantly in conflict with the real knowledge
> which the separate members of the audience derive from their own
> daily occupations. . . . Real life, on the other hand, is so ill understood,
> even by its clearest observers, that no sort of consistency is discoverable
> in it; there is no "natural justice" corresponding to that simple and
> pleasant concept, "poetic justice." . . . But on the other hand, it is
> credible, stimulating, suggestive, various, free from creeds and systems
> – in short, it is real.[5]

Defining the concept of "life" as subject has consistently presented
problems for twentieth-century critics who study realism. George Beck-

er's concise formulation reveals Taine's pervasive influence on realist criticism: "The ultimate subject of a realistic work is a milieu. The question it raises is what are the terms of life in that milieu. The novelistic (or dramatic) strategy is to find a way to answer that question as accurately as possible without resorting to overwhelming documentation."[6] When he approves of the new realistic playwrights' willingness to "wrestle with problems" and to "struggle with motives," Howells is really saying the same thing. The subject of the realist is not only life but also the specific life of his time and place, the objects of his immediate observation.

For American realists, the subject has been more narrowly defined as that emerging from what Edwin Cady calls "common vision," not merely lowlife, or bourgeois life, or aristocratic life, but the "average," common to all yet represented through an individual outlined against his social and physical environment.[7] This is the realistic dramatist's version of "milieu." The "terms of life" are the individual's problems and motives within that milieu, for the realist's investigation has two axes: One is horizontal, directed outward toward problems in the social environment; the other is vertical, boring into the individual's inner being and examining moral and psychological motives. The thought in realistic drama moves along both axes, producing a dynamic tension central to the play's structure.

Two other aspects of Howells's description bear emphasis. The first is his principle of selection for deciding what to represent. The good playwrights "wrestle with problems" and "struggle with motives." They focus on social themes and character. The second is his notion of dramatic form: "To the inward truth, or measure of truth, there is a pleasing response of outward truth; the plays have good form." Howells's notion that dramatic structure was not imposed on the action of a realistic play but grew out of the rhythms of life the playwright was imitating appeared new and startling in the nineteenth century. The idea was a reversal of the Aristotelian theory of plot as it had evolved by way of the neoclassicists, and it flew in the face of the well-made play as conceived by nineteenth-century dramatists seeking to emulate the successful play making of their French contemporaries. Its realism lies in its insistence that even the seemingly artificial construction of a play's plot must imitate "real life," and if it fails to do so, it is bad art.

Howells was not nearly so demanding as his pronouncements make him seem. He believed that the drama of his time was evolving from romanticism to realism, and that the realist must be patient while the process took place:

> The fact is, the two kinds do not mingle well, but for a while yet we must have the romantic and the realistic mixed in the theatre. That is

quite inevitable; and it is strictly in accordance with the law of evolution. The stage, in working free of romanticism, must carry some rags and tags of it forward in the true way; that has been the case always in the rise from a higher to a lower [sic] form; the man on a trapeze recalls the ancestral monkey who swung by his tail from the forest tree; and the realist cannot all at once forget the romanticist. Perhaps not till the next generation shall we have the very realist; which puzzles the groundlings, romantically expectant of miracles that shall clear away all trace of romanticism in an instant.[8]

Henry James, unlike Howells, was not an unswerving admirer of realism. For James the theater was appropriately used in the representation of the traditional "world" of Shakespeare, or even of that stagy world that Shaw described, if it was done in the pure tradition of the Théâtre Français. He objected, in fact, to realism's intrusion on these worlds, and spoke for maintaining their integrity even in the training of the actors: "When you have Shakespeare's speeches to utter, your reality must be a sort of imaginative compromise; you must wind your whole conception to a certain exalted pitch, and there, at that impressive altitude, you may keep among the levels."[9] He admired realism as an artistic aim for an entire dramatic representation, however, and he had fairly clear expectations of the realistic dramatist. He praised Georges Hervieu for clinging to the "line of life" (SA, 327), and he wrote that Dumas *fils's Demi-Monde* was a model for the drama of its time because of the "quiet art with which it is unfolded" and the "naturalness and soberness of the means that are used, and by which great effects are produced" (SA, 279).

Although major differences in the descriptions of dramatic realism emerge from the criticism of Howells and James, the central notion of the imitation of "real life" conveyed in a natural and "quiet" way is common to both. This notion's general currency is clear in the work of several critics and playwrights who were perhaps farther from the sources of realistic theory but closer to the drama, and particularly the theater, than they were. James A. Herne had learned his trade as actor and manager on the job, working his way up from "utility man" in provincial stock companies to leading man and manager of his own company. He had learned play writing in essentially the same way and had developed from an adapter of British plays and novels to an original playwright. It was Hamlin Garland who introduced him to realism and to Howells and who started Herne thinking along the lines that led in 1890 to the writing of *Margaret Fleming,* the play responsible for his sobriquet, the "American Ibsen." In 1897, Herne articulated his principles of dramatic art for the avant-garde magazine *Arena,* in an article entitled "Art for Truth's Sake in the Drama." There he declared, "I stand for truth's sake because it perpetuates the everyday life of its time, because it develops the latent beauty of the so-called commonplaces of life, because it dignifies labor and reveals the divinity of the common man."[10] He goes on to compare the "art for art's sake" of the aestheticist movement with the art for truth's sake that he says "emphasizes humanity":

> It is not sufficient that the subject be attractive or beautiful, or that it does not offend. It must first of all express some *large* truth. That is to say, it must always be representative. Truth is not always beautiful, but in art for truth's sake it is indispensable.
>
> Art for truth's sake is serious. Its highest purpose has ever been to perpetuate the life of its time. . . . But in expressing a truth through art, it should be borne in mind that *selection* is an important principle. If a disagreeable truth is not also an essential, it should not be used in art. . . . In all art, ancient and modern, that which is in touch with contemporaneous life adheres closest to truth, because it is produced through some peculiar social condition.
>
> Art is a personal expression of life. The finer the form and color and the larger the truth, the higher the art.[11]

It is abundantly clear in Herne's plays that realism was a force for him in practice as well as in theory.

Although the realist critics had a consistent notion of representation, they were vague in the use, and imprecise in the definition, of aesthetic and critical terms. In 1886, Howells wrote that Edward Harrigan was "part of the great tendency toward the faithful representation of life which is now animating fiction,"[12] and of Ibsen in 1906 that "the representation of life is his prime business and his main business."[13] But we have already seen him writing of drama as "illustrating" and "reproducing" life. The general idea was clear enough to him and probably to most of his readers, but if the terms "represent," "illustrate," and "reproduce" are held to any degree of precision, they are hardly equivalent. Because this imprecise use of terms presents a genuine problem for the formulation of a clear contemporary statement of literary realism's aesthetic principles for the drama, it is necessary to derive working definitions of the more important terms from the realists' descriptions.

As James describes it, representation is the "attempt to render the look of things, the look that conveys their meaning, to catch the colour, the relief, the expression, the surface, the substance of the human spectacle."[14] This and Howells's warning that "realism becomes false to itself when it heaps up facts merely, and maps life instead of picturing it"[15] are two essential elements of realistic representation: the aim of rendering the "look" of reality and the origin of that "look," in the shaping consciousness of the artist, which makes the crucial difference between "mapping" and "picturing."

One clarification is important at this point. As Francisque Sarcey wrote, "It is inadequate to repeat that the theater is a representation of human life. It would be a more precise definition to say that dramatic art is the sum of those conventions, universal or local, eternal or temporary, which help, when human life is represented on the stage, to give a public the illusion of truth."[16] Howells rejected the obvious conventions of the soliloquy and the aside as disrupting the illusion of reality on the stage, but he seemed unaware of the major convention that framed the representation and that was violated by these disruptions: the illusion of the fourth wall. A contemporary critic who was sharper on this point than the realists described it concisely: "Let it be granted that the auditorium of a theatre constitutes 'the fourth wall' of the room represented in the scene, and that the audience are unobserved hearers and spectators of what is said and done therein."[17]

John Gassner wrote that the fourth-wall convention, the notion that the play is not heard but overheard, is the ruling principle for the medium of realistic drama.[18] From this principle follows the rejection of any aspect of the dramatic medium that is reflexive, that shatters the fourth-wall illusion by calling attention to itself as art, such as rhetorical flourishes in the dialogue, declamatory style in the acting, or manipulating coincidence in the action. From it also follows the use of what Northrop Frye calls the "low mimetic" mode, in which, "superior neither to other men nor to his environment, the hero is one of us: we respond to a sense of his common humanity, and demand from the poet the same canons of probability that we find in our own experience."[19] The dramatic representation, then, may be most simply an attempt at rendering the artist's conception of life, but it takes shape in the very specific medium of men and women in action on the stage within the convention of the fourth-wall illusion and in the low mimetic style.

As Howells saw it, the process of representation has three parts: the subject, "real life," in whatever form that might take; the artistic process of making the text or the theatrical production (he did not distinguish between these two aesthetic activities); and the "illusion of reality" resulting from that process. In theory, the choice of subject is without constraints for the dramatist, as long as it is from "real life." Thus, Howells made no complaints about Edward Harrigan's limited choice of subject matter:

> Mr. Harrigan accurately realizes in his scenes . . . the actual life of this city. He cannot give it all; he can only give phases of it; and he has preferred to give its Irish-American phases in their rich and amusing variety, and some of its African and Teutonic phases. It is what we call low life . . . and it remains for others, if they can, to present other sides of our manifold life with equal perfection; Mr. Harrigan leaves a vast part of the vast field open.[20]

Similarly, he accepted the seeming flaws in Ibsen's art as a truthful reflection of the flaws in the world he sought to represent: "He sees that the world which a wise and merciful and perfect God has created seems full of stupidity and cruelty and out of joint to utter deformity, and he shows it as he sees it. If he is apparently inconsistent, it is because the world is really inconsistent; and if we hold him to any hard and fast rule of logic, we may indeed *have* him, but his best meaning will escape us."[21] According to Howells, the perfection of theatrical art was to be found in those moments when "the illusion is so perfect that you lose the sense of being in the theatre; you are out of that world of conventions and traditions, and in the presence of the facts."[22]

When it came to the medium of the representation, Howells agreed with Joe Jefferson that the art of the drama "could put before the spectator only a few facts, and only the most salient points of these facts. . . . It was a process of selection, and even in the things chosen for representation, the effect was rather suggestion than imitation."[23] Nevertheless, Howells's personal predilection tended toward the literal in theatrical production. He praised the use of fat actors to play the roles of fat men as a help to the theatrical illusion, and he somewhat apologetically defended its realism: "I know this is contrary to the teaching of Mr. Henry James in one of his most subtle and pleasing studies, where a real lady and gentleman are shown failing as models for ladies and gentlemen in illustration; but the presence of real fat people on the stage in the fat character of the drama, has restored my faith in reality."[24]

Edward Harrigan's description of his own practice is a good illustration of Howells's idea of theatrical representation:

> Though I use types and never individuals, I try to be as realistic as possible. Not only must the costuming and accessories be correct, but the speech or dialect, the personal "make-up," the vices and virtues, habits and customs, must be equally accurate in their similarity to the facts. Each drama is a series of photographs of life to-day in the Empire City. As examples, the bar-room in one of the Mulligan series was copied from a saloon in Roosevelt Street, the opium den in *Investigation* from a "joint" in Pell Street, and the "dive" in *Waddy Googan* from an establishment in the neighborhood of the Bowery.[25]

James's "mirror held up to life" had two reflecting sides and, more important, a "crucible of the imagination" between them. His idea of the process of realistic theatrical representation included six rather than three elements: (1) the *subject,* some aspect of "the human spectacle"; (2) the author's *conception* of that spectacle as it exists in his mind or imagination; (3) the *making* of the representation that expresses the author's conception; (4) the author's product, the *text;* (5) the *interpretation* of the text by the theatrical company (for James, chiefly the actors' interpretations of their roles); and (6) the spectacle of the theatrical *production* itself. Although on the one hand he recognized that the playwright "leads us into his own mind, his own vision of things: that's the only place into which the poet *can* lead us" (*SA,* 229), on the other he was able to appreciate the totality of the spectacle created by as good a theatrical representation as the Théâtre Français was able to produce:

> Never has [the spectator] seen anything so smooth and harmonious, so artistic and completed. He has heard all his life of attention to detail, and now, for the first time, he sees something that deserves that name. He sees dramatic effort refined to a point with which the English stage is unacquainted. He sees that there are no limits to possible "finish," and that so trivial an act as taking a letter from a servant or placing one's hat on a chair may be made a suggestive and interesting incident. (*SA,* 72–3)

James's emphasis on the theatrical representation makes for a crucial difference between his conception of the aesthetic process and Howells's. Although Howells considered acting an entirely separate art from the making of the drama, he did not distinguish between the author's vision and the actor's in the *conception* of the theatrical representation. This for him was the playwright's business; the actor simply collaborated in its full realization at a given moment. In essence, the differences between the two critics' versions of representation are differences of complexity in their conceptions of the aesthetic process. They agreed that its ultimate goal was the illusion of reality in a theatrical production; they agreed that the subject of realistic drama was human life; they agreed that the artist's vision of his subject must be rendered as faithfully as possible. James simply recognized that there was more than one artist involved.

STAGECRAFT

In discussing the realists' theory of drama, I have posited six categories that correspond to their major concerns: stagecraft, acting, dialogue, thought, character, and structure. Stagecraft was the first of the drama's parts to receive the label "realism." The "historical" productions of Irving and Mansfield; the detailed reproduction of "real scenes" by Belasco, Harrigan, Herne, and their imitators; the spectacular productions of sawmills, railroad trains, ice floes, and other extravagant effects by Daly, Mackaye, Belasco, and the wizards of the melodrama everywhere – all were well known in the seventies and eighties. To nineteenth-century minds, in fact, realism in a theatrical context meant not the *representation* of reality but the wholesale importation of its furniture onto the stage, a situation that led the realistic actor, manager, and playwright William Gillette to distinguish between "actualism" in stagecraft – the use of real objects for their own sake – and the "artistic representation of reality."[26]

The popular audience had a hard time understanding that the artistic representation of a parlor did not necessarily mean oriental rugs and mahogany furniture, and that oriental rugs and mahogany furniture by no means constituted the artistic representation of a parlor. It became such a commonplace to equate realism in a production with genuine antique furniture and costumes designed from plates in Renaissance books that James was driven to uncharacteristically caustic hyperbole when describing the London theaters in 1877:

> It is a point of honour with the Prince of Wales's to have nothing that is not "real." In the piece now running at this establishment there is a representation of a boudoir very delicately appointed, the ceiling of which is formed by festoons of old lace suspended tent fashion or pavilion fashion. This lace, I am told, has been ascertained, whether by strong opera glasses or other modes of enquiry I know not, to be genuine, ancient, and costly. This is the very pedantry of perfection, and makes the scenery somewhat better than the actors. If the tendency is logically followed out, we shall soon be having Romeo drink real poison and Medea murder a fresh pair of babes every night. (*SA*, 107)

His main complaint about this actualism in scenery concerned the emphasis it was given: "Scenery and decorations have been brought to their highest perfection, while elocution and action, the interpretation of meanings, the representation of human feelings, have not been made the objects of serious study" (*SA*, 165). This, he said, made for serious problems in the drama: "There is evidently a corrosive principle in the large command of machinery and decorations – a germ of perversion and corruption. It gets the upper hand – it becomes the master" (*SA*, 230).

James supported actualism in stagecraft when it served the illusion of the whole, however. He recalled with pleasure a play at the Théâtre Français with "a certain Sunday dinner, in the first act, of which the lavish realism makes the reader's mouth water" (*SA*, 66). More seriously, he praised the actualistic details of Ibsen's staging precisely for their contribution to the play's realism, their expression of the play's meaning through the fuller representation of its world:

> . . . the hideous carpet and wall-paper and curtains (one may answer for them), the conspicuous stove, the lonely centre-table, the "lamps with green shades," as in the sumptuous first act of *The Wild Duck,* the pervasive air of small interests and standards, the sign of limited local life. It represents the very clothes, the inferior fashions, of the figures that move before us, and the shape of their hats and the tone of their conversation and the nature of their diet. (*SA*, 249)

On the whole, Howells paid less attention to setting than James did, and less attention to all of the drama's production elements. When he did mention stagecraft, however, his words echoed James's. When Coquelin appeared in *Thermidor,* "washing his hands at a toilet set which proclaimed itself from Sixth Avenue in stand, basin, and pitcher, and had every effect of having been marked down to ninety-eight cents," Howells seized the opportunity to voice his views in favor of suggestiveness over actualism:

> With the modern luxury of theatrical appointments the play has become a property, and the properties have usurped a dramatic importance. To the true lover of the art the last degree of sketchiness in the *entourage* is consistent with the illusion. Taste must be used; but good taste is not expensive; it is commonly bad taste that is expensive; and a little money will go a great way in realizing all the important effects of a stage background. It should never be more than a background, for the action alone can constitute the picture.[27]

The aesthetic principle here is clear: The function of stagecraft is to assist the illusion – it is suggestive and not simply reflective. And if the real thing does not help to establish the illusion, the real thing is not appropriate to the representation. Steele Mackaye made a concise and intelligent statement on the function of stagecraft in realistic production. His crucial distinction is between the reality of the object for its own sake and the choice of only such objects as support the illusion of reality in the total production:

> In the mechanics of stage setting the greatest law is that which RUSKIN applied to architecture, "Appropriateness, utility, fidelity." Thus, for example, the artisan makes a library scene of impossible painted bookcases, and the furniture of a parlor such as is displayed in an ordinary shop-window. Another artisan presents a ballroom by crowding together as much handsome furniture and useless decoration as the scene will contain. A true artist will have real books and the paraphernalia of scholarship in the one case, and only the furniture and decorations which good manners and common-sense allow in the other.[28]

ACTING

Although they were in fundamental agreement about realistic staging, the realists parted company when it came to acting. James considered the actor's art an integral part of the aesthetic process. Howells, on the other hand, held that acting "is a thing apart and a subordinate affair; though it can give such exquisite joy if it truly interprets a true thing."[29] Far from granting the actor a creative role in the process of representation, he held that it was "the subordinate affair of the actor to adapt himself to the poet's conception, and find it theatricable."[30]

James believed that the actor, like any other artist, must be granted his donnée – in this case, his conception of the character he was to play. It was the actor's task to come up with a conception of the role that was actable, and, indeed, "the most intelligent performer is he who recognizes most surely this 'actable' and distinguishes in it the more from the less" (*SA*, 234). Nevertheless, James maintained, "we are so far from being in possession of a subjective pattern to which we have a right to hold him that he is entitled directly to contradict any such absolute by presenting us with different versions of the same text, each completely coloured, completely consistent with itself" (*SA*, 234). The actor's task was the perfect expression of his role conceived within the context of the total theatrical illusion. To James a bad actor was an actor who failed at any point either in the expression of his conception or in the maintenance of the total illusion. Thus, he spoke of the lesson to be learned from the "finest creations" of Coquelin, "the lesson that acting is an art, and that the application of an art is style, and that style is expression" (*SA*, 200). As for the conception itself, James generally thought that the fuller it was, the better it was, and again his highest praise was for Coquelin. He used Coquelin's Duc de Septmonts, his "finest stroke in the field of a closer realism" (*SA*, 216), as an example of realistic acting par excellence:

> Fine indeed the aesthetic sense and the applied means that can invite, that can insidiously encourage, a conception to so mature and materialize, and that can yet so keep it in the tone of life as we commonly know life, keep it above all "in the picture" in which it is concerned and in relation to the other forms of truth that surround it, forms it may not barbarously sacrifice. M. Coquelin's progress through this long and elaborate part, all of fine shades and pointed particulars, all resting on the keenest observation as well as appealing to it, resembles the method of the "psychological" novelist who (when he is in as complete possession of his form as M. Coquelin of *his*) builds up a character, in his supposedly uncanny process, by touch added to touch, line to line, illustration to illustration, and with a vision of his personage breathing steadily before him. (*SA*, 216)

James's appreciation of realism in the style of the actor was discriminating, however. He praised the "gift of quiet realism, of mingled vehemence and discretion, of impassioned self-control" (*SA*, 48–9) in a young actor, but he objected to "that tendency to underact which is the pitfall of the new generation" (*SA*, 156). Contrasting consciously realistic acting with the older classical style, he complained that "the acting of serious or sentimental comedy and of scenes that may take place in modern drawing-rooms – the acting that corresponds to the contemporary novel of manners – seems by an inexorable necessity given over to amateurishness" (*SA*, 110), and he claimed that "the clever people on the London stage to-day aim at a line of effect in which their being 'amateurs' is almost a positive advantage. Small, realistic comedy is their chosen field, and the art of acting as little as possible has – doubtless with good results in some ways – taken the place of the art of acting as much"

(*SA*, 135). In other words, acting in the new "quiet" style of realism was absolutely necessary to maintain the illusion of reality in modern realistic plays, but it could be inappropriate and useless when the illusion being sought was that evoked by Shakespearean or classical drama. "The truth is," he wrote,

> no artist need expect to play parts demanding style and elevation in this familiar juxtaposition and alternation with the 'realistic' drama of the period. . . . Realism is a very good thing, but it is like baking a pudding in a porcelain dish; your pudding may be excellent but your dish gets cracked. An actor who attempts to play Shakespeare must establish for himself a certain Shakespearean tradition; he must make sacrifices. We are afraid that as things are going, most actors find it easier to sacrifice Shakespeare than to sacrifice to him. (*SA*, 34)

For James, it was the illusion that was crucial, not the style of acting. If the illusion on the stage was perfectly maintained, the acting was good. If the illusion was broken, whether by too studied or stagy a performance in a realistic play or by an "amateurish," too quiet rendering of a romantic role, the acting was bad. Realistic acting was quiet, natural, psychologically complete, and "amateurish" when it came to the subtleties of diction and movement. It was the only thing suitable to the modern realistic drama, and it was not suitable to anything else.

Howells showed a more single-minded devotion to the realistic acting style, as well as to the realistic play. In 1895 he praised Frank Mayo's acting as "of the true school, the only school, to my thinking: quiet, refined, with the repose which is the source of all art, and a sort of dignity born of a worthy conception of a most original, a most native character."[31] Of Annie Russell in Bret Harte's hopelessly artificial *Sue* he said, "She was even in its most artificial phases simple and natural, and where she was suffered the smallest chance for truth she made it tell to the utmost."[32] For James this approach to the part would have been inappropriate, the very naturalness of the acting calling attention to the artificial conventions of the play and thereby breaking the dramatic illusion. Howells stood by the realistic style in all aspects of the drama, however, claiming, "It is always better to underdo than to overdo," though admitting, "It is still better simply to do."[33]

He ascribed the awkwardness in the juxtaposition of realistic acting and artificial drama to the drama's failure to keep up with the actor rather than to the actor's failure to adapt to the drama:

> It has seemed to me that the actor generally, by instinct or inspiration, has now seized the ideal of truthfulness, and that when the author has given him a true thing to do, he has done it well. Whereas, when he has given him a false thing to do, he has seemed embarrassed and helpless. . . . I do not say that he has yet thought out the reason of his

defeat, in such cases, but I will say that the unreality of the work given him was the reason of it. I have fancied him almost pathetically glad of the chance of being natural and lifelike, and when he could not be so because the part given him had no life or nature in it, that he pathetically did his best to put life and nature into it. I speak of him, when I mean her too, and I think it a duty, as certainly it is a pleasure, to bear witness to the general advance of the histrionic art among us. It has advanced because of the refinement and elevation of all art through the insistence on the ideal of truthfulness which most critics of art have contested.[34]

Although they differed in their commitment to the quiet, natural style of realism, the two critics agreed in their fundamental belief that the illusion of truth was crucial to the actor's art. They both approved of the increasing demand being made by the contemporary dramatists for perfection in this illusion, from the broadest sweep of historical verisimilitude to the deepest psychological motives.

DIALOGUE

James and Howells were nearly silent on the subject of dialogue in their drama criticism. This is surprising when one considers the evolution dialogue was undergoing from the stage language of a *Hazel Kirke* to the more natural patterns of speech that Herne and Howells himself attempted during the nineties, not to mention the great interest in dialect that Harrigan touched off, a staple of American drama for fifty years to come. They mention only the stage conventions of the soliloquy and the aside, which they were anxious to see eliminated. Howells made periodic complaints about these disruptions of the illusion of reality, one as late as 1895:

> The soliloquy prevailed, as I notice that it does in most plays new and old. Its prevalence is the most discouraging thing in the work of the playwrights, for it ought never to be, and the smallest art would eliminate it. The soliloquy is of course supposed to represent what is going on in the character's mind; but it always, and at its best, sounds as if he were talking to himself, which would be imaginable and fit in a lunatic like Don Quixote, but in no sane man. It is a little less disillusioning than the aside, but not much less.[35]

He was happy to commend William Gillette two years later for having "wholly cast away these poor crutches, these feeble props of the drama, and required his piece to stand quite on its own feet, as any dramatist addressing a modern audience may and should."[36] These conventions may seem a small matter, but if a play could certainly fail at realism without them, one could by no means succeed at it with them. Likewise, their presence was enough to damn a play in the eyes of a realist, and their absence would signal realism to any reviewer during the nineties.

Although dialogue was not of primary concern to Howells and James, it proved an important element in realistic drama's development. H. A. Kennedy, a contemporary who had observed the function of dialogue in the well-made play and found it wanting, was more specific: "The dialogue in much modern drama is, an inch below the surface, intensely conventional; the words, may be, are colloquial, but the mood of mind, the sequence of ideas, is rhetorical – parliamentary."[37] This is precisely the kind of dialogue Aristotle would have approved of – "language embellished with each kind of artistic ornament"[38] – dialogue with an inherently rhetorical function. The new drama required what, as Kennedy observed, Ibsen was doing for it. With Ibsen, he said, "the anatomy of human discourse is more profoundly understood. . . . only the clever people say clever things, and so dramatically is the dialogue studied that in the strongest situations no rhetorical flourishes are required."[39] Dialogue was seen no longer either as simply a means of moving the plot along by keeping the salient facts of the situation before the audience or as a means of displaying the thought or theme of the piece in as rhetorical a frame as possible, but like dialogue in the realistic novel, as a major means of characterization. The discovery of the simple principle that only the clever people in a play should say clever things was a watershed for realistic drama.

Of course, characterization was not thought of as the sole function of realistic dialogue. Although as radical a realist as Howells would declare that the drama could and should exist solely for the illustration of character, most realistic dramatists were to follow Shaw's lead in making sure that the characters had something to say that was worth listening to. As we shall see, however, even in the primarily thought-centered drama of discussion whose development during and after the 1890s was spurred by Shaw's *Quintessence of Ibsenism,* the realistic dramatist was always careful to work for consistency between character and dialogue. The realistic playwright's stylistic aim for dialogue became chiefly to maintain the illusion that the audience was overhearing a conversation. Not only did the dialogue have to be appropriate to each character, it also had to be believable within the setting of the conversation and its context. Dialect was no longer simply one more trick for the clown to amuse the audience with, but an aspect of human speech to be used for increasing the illusion of reality in the production. Colloquial language and slang became appropriate for the hero and even the heroine as the playwright tried to heighten the sense that his characters were people rather than stock dramatic types. As was true of all the elements of realism, the standards for dialogue were relative, depending on the drama's stage of development, but its major characteristics – appropriateness to character and consistency with the dramatic situation and setting – were part of the realist's goal of maintaining the overall illusion of reality in the production.

THOUGHT

The thought or theme in the drama received a great deal of attention from Howells and James, as well as from other realist critics. They differed in their views on the representation of thought to the extent that they differed in their approaches to didacticism in literature. For James, the subject of a play, like the subject of any other literary work, was the donnée. He objected to any notion that the subject might be interfered with, as in the case of *Hedda Gabler:* "There are many things in the world that are past finding out, and one of them is whether the subject of a work had not better have been another subject. We shall always do well to leave that matter to the author (*he* may have some secret for solving the riddle); so terrible would his revenge easily become if we were to accept a responsibility for his theme" (*SA,* 251). For James, "In a drama the subject is of the essence of the work – it *is* the work. . . . if it is shapeless, the work must be amorphous."[40] Indeed, as he said of Ibsen's work, it is the subject that generates the structure: "His violent substance imposes, as it were, his insidious form; it is not (as would have seemed more likely) the form that imposes the substance" (*SA,* 291). It is important to remember, though, that in James's opinion a play's *quality* was dependent not on the quality of its thought but on the thought's aesthetic development. Vehemently rejecting the notion that a play could be a bad work of art because it embodied bad morality, he declared that "the only immorality I know on the stage is the production of an ill-made play" (*SA,* 108), and that "the highest morality, for a play, is that it be very well made" (*SA,* 114).

On the whole, Howells had less trouble seeing a fundamentally didactic mission for the drama than James did. He admired the British "problem playwrights" greatly, and he held that "we shall never have a national drama till our playwrights approach social and psychological problems in the spirit of their liberal art, and deal with them as simply, freely, and faithfully."[41] An early champion of Ibsen, Howells defended the moral and sociological emphasis of his problem plays against those who said that such subject matter had no place in the drama:

> A great many good, elderly minded people think it dreadful Ibsen should show us that the house we have lived in so long is full of vermin, that its drainage is bad, that the roof leaks and the chimney smokes abominably; but if it is true, is it not well for us to know it? It is dreadful because it is so, not because he shows it so; and the house is no better because our fathers got on in it as it is. . . . It is really no concern of

mine whether he solves his problems or not; generally, I see that he does not solve them, and I see that life does not. . . . It is not by the solution of problems that the moralist teaches, but by the question that his handling of them suggests to us respecting ourselves. Artistically he is bound, Ibsen as a dramatist is bound, to give an aesthetic completeness to his works, and I do not find that he ever fails to do this; to my thinking they have a high beauty and propriety; but ethically he is bound not to be final; for if he forces himself to be final in things that do not and can not end here, he becomes dishonest. [42]

Although he could separate "aesthetic completeness" from ethical or moral completeness, Howells held that "art and truth are forever bound up in each other,"[43] and therein lay an inconsistency. On the one hand, because he believed that art and truth were inseparable, he had to maintain theoretically that aesthetic form *is* truth. But because, as he said, life does not solve moral problems, and thus does not provide closure to human experience, any work of art that did so artificially in order to be satisfying aesthetically would fail at being true to human experience, and thus be bad art from a realist's point of view. He laid out the problem without producing any clear resolution during his discussion of a British problem play:

The play left me with some very grave misgivings as to the usefulness of the moral problem in the drama. That is, it gave me question whether it could well be made the chief interest of a play; for there is great danger that it may be falsely solved, or else shirked, which is nearly as bad. I asked myself whether the play would not be better to be simply a picture of life, resting for its success upon incident and character, without those crucial events which in life are so rarely dramatic, but which, when they come, arrive with as little ceremony as the event of dinner or of death. I said that, after all, morality is an affair of being, rather than of doing, that the same action was not always as bad or as good at all times or for all persons; and that without more room than the drama can possibly give itself, it cannot be shown in its real relation to life, in its proportion, its value. [44]

Howells never achieved a satisfactory resolution of the form–content problem. Dramatic structure as he knew it remained a procrustean imposition on human experience, one that was not true to the rhythms of life and that was, therefore, inadequate to the task of depicting character in its sociological as well as its psychological and moral dimensions. On the other hand, he tried to analyze dramatic structure in terms of life, wherever possible making the connection between the particular way of life that was the play's subject and the dramatic structure that rose out of it. One of his major interests, the contrast between the British and American societies, led to an interesting perspective on the drama. Generalizing about the British and American plays of the 1903–4 season, Howells drew some sociological conclusions about their thought:

> The English plays have to do with man as a society man, both in the narrower and the wider sense, and the American plays have to do with man as a family man; and I hope that a little thought about them will confirm the reader in any impression he may have that with us the main human interest is the home, and that with the English the main human interest is society. But lest we should be unduly proud of our difference from the English in this point, I hasten to suggest that this is because in the narrower English sense we have no society, and if we have a great deal of home, it is because we are still almost entirely rustic in origin, and preponderantly simple in our conceptions of happiness. In the wider sense we certainly have society; and it is a defect of our playwrighting that it does not carry over from the home to humanity. Its interest does not live from man to man, but from men to women, and from women to men; it has no implications; its meanings are for the given time and place only.[45]

Howells's assumed connection between form and meaning is obvious in his remarks about the dramatic forms produced by the two countries:

> To go from the American to the English plays is to pass from clever sketches, from graphic studies, brilliant suggestions, to finished pictures. It may be that we shall never produce such finished pictures as the English, at least till our conditions have lost their provisional character. Perhaps our drama is the more genuine in sympathizing with the provisionality of our conditions, and it may be that our success is still to be in the line of sketches, studies, suggestions.[46]

Despite the inconsistencies that arise in a theory that must be gleaned from occasional writings on the drama over a fifty-year period and, to be fair to both James and Howells, was not intended as a unified statement, it is clear that both realists believed in an inherent connection between structure and meaning. It is equally clear that they differed about which of these deserved more emphasis. For Howells, the subject, by which he sometimes also meant the depiction of character, was of prime importance; for James, it was the dramatic structure. Howells saw the drama as depicting and thereby serving society. James saw it as serving society by being good art. The difference in emphasis is obviously crucial. As we shall see, some realistic playwrights chose to emphasize structure; some, to emphasize character and thought. The most successful were to achieve balance through the integration of these three important elements.

CHARACTER

As might be expected, although there is a fundamental agreement about the realistic depiction of character in the writings of the two critics, there is a difference in emphasis. Although James was more concerned with the actor's conception of his role than with the dramatist's conception of the character, he did insist that the character must be a psychologically believable individual at the same time that he must be a recognizably conventional type. In other words, character, in the Aristotelian sense of the human qualities that precipitate action, must be easily recognizable in the shorthand of theatrical convention, but characters must also be recognizable as people who perform the actions of real people in real life. The character should operate both in the code of the text (the dramatist's representation of the "real world") and in the conventional theatrical code of the production. This required a fine sense of balance on the playwright's part, and James the reviewer was quick to object when it was thrown off in either direction. For example, he complained that George Alexander as the forsaken young lover in *Young Folks' Ways* "rather neglects the realities of the part, scantily as they are indicated in the drama. He has not had enough in his eye the particular young man whom Miss Rogers would have been likely to be engaged to. . . . The part, in truth, however, strikes us as vague and false" (*SA,* 196–7). But too much individual and too little type was an error at the other end of the scale, and he complained about Ibsen's "habit of dealing essentially with the individual caught in the fact": "Sometimes, no doubt, he leans too far on that side, loses sight too much of the type-quality and gives his spectators free play to say that even caught in the fact his individuals are mad. We are not at all sure, for instance, of the type-quality in Hedda" (*SA,* 255).

Howells, who came down firmly on the side of the individual as opposed to the type, was more likely to complain that "there is often more of type than of character in [Ibsen's] personages."[47] For him character in the drama meant not so much qualities as personality, and he was quite clear about the centrality of its depiction in the drama: "What gives us most pleasure in a play is, I am sure, the representation of character, of mere personality, if that is something less than character. What we enjoy is Mr. Jefferson's quality, Mr. Wilson's quality, Mr. Drew's quality, in the expression of this or that type."[48] Not only did he reject James's distinction between the world of the theatrical representation and the "real" world, he also rejected a distinction between the character and the actor. As long as the illusion of a "real person" was complete on the stage, it made little difference to him whether the personality originated from the playwright's conception, the actor's conception, or the actor's unconscious presence as himself on the stage. He was concerned with nuance in the illusion, however, for he thought that "nothing could be better than the neatness, the fineness, with which the shades of character are given in Mr. Mulligan's Irish people; and this literary conscientiousness is supplemented by acting which is worthy of it."[49]

Fine shades of character were not enough for Howells, however. He complained of *The Governor of Kentucky* that although "the people are mostly live people . . . they behave with the motives and emotions of the immemorial puppets of the stage."[50] For him the character must be a complete and finely drawn individual, psychologically believable and recognizable as a "personality" in real life. Far from seeking the balance between individual and theatrical type that James was after, Howells rejected any use of dramatic action inconsistent with the personal psychological motives of the characters. The shorthand of dramatic convention was as antirealistic to him as the stage heroes, heroines, and villains created to experience the stage jealousy, passion, revenge, and rage that kept the typical nineteenth-century melodrama moving along.

Again the difference between the two points of view reflects the difference in emphasis of the two critics. For James, who saw the plot as central, characters were important largely as forces that motivate purposeful action, the Aristotelian notion of *praxis*. Howells, who wished to deemphasize plot, put the reflection of character, viewed as individual personality, at the center of the drama. In fact, he suggested that his favorite, Harrigan, should have as little of anything else as possible in his plays, declaring that "the plot, as the stage understands it, is purely mischievous for him. . . . Why will not he persuade himself that all he needs, and that all his lovers desire, is the simplest and openest scheme, the merest uninvolved and commonest incident round which his characters can play?"[51]

STRUCTURE

The nineteenth-century realists would have been bewildered by a discussion of literary structure in the critical terms of the 1980s. They made few distinctions among the literary genres of drama beyond the traditional categories of tragedy, comedy, and melodrama. Not only did they not concern themselves with niceties of distinction among such terms as *fabula* and *sjuzet, mythos* and *praxis,* "genre," "form," "plot," "linear structure," "narrative sentence," and so on; they tended to use such terms as "plot," "form," "structure," "incident," and "action" with a loose interchangeableness that can make translating their ideas about structure into contemporary critical language rather difficult. Nevertheless, it is important to define the issues that existed for them and to get as clear a sense as possible of how they expected a playwright to conceive of realistic dramatic structure.

In his little dramatic sketch "After the Play" (1889), James defined the central point of the controversy over structure. Referring to a production of *Duc d'Enghien,* one character says, "It appealed to me, touched me,

offered me a poignant suggestion of the way things happen in life."
Whereupon another character retorts, "In life they happen clumsily,
stupidly, meanly. One goes to the theatre just for the refreshment of
seeing them happen in another way – in symmetrical, satisfactory form,
with unmistakable effect and just at the right moment" (SA, 227–8). It is
tempting to see Howells and James in the roles of these two characters,
although neither's conception of dramatic structure was as simple as
those the characters express. The question lurking behind the disagreement is simply, What *is* dramatic structure? Is it a single and specific
pattern of events with a recognizable "organic" form ("all one and continuous," as James said of fiction), or can it be a loosely connected series
of situations displaying the characters and the social conditions in which
they function? James, on the whole, expressed faith in the existence of a
recognizable dramatic form. His rather rigid notion of form emerges
from his review of Tennyson's *Queen Mary*, often quoted as evidence of
his infatuation with the French well-made play:[52]

> The five-act drama – serious or humorous, poetic or prosaic – is like a
> box of fixt dimensions and inelastic material, into which a mass of
> precious things are to be packed away. The precious things in question
> seem out of all proportion to the compass of the receptacle; but the artist
> has an assurance that with patience and skill a place may be made for
> each, and that nothing need be clipped or crumpled, squeezed or
> damaged. The false dramatist either knocks out the sides of his box or
> plays the deuce with the contents; the real one gets down on his knees,
> disposes of his goods tentatively, this, that, and the other way, loses his
> temper but keeps his ideal and at last rises in triumph, having packed his
> coffer in the one way that is mathematically right. It closes perfectly,
> and the lock turns with a click; between one object and another you
> cannot insert the point of a penknife.[53]

James made no secret that he thought this restrictive form "almost
intolerable" (SA, 64) and that he thought it was often necessary to sacrifice "the highest advantage of the literary" to it (SA, 273). Nevertheless,
he confessed to his brother William that "as for the form itself its honor
and inspiration are its difficulty. If it were easy to write a good play I
couldn't and wouldn't think of it; but it is in fact damnably hard."[54] And
he considered Ibsen's mastery of form his major accomplishment:

> He arrives for all his meagreness at intensity. The meagreness, which is
> after all but an unconscious, an admirable economy, never interferes
> with that: it plays straight into the hands of his rare mastery of form.
> The contrast between this form – so difficult to have reached, so civi-
> lized, so "evolved," – and the bareness and bleakness of his little north-
> ern democracy is the source of half the hard frugal charm that he puts
> forth. (SA, 293)

For all his emphasis on form, however, it was the purposed action that was the absolute heart of the drama for James, as he wrote in a letter in 1909:

> A play appears to me of necessity to involve a struggle, a question of whether and how, will it or won't it happen? And if so, or not so, how and why? – [in] which we have the suspense, the curiosity, the anxiety, the *tension,* in a word of seeing; and which means that the whole thing shows an attack upon oppositions – with the victory or the failure on one side or the other, and each wavering and shifting from point to point.[55]

In the context of realism's development in the theater, James's notion of dramatic structure must be recognized as fundamentally Aristotelian and conservative. Howells's notion was at the opposite end of the spectrum. Because he believed that drama should be precisely the representation of a condition or of a character and not of an action, he rejected what he saw as the artificial imposition of traditional dramatic structure on human experience. He objected strenuously to the critical adulation of the French, and voiced contempt for the well-made play:

> Many [critics] know what a French play is, for they have seen enough adaptations of French plays to have learned to admire their extremely neat carpentry, and their carefully adjusted and brilliantly varnished sections, which can be carried to any climate, and put together and taken apart as often as you like, without making them less representative of anything that ever was in the world. They have been struck with the ingenious regularity of the design in these contrivances; they have seen how smoothly they worked, and they have formed such dramatic theories as they have from dramas in which situation links into situation, and effect into effect, upon lines of such admirable rigidity that it is all as unerring as making up a train of cars with the Miller Coupler and Buffer.[56]

Howells not only pointed out the error of his ways to any otherwise realistic playwright whose work showed a trace of the coupler and buffer, he even claimed that "the effort to work out a plot of the sort supposed essential to a play warped [Harrigan] from his true function as a painter of life, and merged in the coarse colors of a melodrama the delightful *nuances* with which he realizes character both in his writing and his acting."[57] He suggested that, in the place of the old artificial structures, the playwright commit himself to Harrigan's usual " 'prolongation of sketches.' People may or may not call it a play: we are sure it will be a charming piece of dramatic art."[58] In short, he sought the playwright's "liberation"[59] from all the conventions of plot, and the establishment of a drama that took its structure not from the artificial conventions of the theater but from the natural rhythms inherent in life. As for the problem of aesthetic completeness, he believed there was an inherent unity in life that could be derived *from* men-in-action rather than imposed *on* it. Harrigan's "prolongation of sketches" was the best the new realism had so far evolved in the way of structure, but Howells had hopes. Charles Klein's *Maggie Pepper* had unified a "succession of situations to 'one divine far-off' event . . . transferring from nature those wilding growths of our new conditions which we have but to see with the vision of art to know for fresh and wonderful."[60] As we have seen, Howells also thought it in keeping with sociological reality that the British could produce a "finished picture" whereas the Americans could only manage a sketch. America's freer social conditions were reflected in free literary forms; and Britain's elaborate social institutions, in elaborate literary forms.

An interesting offshoot of Howells's notion that dramatic form imitates content is his attitude toward the "dramatic unities" as enunciated by the neoclassical school. Far from considering unity of time, place, and action artificial restraints imposed on the playwright, he approved of them precisely because he saw them as developing directly from the rhythm of life and therefore coming to the playwright instinctively. Speaking of *Secret Service,* Howells said, "I do not know whether Mr. Gillette bothers himself much about the classical unities . . . but I was vastly interested to see how closely, with or without knowing it, he had observed them."[61] In a later article, he called the unity of time an "instinctive concession to probability" and hypothesized that "deep in the heart perhaps is the wish to see a play which should be confined in the action not only to twenty-four hours, but to just the time that it would take for the events really to happen. This alone would satisfy Nature, however lenient Aristotle might be."[62]

Howells's notion of dramatic structure is by far the most radical, and also the most naive, of those held by the nineteenth-century realists. If he could entirely have done away with structure as the theater knew it, and simply had a genuine slice of life represented for three hours on the stage, he would have been happy, so long as he thought it recognizably true to psychological and sociological reality. Of course, his naiveté was in some sense prophetic. Doing away with the artificial structures of theatrical tradition was also freeing the drama for the structures that eventually did arise from the rhythms of life after the turn of the century.

The two basic notions about dramatic structure that arise from realist criticism seem to conflict. James's idea was that a play must "of necessity . . . involve a struggle, a question of whether and how, will it or won't it happen" – that is, *praxis,* or, as S. H. Butcher defined it, a "psychic energy working outwards"[63] – and that the struggle must be confined with effort into a structure that is "like a box of fixt dimensions and inelastic material." This notion seems radically opposed to Howells's idea of a "prolongation of sketches" for the illustration of character, or an "outward truth" to match the "inward truth" of the play's reflection of life, as well as with James's own statement that the "substance" imposes the form. Nor is the apparent contradiction between the imposition of a fixed structure and the reflection of a pattern from the events in life simply a problem with these two critics. The two apparently conflicting assumptions that realism has a fixed, "well-made" structure and that its structure is based on the reflection of life are apparent even in modern critical works such as John Gassner's otherwise acute study *Form and Idea in Modern Theatre*. There they make for such contradictory statements as that "in the writing of the new-fashioned realistic plays after 1875 there was, indeed, virtually a return to neoclassic structure"[64] and, within a few pages, that "the good realistic playwright has not felt constrained to adhere to rules of neat packaging."[65]

But perhaps the two notions are not as antithetical as they appear. Two principles are involved in the shaping of the realistic work of art, Aristotle's *mimesis* and *harmonia,* imitation and harmony. Harry Levin has noted that Aristotle "authorizes us, if we seek the sanction of classical authority, to require of a work of imagination not only that it be true to life but that it shape life into a pattern, that it stylize its mimicry."[66] In other words, two separate processes are involved in the making of a plot: the reflection of the subject – in this case, the psychological and social life of real people in contemporary society – and the imposition of a pattern on that reflection.

Paul M. Levitt has worked out this distinction neatly as that between form, "the ultimate organization, the appearance of the whole, the overall pattern which results from the conjunction of the parts of a play,"[67] and structure, "the place, relation, and function of scenes in episodes and in the whole play."[68] To put it another way, realistic dramatic *form* is the overall shape of experience derived from the imitation of life in the drama; realistic dramatic *structure* is the specific patterning of events or episodes within that form. The problem for the study of dramatic realism is not so much whether the views of Howells and James can be resolved as whether a dramatic structure that embodies form derived from the observation of human experience was in fact created by realistic dramatists. Or it might be more accurate to ask, Can the free form of human experience accommodate an artistic dramatic structure? According to Emile Zola, "Nature is all we need; it is necessary to accept her as she is, without modifying her or diminishing her in any respect; she is sufficiently beautiful and great to provide a beginning, a middle, and an end."[69] Howells obviously agreed, but more conservative critics like James remained skeptical.

The disagreement over the primacy of character versus the primacy of structure raises a similar question. As we have seen, Howells tended to talk about the drama as a series of incidents for the illustration of character; James, as a continuous action. The crucial point is that emphasizing character does not necessarily mean doing away with plot. As Harold Kolb puts it, "The realists prefer character analysis to gunfights off the Barbary Coast, but they do not accept the seesaw theory of plot and character in which one goes up as the other goes down. Plot for the realists is inextricably linked to character; narrative action is a result of character; people make events."[70] Of the drama, Northrop Frye wrote, "as an imitation of life, drama is, in terms of *mythos,* conflict; in terms of *ethos* [character], a representative image; in terms of *dianoia* [thought], the final harmonic chord revealing the tonality under the narrative movement, it is community."[71] It is essential, both to realism as a literary theory and to drama as a genre, to view the various parts of the play not in isolation but in relation to one another. As James often said of fiction, incident illustrates character; character determines incident.

It was natural at a time when diagrams of rising and falling action seemed to define the drama that a realist like Howells should emphasize the depiction of character in the drama as he did the treatment of social issues. It was probably also natural for writers like Howells and James, primarily novelists, to see the relatively overstructured drama of their day as an unnatural manipulation of human experience. They tended to overlook the fact that in the drama as in the novel, the structure could be built up *in terms* of the characters, thus producing a much more natural piece of work than one in which incidents were structured arbitrarily and conventionally to achieve the emotional effect they were seeing in the melodrama and the well-made play. It is possible, as J. A. Withey has demonstrated, to base a theory of dramatic structure on characters and their relationships, one in which a scene is defined as a "language unit that is complete when there is a change of relationship between characters in the course of the dramatic action," and in which "what the scene describes is a relationship integral to the total human experience that is the play."[72] This is precisely what the twentieth-century American realistic playwrights achieved when, at their best, they wrote plays in which all the parts worked in one harmonious design of reflecting reality in dramatic form. The dramatic action arose from the informing principle of the thought; it developed in terms of the character; and its stagecraft produced as complete an illusion of reality as was possible within the technical limits of the theater. But the evolutionary process that produced this drama was a slow one, and it was four decades before the drama imperfectly envisioned by the literary realists of the 1880s reached its full development.

On this issue of dramatic form, Howells and James seem to represent two opposing camps in the criticism of those committed to the cause of realism. The more traditional writers held out with James for the centrality of action and structure in the drama, and the radicals looked with Howells for ways of structuring the action that emphasized character and setting. Brander Matthews held that the organic unity of the play made good depiction of character impossible without what he called a "sound" structure: "If a drama have not the well-knit story and the artful sequence of situation which permit the characters to reveal themselves decently and in order, no meteor flashes of poetry, no aurora borealis of eloquence, can save it from the deep damnation of its taking off the boards."[73] But he contradicted himself by acknowledging the completeness with which the American characters like Davy Crockett, Rip Van Winkle, Colonel Sellers, and Joshua Whitcomb had been depicted in plays that were often "feeble, forced, and false, shabby in structure and shambling in action."[74]

From Herne and Harrigan, working playwrights and conscious followers of Howells, one gets a practical sense of what plot was on the nineteenth-century American stage, and what changes realism could make in its conventions. Herne compares the situation in 1897 with that of twenty years before:

> We had tragedy, melodrama, domestic drama, spectacle, and farce. The standard drama of that day was a drama of plot rather than of purpose. The dramatist was concerned first of all with his plot. A play without a plot could not have obtained a hearing twenty years ago. In fact it is pretty hard work today to get a hearing for a play based upon theme and character, and depending upon treatment and not upon plot; but twenty years ago such a thing would have been impossible.[75]

For Herne, the reversal of emphasis from plot to character had been a major accomplishment and meant that the drama was making progress toward less artificiality. A more specific description of the unstructured realistic play comes from Harrigan's response to the Palmer charge that he wrote not plays but prolongations of sketches:

> The phrase, a prolongation of sketches, coined by Mr. A. M. Palmer, is not well put regarding my plays. I would say a continuity of incidents, with some simple reason for their dovetailing, and each link on the string sustained by some natural motive that calls for the building of the entire stage structure. In this principle of playmaking, or sketch-prolonging, we find reason for the character-drawing which should be the one great aim of the dramatist.[76]

Whether these playwrights really did what they said they were trying to do is another issue. There is no question that their statements contributed to the theater's development and that there were many serious young playwrights of the next generation who tried to do what they said regardless of what they did.

The realistic theory of drama had its variations, but all the versions shared an assumption of what drama in the realistic mode should be: a representation of the playwright's conception of some aspect of human experience in a given milieu, within the fourth-wall illusion and in the low mimetic style. It should have characters who were individuals as well as social types, a setting that aimed at producing the illusion of the milieu as fully as possible rather than simply importing "real" objects onto the stage, thought that expressed the social issues of the milieu and the psychological conflicts of the characters in dialogue they would naturally speak, a form that was derived from the human experience being depicted, and a structure designed to produce the fullest illusion for the audience that the action onstage was taking place in reality. This notion came to dominate the American theater during the twenties and thirties, but as we shall see, it took a full forty years for it to be established.

3

The Literary Realists as Playwrights

In the essay he wrote about Bret Harte in 1906, Mark Twain recalled his experience as a reporter for the *San Francisco Morning Call* forty years earlier:

> At night we visited the six theaters, one after the other: seven nights in the week, three hundred and sixty-five nights in the year. We remained in each of those places five minutes, got the merest passing glimpse of play and opera, and with that for a text we "wrote up" those plays and operas, as the phrase goes, torturing our souls every night from the beginning of the year to the end of it in the effort to find something to say about those performances which we had not said a couple of hundred times before. There has never been a time from that day to this, forty years, that I have been able to look at even the outside of a theater without a spasm of the dry gripes, as "Uncle Remus" calls it – and as for the inside, I know next to nothing about that, for in all this time I have seldom had a sight of it nor a desire in that regard which couldn't have been overcome by argument.[1]

Writing to his brother William in 1894 of his decision to give one more try to writing plays, Henry James complained, "The whole odiousness of the thing lies in the connection between the drama and the theatre. The one is admirable in its interest and difficulty, the other loathesome in its conditions."[2] Even the gentle Howells complained to James, "It is strange how the stage can keep on fooling us; what the burnt child does *not* dread is the fire, or at least the blue fire of the theatre"[3] (Howells's emphasis).

Despite their vehemently declared antipathy to the theater, these realists were far from closet dramatists. In fact, they were so eager to get their plays on the stage that they were involved in negotiations with a veritable who's who of the American theater at the turn of the century.

James, Howells, Mark Twain, and Bret Harte all had dealings with Augustin Daly, who wanted to produce American plays of literary worth. Howells, James, and Mark Twain also dealt at one time or another with nineteenth-century America's most powerful producer, Daniel Frohman. Howells, like Hamlin Garland, had business dealings as well as a long friendship with James A. Herne. In addition, all of these writers struck close connections with actors and managers in order to get their plays produced: Harte, with Dion Boucicault, C. T. Parsloe, Stuart Robson, and Charles Frohman; Mark Twain, with Parsloe, John T. Raymond, and A. P. Burbank; Howells, with Ellen Terry, Lawrence Barrett, Madge Kendall, William Gillette, A. M. Palmer, and W. H. Crane; James, with Edward Compton, Elizabeth Robins, Genevieve Ward, John Hare, George Alexander, Ada Rehan, Ellen Terry, Harley Granville-Barker, G. B. Shaw, and Charles Frohman. Among them, Mark Twain, Harte, James, and Howells wrote more than sixty plays, either alone or in collaboration. In short, despite their disclaimers, their overall lack of theatrical success was not for lack of trying, and trying hard.

It took some coaxing to get them started, however. According to his biographer, as soon as Augustin Daly's New Fifth Avenue Theatre opened in 1873, he "was active in exciting among the literary Americans of the day the ambition to win fame as playwrights,"[4] and the correspondence quoted in his biography records his substantial efforts as well as the squeamishness of the "literary Americans." Mark Twain expresses interest but time and again pleads pressing work, and finally suggests Howells. Howells confesses that he has "long had the notion of a play," as well as a "farce or vaudeville of strictly American circumstances," but concludes, "of course I'm a very busy man, and I must do these plays in moments of leisure from my editorial work."[5] When Daly finally succeeded in eliciting Bret Harte's interest, he found he had gotten himself a short-story writer when he needed a playwright, for Harte had no notion of dramatic structure. Accustomed to the need for play-doctoring, Daly brought in Dion Boucicault, who agreed to help Harte not only to "reshape Acts 1 and 2" of his projected play but also "to construct in detail Acts 3 and 4, which so far have not been shadowed, much less written."[6] Boucicault's reports to Daly reveal the professional playwright's exasperation with the rather cavalier Harte: "Harte is dilatory and erratic. He is very anxious to get the work done – but thinks we can scurry over the ground more rapidly than is consistent with safety. For your sake – as well as for ours – the piece should be carefully done."[7] The result of this uneven collaboration, a play called *Kentuck,* survives only in the inimitably Boucicault *cast raisonée.* The play never made it to the stage.

BRET HARTE AND MARK TWAIN

Once Daly had started him off, Harte never stopped trying to become a successful playwright. His *Two Men of Sandy Bar,* a play loosely based on his short stories "Mr. Thompson's Prodigal" and "The Idyl of Red Gulch," was produced at the Union Square Theatre in 1876. A year later, his ill-fated collaboration with Mark Twain, *Ah Sin,* was produced at Daly's Fifth Avenue Theatre. After Harte moved to England, he collaborated on a number of adaptations of his stories. Arthur Hobson Quinn mentions dramatizations of *Jeff Briggs' Love Story, Thankful Blossom, The Luck of Roaring Camp, Clarence,* and *A Blue Grass Penelope.*[8] Harte's biographer T. Edgar Pemberton says that he and Harte collaborated on "several other plays,"[9] but the only one that saw production was *Sue* in 1896, a play whose moderate success resulted mainly from Annie Russell's portrayal of the title role.

Harte's collaborator Mark Twain was similarly productive. Before he got together with Harte to write *Ah Sin,* Mark Twain had had considerable financial success with an adaptation of *The Gilded Age,* which he had bought from an obscure playwright named Gilbert Densmore and revised, essentially grafting his dialogue to Densmore's plot.[10] In the hands of John T. Raymond, the play was a successful one-character piece, and Mark Twain's delight in the substantial profits – recorded for posterity in Howell's *My Mark Twain* – prompted him to seek further profit and glory from the drama. He tried first, in 1875, to get Howells to help him with a dramatization of *Tom Sawyer,* but the collaboration never came off, although he submitted a play to Daly in 1884 that Daly's biographer remembered as "Bob Sawyer's Adventures."[11] In October 1876, Mark Twain wrote to Howells, "Bret Harte came up here the other day & asked me to help him write a play & divide the swag."[12] The play was *Ah Sin,* the wedge that severed for good the uneasy friendship between its authors. Undaunted either by the play's failure or by the emotional toll it took, Mark Twain set to work on a new play, *Cap'n Simon Wheeler, Detective,* with enormous energy and enthusiasm. "I have not written less than 30 pages any day since I began," he wrote to Howells. "Never had so much fun over anything in my life – never such consuming interest & delight."[13] His interest flagged, however, and he decided the play needed doctoring, which he planned to get from Howells. Then, early in 1879, he wrote to Howells that he was not going to send him the play after all: "I couldn't find a single idea in it that could be useful to you. It was dreadfully witless & flat. I knew it would sadden you & unfit you for work."[14]

It was not until 1883 that Mark Twain and Howells finally got together for their dramatic collaboration. The play was a sequel to *The Gilded Age* variously entitled *Orme's Motor, The Steam Generator, The*

American Claimant, and *Colonel Sellers as a Scientist,* the title under which it now appears in *The Complete Plays of W. D. Howells.* The Mark Twain–Howells partnership was much more pleasant than the Mark Twain–Harte one had been, but it eventually resulted in a misunderstanding about the proposed production of the play arranged between Mark Twain and A. P. Burbank in 1886, and withdrawal of the play because of Howells's cold feet, at a cost to each playwright of $350. Undaunted, Mark Twain suggested further dramatic experiments with Howells, including a tragedy about Oliver Cromwell and a "Sandwich Island play,"[15] and he made separate arrangements to have the Sellers play produced as *The American Claimant, or, Mulberry Sellers Ten Years Later* at the Lyceum in 1887.

Despite the success of the first Sellers play and of *Sue,* both Harte and Mark Twain would have to be classed as failures at play writing. That their moderate success came in collaboration with others and that they met overwhelming failure when they worked together suggest the source of the problem. When Harte worked wth Boucicault, he mainly provided the local color while Boucicault did the scenario. Howells remarked in *My Mark Twain* that the "structure of [*The Gilded Age*] as John T. Raymond gave it was substantially the work of this unknown dramatist [Densmore]. Clemens never pretended, to me at any rate, that he had the least hand in it; he frankly owned that he was incapable of dramatization."[16] Likewise, as Howells remembered the collaboration on the Sellers sequel, Mark Twain summoned Howells by telegram to Hartford for work on a play before he had any idea what form it would take. Upon his arrival, as Howells recalled:

> I found him with no definite idea of what he [Mark Twain] wanted to do with him [Sellers]. I represented that we must have some sort of plan, and he agreed that we should both jot down a scenario overnight and compare our respective schemes the next morning. . . . I felt authorized to make him observe that his scheme was as nearly nothing as chaos could be. He agreed hilariously with me, and was willing to let it stand in proof of his entire dramatic inability.[17]

As Mark Twain remembered it thirty years later, the work of structuring *Ah Sin* had been left to Harte:

> I named my characters and described them; Harte did the same by his. Then he began to sketch the scenario, act by act, and scene by scene. He worked rapidly and seemed to be troubled by no hesitations or indecisions; what he accomplished in an hour or two would have cost me several weeks of painful and difficult labor, and would have been valueless when I got through. But Harte's work was good and usable; to me it was a wonderful performance.[18]

This view was not shared by actor C. T. Parsloe and manager Augustin Daly when it came to producing the piece, as Mark Twain's opening-night curtain speech revealed:

> When this play was originally completed, it was so long and so wide and so deep (in places) and so comprehensive that it would have taken two weeks to play it. And I thought this was a good feature. I supposed we could have a sign on the curtain, "To be continued," and it would be all right; but the manager said no, that wouldn't do; to play a play two weeks long would be sure to get us into trouble with the Government because the Constitution of the United States says you shan't inflict cruel and unusual punishments. So he set to work to cut it down and cart the refuse to the paper-mill. Now that was a good thing. I never saw a play improve as this one did. The more he cut out of it the better it got right along. He cut out, and cut out, and cut out, and I do believe this would be one of the best plays in the world today if his strength had held out, and he could have gone on and cut out the rest of it.[19]

Considering the play, this isn't a bad piece of drama criticism. As Frederick Anderson remarks in the Preface to his edition, "While *Ah Sin* is not the poorest work by either man, it is not far from it."[20] And its greatest weakness is its structure. Each of them wrote plays with an amazing amount of activity but little sense of structure. *Ah Sin*'s plot is a conglomeration of most of the conventions known to both comedy and melodrama. Its dramatic structure certainly does not originate in any impulse toward realism. It arises from the opposite impulse: to represent as manipulated and convoluted a set of actions as is possible within the confines of conventional form, with the apparent object of removing the play as far from the commonplace action of real life as an active imagination can take it. The realistic dimension in *Ah Sin*, as in *Two Men of Sandy Bar* and *Sue*, is similar to that in the early fiction of Harte and Mark Twain. It consists of the local-color elements of setting, dialogue, and character type. Both authors were keenly aware of the opportunity to exploit the settings of their stories in the plays. Both made full use of the mining camp, and Harte also used a ranch and a San Francisco mansion in *Two Men of Sandy Bar*.

The dialogue similarly juxtaposes disregard for the effect of reality in the total representation with concern for consistency in details. Both writers' plays are full of soliloquies and asides, but they are also full of carefully written dialect suitable both to the milieu and to the character's background and social position. In *Sandy Bar*, Hop Sing speaks in Harte's version of Chinese English – a local-color attempt at humor: "Me wash-ee shirt flo you, flowty dozen hab. You no payee me. Me wantee twenty dollar hep. Sabe."[21] The dialogue is not deeply rooted in the characters, however. Acting for his banker father, Sandy Morton says things like "You have asked for me, sir: may I inquire your business?" (411). On his own at the ranch, he talks to himself in dialect: "I reckon the old man's at his siesta yet. Ef he'll only hang onto that snooze ten minutes longer, I'll manage to let that gal Jovita slip out to that yer fandango, and no questions asked" (311). And when it comes to the love scenes, the dialogue is as conventional as the action. The frontier gambler Oakhurst says in a tender moment, "Still silent? Poor dove! I can hear her foolish heart flutter against mine. Another moment decides our fate" (338).

Mark Twain was more interested than Harte was in creating realistic dialogue. As Anderson notes, "Clemens's chief contribution to *Ah Sin* was his effort to render accurately the rhythms and vocabulary of actual speech, since Harte's dialogue in this play, as in most of his writing, was conventionally stilted and romantic."[22] As evidence for his statement, Anderson cites a number of alterations made by Mark Twain, such as changing Harte's line "I know not what to say" to "Well, I don't know of anything further to say." Thus the dialect that Harte saw as a device to use for a special effect, Mark Twain saw as a vital aspect of dramatic dialogue. His concern for natural cadence did not extend to the use of speech natural to the situation, however. An example of the awkward dialogue resulting from a clumsy attempt to use soliloquy for exposition and characterization occurs in the first scene of *Ah Sin,* when the villain Broderick is alone on stage and says:

> The stage coach broken down, eh? I'm glad of that; it never brought *me* any good. Hello! (*looks off R*) there's that old liar Plunkett, and with a woman in tow. I wonder who she is? One of his family come from the states may be. I don't want to meet any more of the Plunkett tribe. I'll step aside![23]

No doubt Mark Twain would have considered this absurdly clumsy method of characterization and exposition a "literary offense" had it occurred in fiction.

When Mark Twain worked with Howells rather than Harte, his dialogue made a much closer approach to the illusion of reality. In *Colonel Sellers as a Scientist,* the dialect is not a local-color curiosity but is simply speech appropriate to the various character types, including the "Southern colonel," the Negro servant, and the English gentleman. Where there is humor in the dialogue, it resides in the character rather than in a trick of speech, as is the case with Harte's Colonel Starbottle. The only departures from the illusion of the fourth wall in dialogue are occasional asides or soliloquies to indicate a character's process of thought, not to provide exposition.

Like Edward Harrigan's, the characters created by Mark Twain and Harte are a combination of the conventional types of the drama and the local-color types familiar from their fiction. In *Sandy Bar,* for example, Starbottle is the immemorial pedant of comedy with the dress and accent of the Southern colonel; Harte's recognizable "Western" types – the gambler, the drunken but loyal miner, the innocent schoolteacher, the prostitute with the heart of gold, the humorous "Chinaman," the hot-blooded aristocratic Spaniard – fit into their places as heroes and hero-ines, heavy father, scarlet woman, and scheming servant. The same is true of *Ah Sin's* characters. The formula for these local-color dramatists was to graft onto the dramatic stereotype a few recognizable details specific to the place and time, thus producing an agreeable sense of immediacy in the actions of characters whose habitual behavior was as predictable as the eventual outcome of the convoluted plot. In other words, the realism was all on the surface in these plays – in the external codes of costume, diction, and stagecraft.

HENRY JAMES

On the whole, Henry James and William Dean Howells took their play writing much more seriously than Harte and Mark Twain did. Leon Edel has clearly demonstrated James's fundamental tension be-tween enthusiasm for the drama as a literary form and contempt for the theater as a vulgar business.[24] Howells's attitude embodied a similar ambivalence. But both men saw the writing of plays as a literary endeav-or, and a great deal can be learned from the more than fifty plays they wrote between them. James's plays, written over a period of forty years, from 1869 to 1909, provide an interesting parallel to the literary develop-ment of the American theater.[25] During most of those years, he was living and writing in England, and his immediate influences, after he had outgrown his infatuation with the Théâtre Français, were British. Yet six of his fifteen plays are about Americans, and many were written with American actors and managers, and thus the American theater, in mind.

In a sense, James was a striking individual instance of the serious American playwright in the nineteenth century – an American writer with an American audience, an interest in American subjects, and Euro-pean dramatic influences.[26] Like the American theater at large, James went through a series of stages in his dramatic composition. His many experiments with form and structure resulted eventually in drama that combined his own realistic thinking with the influences of Ibsen and Shaw and the sense of tight construction learned from the French and from such British contemporaries as Henry Arthur Jones, Arthur Wing Pinero, and – whether James liked it or not – Oscar Wilde. Leading up to his full development as an original dramatist, James's plays appeared in five fairly distinct phases: early experiments, mixed forms, well-made comedies, Ibsenist melodramas, and Shavian discussion plays.

In one sense, the early experiments are the most interesting of his plays, for they are most purely the work of Henry James, with the fewest preconceptions about what makes a play either theatrically successful or literarily respectable. *Pyramus and Thisbe*, a one-act play written in 1869, embodies a Howellsian realism unheard of in the drama of its time. It has an extremely simple plot about two lonely young residents of a boardinghouse who fall in love, and its action consists entirely of the characters' conversations. Its single dramatic "event" is the realization that the landlord is forcing the young people to leave the boardinghouse, which precipitates their admissions that they care for each other. The revelation of the two characters' feelings takes place simultaneously for the characters and the audience. James does make rather liberal use of soliloquy in the play, but he maintains a hold on the illusion of the fourth wall with the assumption that his heroine, accustomed to living alone, has a habit of talking to herself. At no time does the character break the fourth-wall illusion in order to take the audience into her confidence. The dialogue itself realistically represents the verbal sparring of a bright young mid-century couple who are just beginning to fall in love, with none of the "literariness" that critics like Shaw complained of in James's later dialogue.

Perhaps the most realistic element of the play, however, is James's successful evocation of the boardinghouse milieu without any local-color tricks. The setting is simple but realistic: "*Miss West's apartment; plainly but comfortably furnished; a few prints and photographs on the walls; a sofa, a piano.*"[27] The loneliness and dreariness of the boardinghouse background come out only by allusion in the conversation between the two characters. Invited to stay to tea, Stephen responds, "It's something I never have at all. I dine at six, at an eating-house, where I take a very bad cup of coffee" (80). The audience is led into the milieu when Stephen's description of the "musty, dusty, absolutely naked little hole on the other side of that wall, in which I spend my days and nights" (82) invites its imaginative construction:

> In the middle, a rickety table, with a book under one foot to keep it steady, littered with the direst confusion of dust-covered books and papers, and literally constellated with an infinite diversity of ink blots. A row of bookshelves, with the books thrust in any way but the right way; a cane-seated armchair, a stuffed ditto, a stove, a bed, a washstand, a trunk, a window, four walls, a ceiling and a floor. There you have a complete inventory. That is, it would be complete if I could represent, by any form of words, the lonely, grimy, dingy, late-of-a-November-afternoon expression of the whole place! (82)

This one-act play was precisely the sort of dramatic experiment for which Howells would soon be calling. But James left for Europe shortly

before the play appeared in *Galaxy,* and there he encountered in the
Théâtre Français the shaping influence for most of his early dramatic
work. The other two experiments of his twenties, *Still Waters* (1871) and
A Change of Heart (1872), constituted a step backward in realistic representation as well as in dramatic subtlety. Both plays have unnatural
soliloquies and reflexive asides. Their dialogue has slipped from the natural conversation of *Pyramus and Thisbe* to an unreal "literary" discourse
using elaborate rhetorical figures to embody extraordinary flights of
fancy. They also suffer from James's clumsy use of soliloquy for exposition and straightforward characterization. In *A Change of Heart* he actually uses a soliloquy to report a conversation. The greatest departure
from realism, however, occurs when James rejects the simple linear plot
of the first play – which depicts an action that is a natural outgrowth of
the situation in which the two characters find themselves – to attempt the
unnatural manipulation of the dramatic action demanded by the configu-
ration of characters in the French triangle.

It was not until ten years after these early efforts that James returned to
the drama. His 1882 dramatization of *Daisy Miller* was his first full-
length play, and his first written with theatrical representation directly in
mind. *Daisy Miller* was written for the American theater and *The American* (1890), for the British, but the two adaptations have a great deal in
common. They are the first examples of James's mixture of comedy with
the French *drame bourgeois,* the serious play about middle-class people.
The adaptations of his two novels provide a unique insight into James's
attitude toward the drama, and some good clues about what was going
wrong when he tried to work in that medium.[28] James's advice to
William Heinemann "Forget not that you write for the stupid"[29] has
been cited as evidence of his contempt for the theater audience.[30] Leon
Edel notes James's idea that he must create from *The American* the "simplest, strongest, boldest, most rudimentary, at once most humorous and
most touching play," adding, "Oh how it must not be too good and
how very bad it must be."[31] It was partly this attitude that led him to
supply his two novels with comic endings when he made them into
plays, thus lowering their complex depictions of characters and human
relations to the level of timeworn theatrical convention.

The imposition of comic form on the two novels had three major
effects. It led to a mixture of tones in the plays, and a consequent confu-
sion of thought; it reduced the complex characters of the novels to types;
and it led to a general oversimplification of the stories. By having Daisy
recover from her illness to marry Winterbourne, James turned a serious
realistic story into a sentimental comedy, establishing a lighter tone,
which he reinforced by introducing Miss Durant and Reverdy, a pair of
juvenile lovers. In order to fill out his slim plot, however, he also intro-

duced Madame de Katkoff as the *intrigante* and made the evil that Daisy is
up against more patent by turning Eugenio the courier into a melodramatic villain. Thus all the characters were either developed from or made
over to the types of melodrama and comedy.

The biggest changes are in Daisy and Winterbourne. In having Daisy
recover from her illness, James also has her undergo a complete change
of character. While she is recovering, she soliloquizes:

> It's hard to be sick when there's so much pleasure going on, especially
> when you're so fond of pleasure as poor silly me! Perhaps I'm too fond;
> that's one of the things I thought of as I lay there. I thought of so many
> – and some of them so sad – as I listened to the far-away Carnival. I
> think it was this that helped me to get better. I was afraid I had been
> bad, and I wanted to live to be good again. (163)

This is hardly the Daisy Miller of the novella. And by making Daisy
conventional, by having her capitulate to the very forms of society
fiercely resisted by the character in the story, James reduces the play to
action without significant thought. Similarly, Winterbourne, the most
fully developed consciousness in the novella, is reduced to a young man
who is completely at the mercy of his hormones. Although he is in love
with Daisy, one word from Madame de Katkoff quickly sets him off his
course, and the reappearance of Daisy just as quickly sets him back on it.
His action is completely predictable by theatrical convention, but it is far
from understandable in the Winterbourne whose character James drew
so carefully in the novella. Finally, the sense of evil in the corruption and
decay of the old culture, suggested so subtly in the story, is embodied
simplistically in the courier Eugenio's self-interest and Madame de Katkoff's weakness under the threat of blackmail. Reducing the depths of
evil to the person of one easily defeated villain reduces the play to melodrama and reduces the quality of its thought accordingly. In place of his
subtle exposure of complex European corruption through its contact
with American innocence, James repeats melodrama's simplistic formulation that the world is full of good guys and bad guys, and eventually
the good guys will win. There is no mistake here that James was writing
for the "stupid."

The imposition of a happy ending also oversimplified *The American*.
Here James reduced the Bellegardes' complex corruption to self-interest
– they are selling Claire to the highest bidder – and made Christopher
Newman into the American hero come to save Claire from the European
dragons who imprison her. Again the quality of the novel's thought
suffered. By saving Claire from her ancestral evil, Christopher is effect-
ing the easy victory of the New World over the Old, of American optimism over European pessimism, hardly a Jamesian thematic
statement.

An even more difficult problem with *The American* arises from its mixture of the serious tone of melodrama with the lighter tone of comedy of manners. There is a sense of evil and danger in the play. The Bellegardes use secret and ghastly mental torture on Claire; Valentin is killed in a duel; the servant reveals that Mrs. Bellegarde has murdered her husband. On the one hand, Christopher is the heroic figure who can win Claire and rescue her from this corruption. But on the other, he is nearly a caricature of the American tourist, complete with tag line – "That's just what I want to see" – and, in the Compton production that James oversaw, a "Noah-ark coat of yellowish brown, with blue facings and mother of pearl buttons almost as large as cheese plates."[32] So great was the sense of incongruity that Compton finally persuaded James to write a new fourth act in which Valentin lives, and the tone is more uniformly light and humorous. But the tension between the two impulses – the serious attempt to express the theme of the novel and the attempt to reduce it to the level of the "stupid" – remained unresolved in the play. In both *Daisy Miller* and *The American,* James's comic form and strained lightness of tone continued to be at odds with the serious thought he tried to subvert for them.

Because it was the occasion of James's great humiliation on the stage, *Guy Domville* (1893) has received more than its share of critical attention.[33] It is not necessary to tell a James scholar that this play shares a fatal inconsistency of tone with the two adaptations. Mixing the form of comedy, the sentiment of the *drame bourgeois,* and an oversimplified version of his realistic characters and motives, he ended up with a hybrid play that was inadequately comic, sentimental, and realistic.

When he was able to drop one of the elements of his unstable compound, James began to have more success. During the nineties, he wrote four plays that were intended for production but for one reason or another didn't receive it. He subsequently published them in two volumes, *Theatricals: Two Comedies* (1894) and *Theatricals: Second Series* (1895). According to James, the plays were "experiments in the line of comedy pure and simple,"[34] and there is no doubt that all four plays have straightforward comic form. In the first of them, however, a play called *Tenants,* an extra twist to the plot and a flight of sentiment mitigate the comic perspective slightly in the last act. There is also an undertone of melodrama in the insidious evil of the character Lurcher and his expulsion from the group at the end, the impulse of comedy being to reform the villain and include him in the new order rather than to punish and exclude him, but on the whole James has a much firmer control of his comic form in this play than in the earlier ones, and a much clearer sense of its thematic implications.

In his study of Shaw and the nineteenth-century theater, Martin Meisel identifies a form of comedy popular on the London stage during the eighties and nineties:

> Domestic Comedy was an intermediate kind of play which lacked the frightening amorality of Sex Farce and still supplemented with lighter tones the more "tragically turned" studies of sexual misadventure. In the plays of this middle range, a domestic triangle invariably ends in the defeat of the lover by the husband. Domestic Comedy is, in a sense, the obverse of the domestic magdalen play, for the adultery is always unconsummated, though the possibility provides the interest and the intrigue. It is in a sense the reverse of Sex Farce, for domesticity triumphs and morality reigns.[35]

Domestic comedy was a natural for the Anglo-American theater of the nineties, for it allowed the playwright to poke fun at the flaws in societal and familial structures while providing the audience, and the Lord Chamberlain's office, with the comfortable sense of affirmation provided by the comic form. It was a favorite of Shaw's and Oscar Wilde's, and in 1892 it became a vehicle for Henry James. The second of James's "theatricals," *Disengaged,* was inspired by "an anecdote told James some years earlier by Fanny Kemble concerning a young and wealthy member of the diplomatic corps in Rome who was talked by some mischievous companions into believing that he had compromised a young girl and thereupon proposed to her and in due course was married to her."[36] James developed this anecdote first into a story called "The Solution" and then into a play he wrote for Augustin Daly's star Ada Rehan.

Disengaged is interesting for a number of reasons. It is James's first play to be entirely free from disruptions of the fourth-wall illusion such as asides and soliloquies, and it has the extended stage directions typical of Shaw to indicate setting, character, psychological reactions, and stage business. In other words the play is James's first attempt to produce a completely integrated, authorially controlled theatrical representation. The control extends to the structure and tone as well. With its humor of situation, its volatile, unpredictable action, its amoral, fantastic atmosphere, and its titillating subject of sexual misbehavior, the play is rooted in farce, and as such it attacks social convention by burlesquing it, but James ultimately domesticates his farce by restoring morality to his characters in the end. In the domestic comedy of *Disengaged,* it seems that James had finally found a comic form that he could work with, and a tone that would express his perspective on society, or at least on some carefully chosen aspects of it.

In his Preface to the second series of "theatricals," *The Album* and *The Reprobate,* James remarks picturesquely that at the time, the dramatist's effort "seemed most securely to lie in the uttermost regions of dramatic amiability, the bland air of the little domestic fairy-tale, a species of which we had recently enough welcomed, with wonderment and envy, sundry successful specimens."[37] In setting out to "master the specific type," he wrote, the dramatists had to summon the aid of the "fairy Genial" and the "fairy Coincidence," but that the "fairy Sentiment" must be under the eye of the "foul fiend Excision." Then "the mixture was to be stirred to the tune of perpetual motion and served, under pain of being rejected with disgust, with the time-honoured bread-sauce of the happy ending."[38] Whereas his first two comedies had departed a little from the recipe in their degree of sentiment, his next two were nearly perfect specimens of domestic comedy. *The Album* is a "fairy-tale" with the age-old moral of the reforming power of love. It has the hard, epigrammatic style and the atmosphere of "perpetual motion" that James was seeking, and his structuring of the comic action is a neat manipulation of rhythm and incident, complete with a last-minute counterturn in Act III that is worthy of Molière.

The Reprobate has an equally neat comic structure, expressing an equally traditional comic theme, but it embodies a more subversive comment on Victorian society. The story is based on the actual condition of a cousin of James's who was restricted to ten cents a day for spending money out of fear that he was the slave of passions that would run amok if he had the wherewithal to indulge them. In the play, Paul Doubleday, who has had a liaison with an actress in his early youth, is kept under the eye of his stepmother and his guardian, Mr. Bonsor, for fear that his dreadful weakness will take hold again and lead him inexorably down the path to dissolution. The play's comic form neatly reverses the Victorian notion of moral reformation. Paul undergoes the comic hero's archetypal experience by achieving his maturation when he frees himself from the restrictions – and by implication from the moral code – imposed by the older generation, his stepmother and Bonsor. He proves that he is not evil but merely natural. Once he achieves his manhood through his rebellion, he assumes his place as head of the family and wins the love of the heroine. In the true comic spirit, it is his stepmother's suitor Chanter and Mr. Bonsor's protégé, hypocritical representatives of the prevailing Victorian moral order, who are exposed as the reprobates. But it is also in the comic spirit that they are included in the freer new order rather than excluded, as they would be by the narrow limits of Victorian morality, after the truth about them has been revealed.

In *The Reprobate,* James displays masterly control of the comic form and its thematic implications, stripping it down to the essentials of the coming-of-age motif, the exposure of corruption in the old order, and the establishment of a new, freer, and more natural order around the hero. James's "fairy-tale" expresses the comic spirit of optimism. Victorian society is rotten, it says, but it is not the last word. Our hope for the future lies in the next generation, just now preparing to throw off the hypocritical moral strictures of Victorian society and establish new values that are more natural, more honest, and more human.

In *The Reprobate,* James took domestic comedy as far as it would go in his hands. His next comedy, a one-act play written in 1895 for Ellen Terry, who wanted to portray an American heroine, was *Summersoft.* It represents a reversal of James's earlier "international theme" in that it centers on the efforts of Mrs. Gracedew, an American woman of "Taste," to persuade Captain Yule, a young Liberal member of Parliament, that he has a duty to hold on to his old family estate for the sake of beauty and tradition. In form, the play is traditional comedy, with the inevitable marriage of Yule and Mrs. Gracedew temporarily blocked by the efforts of Mr. Prodmore, the owner of the mortgage on Yule's ancestral estate. Prodmore proposes to let Yule have the estate if he will marry Prodmore's daughter and renounce his Liberal principles. Yule objects to both conditions but is persuaded, mostly through the force of the influence that Mrs. Gracedew's personality has on him, that he should save the estate, even at the cost of his principles. When Mrs. Gracedew finds out about the other condition, she thinks better of her stand and discusses honor with Yule, who changes his mind. When Prodmore's daughter Cora confides to Mrs. Gracedew that she is unwilling to marry Yule, because she loves another, Mrs. Gracedew confronts Prodmore with the facts, buys the mortgage from him, and sets out to save both the estate and Yule, who now proposes to her. Thus Prodmore is defeated, the two couples are united, Yule keeps his principles intact, and the estate is saved.

Although the play is certainly a normal comedy in form, with the action and the structure proceeding from the love story, it contains within its dynamics the new Shavian element of the discussion of an issue. The plot hinges on Mrs. Gracedew's convincing Yule that he must save the estate, and the discussion is a crucial part of the action. In *The Quintessence of Ibsenism* (1891), G. B. Shaw referred to "a new technical factor in the art of popular stage-play making which every considerable playwright has been thrusting under [the audience's] noses night after night for a whole generation," meaning the discussion: "Formerly you had in what was called a well made play an exposition in the first act, a situation in the second, and unravelling in the third. Now you have exposition, situation, and discussion; and the discussion is the test of the playwright."[39] James's comedy was much closer to the well-made play than to the new play Shaw described, but its short discussion scene was important. Although the comic love story impels the action of *Summer-*

soft, and it is at bottom Yule's attraction to Mrs. Gracedew that causes his capitulation to her argument, the argument itself holds a conspicuous position in the play. Mrs. Gracedew's appeal is nothing if not rhetorical:

> What do politics amount to – compared with *religions.* Parties and programmes come and go, but a duty like *this* abides. There's nothing you can break with that would be like breaking *here,* the very *word's* a violence – a sacrilege: your house is a kind of altar! You *must* have beauty in your life – that's the only way to make *sure* of it for the life of others. Keep leaving it to *them,* and heaven knows what they'll *do* with it! Does it take one of *us* [Americans] to feel that? – to preach you the *truth?* Then it's good we come *over,* to see what you're about! We know what we *haven't* got, and if *you've* luckily got it, you've got it also for *us.* You've got it in *trust,* and oh! we have an *eye* on you. (538)

Yule's response indicates what the audience's should be: "(*Strongly troubled, rendered nervous and uncertain by her appeal; moving restlessly about.*) You have a strange eloquence" (538). The comic outcome, the union of the lovers, the institution of a new and better order of things, depends on Yule's accepting Mrs. Gracedew's argument, and thus the comic structure rests on the discussion's success at conveying James's thought.

Reactions to the unproduced play indicate that James's first use of the drama of discussion was not successful. In the opinion of the actors and managers who rejected the play, Yule's capitulation to Mrs. Gracedew's point of view simply could not be believed. Edel reports in his introduction to the play that William Archer considered Yule's capitulation the "single flaw" in a play that was a gem, for it was "utterly implausible, and . . . in real life would make a political figure the laughing-stock of all England" (523). In the reaction to *Summersoft,* James came face to face with the new spirit of realism that was animating the Anglo-American theater. While he had been straining for five years to master the "fairy-tale" unreality of domestic comedy, the presence of Ibsen and Shaw had been changing the rules of the drama. The artificial impulse of fairy-tale comedy had to be replaced by the impulse of real ideas with psychologically believable responses to motivate action. It was twelve years before James took advantage of the changes to construct dramas that were more believable psychologically, more thought-centered, and more in keeping with his artistic strengths than those he had felt compelled to construct before.

The changes he made as he rewrote *Summersoft* into *The High Bid* (1907) are an excellent index of the influence that Shaw and the new drama eventually had on James, who expanded the stage directions considerably to include, as Shaw was doing, not only details of the set but also full characterizations and minute descriptions of costumes. He also extended his tendency to direct reaction and stage business to the point of maintaining tight control of the portrayal of his characters, right down to the tones of their speeches. The new version of Mrs. Gracedew's first meeting with Yule contains more direction than dialogue, as she asks permission to explore the house:

> Don't tell me I *can't* now, because I already *have;* I've been upstairs and downstairs and in my lady's chamber! – I'm not even sure I haven't been in my lord's! I got round your lovely *servant* – if you don't look out I'll *grab* him! (*Then as if fairly provoked to the last familiarity by some charm in the very stare with which he meets her amazing serenity.*) If you don't look out, you know, I'll grab everything! (*She gives fair notice, she plays with his frank stupefaction.*) That's what I came *over* for (*she explains*) just to lay your country *waste.* Your house (*she explains further*) is a wild old dream; and besides (*dropping, oddly and quaintly, into real responsible judgment*) you've got some quite good things. (570)

If James seems to be usurping the actor's interpretive role here, it's also clear that his characters are obviously, to him, real people with psychological depths, whims, manners, and tones of voice. His characterization is a matter of realizing these people on the stage, not of grafting some human characteristics on to the conventional types of the drama.

The other major development from *Summersoft* to *The High Bid* is the elaboration of the discussion from essentially one speech by Mrs. Gracedew to an entire scene, in which Yule answers her pleas for beauty and tradition with a stand arising from his Liberal principles:

> One's "human home" is all very well – but the rest of one's humanity is better! (*She gives at this a charming wail of protest; she turns impatiently away.*) I see you're disgusted with me, and I'm sorry; but it's not my fault, you know, if circumstances and experience have made me a very modern man. I see something else in the world than the beauty of old show-houses and the glory of old show-families. There are thousands of people in England who can show no houses *at all,* and (*with the emphasis of sincerity*) I don't feel it utterly shameful to share their poor *fate.* (581)

The chief problem with the play was that audiences found Yule's position much more eloquent and moving than Mrs. Gracedew's rejoinder: "We share the poor fate of humanity whatever we do, and we do much to help and console when we've something precious to *show*" (581). Gertrude Eliott, who played Mrs. Gracedew in the Forbes-Robertson production of the play, wrote to James: "From the general audience's point of view Mrs. Gracedew's appeal for beauty is not so fine as Yule's point of view that it is his duty to throw in his lot with the needy. . . . I used to be very worried about it because it is the crux of the play and if she is not convincing to the audience at that point, they can't understand why a man of radical views should renounce them so quickly."[40] James's response, completely consistent with the Jamesian aesthetic, goes far to explain why he did not have as much success with his audiences for the discussion play as Ibsen and Shaw did: "My small comedy treats its subject – and its subject is Mrs. Gracedew's appeal and adventure – on Mrs. Gracedew's grounds and in Mrs. Gracedew's spirit, and any deflection from these and that logic and consistency would send the whole action off into a whirlwind of incoherence."[41] We've seen that many critics think James the dramatist was out of touch with his audience, but perhaps an even stronger reason for The High Bid's ultimate failure was his refusal to turn it into polemical drama. Consistency between dialogue and character was more important to him than a rhetorically convincing argument for this point of view.

Two years later he was able to write a play that integrates an idea sympathetic to his audience, an effective discussion of the problem arising from it, and a comic form. The Outcry (1909) was written for a London season produced by Charles Frohman, which enlisted the efforts of Harley Granville-Barker, John Galsworthy, G. B. Shaw, Somerset Maugham, and John Masefield, as well as James. It is a discussion play built around the issue of whether England's works of art should be used for the good of the aristocracy that owns them or for the good of all the British people. James manages to integrate the discussion with the action of the comedy so that the union of the romantic couples at the end is a celebration of community for England as well. The combination is complicated, of course. The strain that results from the heroine's capitulation on the issue in order to marry the hero undermines the force that the supporting structure lends to the discussion, and her father's final act of acquiescence comes out of self-interest rather than altruism like that of the young people. These departures from resolution by discussion may simply be James's ironic comment on the naïveté of the Shavian point of view. At bottom, the play suggests, actions are much more likely to be motivated by self-interest or sexual love than by one's rational conviction of their justice. In a sense, The Outcry is James's answer to the public criticism of The High Bid. If Mrs. Gracedew's desire to hold on to Yule's estate seemed to smack of self-interest, here was the father's completely selfless gesture, actually donating a valuable work of art to the nation. But just as Mrs. Gracedew's seeming self-interest could have higher aesthetic motivations, so Lord Theign's extravagant gesture of altruism could have baser personal motives. In any case, The Outcry shows that James had a sophisticated sense of the drama of discussion and of how to manipulate the conventions of comic form to support or punctuate the discussion. Forty years after he had begun seriously to write plays, he had found a genre suited to his talents.

The other great influence on James's later plays has provoked more critical interest and more disagreement than that of Shaw. While one critic can maintain that the Ibsen influence helped James to "crystallize his aesthetic theories as antithetical to Ibsen's work,"[42] another can claim that *The Other House* (1908) is "pure Ibsen, unalloyed, undistilled and hawked directly from the pages of *Hedda Gabler* and *Rosmersholm*."[43] Somewhere between these extreme statements lies the truth. James's letters to Edmund Gosse show his reservations about Ibsen, whereas those to Elizabeth Robins show his enthusiasm. Both responses come out in his critical pieces on *Hedda Gabler*, *The Master Builder*, *John Gabriel Borkman*, and *Little Eyolf*.[44] In any case, *The Other House*, which James originally conceived in 1893, the year in which he wrote an essay praising Elizabeth Robins's production of *The Master Builder*, and "the height of the struggle for Ibsen in the London theatre,"[45] clearly shows "the Ibsen influence." The play's central motive is similar to the one James discussed in his essay on *Hedda Gabler*, the study of an *"état d'âme."* In this case, James presents a woman who is acting out passions beyond her control. Rose Armiger, in love with her friend's husband, Tony Bream, is prevented from pursuing him after the friend's death by his promise not to marry again while his daughter Effie lives. The convoluted plot begins as melodrama, with Rose as the evil principle out to destroy anyone who approaches too close to Tony. The melodramatic principle of innocence resides in Effie and in Jean, the young woman who becomes a surrogate mother to Effie because she loves Tony. The melodrama reaches its height when Rose drowns the child and tries to arrange the circumstances to implicate Jean.

Like Ibsen's plays, however, *The Other House* moves beyond the simple opposition of good and evil in its melodramatic form to present a more complicated version of reality. Like Hedda, Rose cannot be dismissed as motiveless evil that ought to be destroyed by the forces of good. Her case is more complicated. Rose is pathological, and throughout the play James makes it clear that the real drama is not in the physical actions that proceed from her state of mind but in the drama of that state itself. Early in the action, the audience, along with Tony, is given a glimpse of her inner state:

> He catches himself up: the face offered him is the convulsed face ROSE has managed though only comparatively to keep from her love. She literally glares at him; standing there with her two hands pressing down her agitated breast and something in all her aspect like the first shock of a great accident. What he sees, without at first understanding it, is the final snap of tremendous tension, the end of her wonderful false calm; which makes him instantly begin, dismayed and disappointed, to guess and spell out, as it were, quite misunderstandingly, the real truth of her situation. (696)

It is the recognition of moral ambiguity that raises James's play above the level of melodrama. The center of *The Other House*, like the center of *Hedda Gabler*, is in the characters, not in the action. It is precisely when the play departs from the simplistic moral assumptions of melodrama in order to accommodate the complex psychology actually involved in moral decisions that it takes a step toward realism. Here James changes his form to fit his psychological investigation rather than reduce his characters to the "immemorial puppets of the stage" in order to fit a preconceived form. The shift from primary interest in structure to primary interest in character was crucial in the drama's development toward realism, as it was in James's development as a dramatist.

In his last play, an adaptation of his *Owen Wingrave* (1892) called *The Saloon* (1908), James combined elements of the Shavian discussion play with elements drawn from Ibsen and a uniquely Jamesian tone and structure. Not surprisingly in a work of the "major phase," and an adaptation of a story, James's stage directions in *The Saloon* out-Shaw Shaw in their inclusiveness. He gives full descriptions of the set, characters, costumes, and business, as he does in the other late plays, but here he so controls the psychological action on the stage that the meaning in the play is signified as much by gestures and facial expressions as by words. The play's theme is conveyed in a number of ways, which combine the modes of Ibsen, Shaw, and James.

At one level, the play is a drama of discussion, its action consisting of Owen's attempt to convince his family and his fiancée that his decision to abandon the traditional military career of the Wingraves in favor of his new pacifist principles is a good one. Like that of any discussion play, *The Saloon*'s success depends a great deal on the audience's being convinced by the arguments Owen uses against his fiancée's defense of conventional "honour" and "heroism." But the play moves into another realm, which caused Shaw considerable consternation when it was submitted to the Incorporated Stage Society in 1909. The problem came with James's use of the supernatural in the play. Owen's final action is to die while confronting the family specter, thus exorcising the war spirit and securing his final triumph; Shaw, however, held that Owen's death gave the victory to the specter and thus undermined the discussion in the play. He wrote to James:

> It is really a damnable sin to draw with such consummate art a houseful of rubbish, and a dead incubus of a father waiting to be scrapped; to bring on for us the hero with his torch and his scrapping shovel; and, then, when the audience is saturated with interest and elated with hope, waiting for the triumph over victory, calmly announce that the rubbish has choked the hero, and that the incubus is really the strong master of all our souls. Why have you done this? If it were true to nature – if it were scientific – if it were common sense, I should say let us face it, let us say Amen. But it isn't. Every man who really wants his latchkey gets it. No man who doesn't believe in ghosts ever sees one. . . . Why do

you preach cowardice to an army which has victory always and easily within its reach?[46]

James replied, characteristically, that his subject was his subject and his form was his form, and Shaw had no right to suggest that he change them. When Shaw wrote back, "You cannot evade me thus. . . . you can give the victory to one side just as artistically as to the other," James replied:

> There was only one question to me, that is, that of my hero's . . . *getting the best of everything*, simply; which his death makes him do by, in the first place, purging the house of the beastly legend, and in the second place by his creating for us, spectators and admirers, such an intensity of impression and emotion about him as must promote his romantic glory and edifying example for ever. . . . He wins the victory – that is he clears the air, and he pays with his life[47] (James's emphasis).

It was here that James and dramatic realism parted company. The play's structure is not that of the discussion play but of what Northrop Frye calls the final phase of comedy, "the phase of the collapse and disintegration of the comic society."[48] In this phase, "the social units of comedy become small and esoteric, or even confined to a single individual," and the mood becomes pensive, accommodating "the love of the occult and the marvellous, the sense of individual detachment from routine existence." In short, "in this kind of comedy we have finally left the world of wit and the awakened critical intelligence for the opposite pole, an oracular solemnity which, if we surrender uncritically to it, will provide a delightful *frisson*. This is the world of ghost stories, thrillers, and Gothic romances."[49]

In *The Saloon*, James's new order is confined to the single consciousness of Owen; and its triumph, to a transcendence of the old, ending in death. The circumstances of Owen's death remain ambiguous, but his legacy for the new order is clear. His death is a heroic rejection of the order that glorifies "the Bully, the Beast and the Murderer" (664) through its institutionalization of war, and an homage to what he calls *his* view of "honour – which is not to go in for the consecration of the Brute but for the affirmation of the Man and the liberation of the Spirit" (665). So strong is the hold of the old order on the living world that Owen's spirit can be liberated only through death, but in his death he leaves behind the knowledge of his statement, and this, to James, represents triumph. Owen's refusal to capitulate to the family war specter has "purged" it from his house and taken the world one small step closer to harmony and peace.

James's chosen form in *The Saloon* is far from realistic. The comedy of disintegration is as close as one can get to romance on the stage. But the fusion of the romantic form, and its accompanying tone of "oracular solemnity," with the psychological detail in the characterizations of Owen, Kate, and even the play's minor characters, and the clear discussion of an immediate social issue, was a uniquely Jamesian feat. *The Saloon* shows the impulse of realism in focusing on Owen's internal dilemma, and in using the articulation of that dilemma as discussion to propel the action of the play, but the realism is used in the service of what James saw as a higher aesthetic vision. In his "final phase," he had mastered the techniques of dramatic realism sufficiently to be able to manipulate them as handily as he did those of fiction. He had passed from a drama that was pure imitation of convention, through the realistic drama of discussion and Ibsenist melodrama, and into a new mode that was inimitably Henry James. Although we need not follow him into that neoromantic Jamesian final phase, it is important that we recognize the realistic techniques that ground his later works in reality, and thus intensify the *frisson* of his gothic flights.

WILLIAM DEAN HOWELLS

In his *History of the American Drama,* Arthur Hobson Quinn wrote that "one of the common errors in the discussion of American drama is to assume its divorce from the main currents of our literature."[50] Quinn made a point of correcting this error partly by taking the efforts of Harte and Mark Twain seriously but mainly by devoting a whole chapter to William Dean Howells because he felt Howells demanded "special treatment, on account both of his achievement and of his influence upon others. The leader in the realistic treatment of familiar life, his example and his critical judgments and inspiration, guided and encouraged Harrigan, Herne, Thomas, and Fitch."[51] We have already seen support for Quinn's view in the theoretical writings of Edward Harrigan and James A. Herne. Clyde Fitch, writing in 1904 to thank Howells for a favorable review, expressed his indebtedness in the exuberant Fitch style: "You see I really represent the *Howells' Age!* by wh I mean when you were in the first glory & fight of yr success, I was a boy beginning to 'take notice,' – never in a scholastic sense either, entirely from instinct & the impulse of my nature – or I might leave out the 'my.' I grew up on YOU!"[52] In a more subdued tone, Augustus Thomas remembered that Howells's farces "were very educational suggestions to a young writer as to what could be done in the theatre with restraint joined to precision."[53] In short, Howells was a more significant force in the American theater than the other realistic writers because he earned the respect of the working playwrights, not only through his critical writings but also through his own dramatic efforts, and he exerted a strong, native aesthetic influence on an American theater that tended otherwise to function very much in the shadow of European ideas. Howells's influence, needless to say, was always toward the establishment of a more thoroughgoing realism in drama.

Although they are by no means great dramatic works, Howells's plays have many of the strengths of his realistic convictions. Quinn commented that "the dialogue is never 'literary' – it is just that compromise between actual conversation and perfect English which is suitable for the stage."[54] Walter Meserve has added that "Howells wrote brilliant conversations, far more witty and clever than anything being written in American drama of his time."[55] Other strengths of Howells's plays are psychological but economic characterization; settings that are typical of the middle-class life he wrote about, such as the summer hotel, the sleeping car, parlor car, or smoking car of a train, the railroad station, the elevator, the florist's shop; and the discussion of issues that had import for the life of his time, such as class snobbery, the Victorian glorification of needless self-sacrifice, and the sentimental "idealism" that Howells opposed all his adult life. Also, as Quinn noted, his use of extensive stage directions anticipated the practice of Shaw and his followers.

Howells breathed the new air of realism into all aspects of the drama, but the uniqueness of his work in its place and time lay in his concern with form rather than structure.[56] Amateurs like Harte and Mark Twain concentrated on elaborate structures while they were only dimly aware of a play's overall form. A playwright with the reverence for the traditional forms that James had concentrated on manipulating the structure with as much ingenuity as possible within a form he assumed was given. Howells tried to put realism into the dramatic form itself, and although most of his plays are either farces with simple linear structures or straightforward comedies, he also experimented with the discussion play (*Out of the Question*), the drama of pathos (*Bride Roses*), the philosophical dialogue (*The Mother and the Father*), the burlesque (*Saved: An Emotional Drama*), and two original forms he called the "mystery play" (*The Impossible*) and the "farce tragedy" (*Self-Sacrifice*). Some of these experiments are interesting only for the ingenuity of the enterprise, but Howells's work with the discussion play, the farce, and the comedy was important for American drama's development toward realism.

One perennial critical problem in dealing with Howells's drama arises from his having written so many one-act plays. For the author, the obvious problem that arose from this choice was the practical one of getting the plays produced. The period of Howells's greatest productivity, the eighties and nineties, was the time when the custom of the one-act curtain raiser was falling into disuse, and it was still far from the time when the one-act play would be the genre of serious experimentation that could make a reputation, as it would for the Provincetown Players

during World War I. For literary critics, the chief problem arising from
this theatrical situation has been the generic classification of Howells's
one-act plays. As Meserve observed, "Howells subtitled most of them
farces, but such able critics of the drama as G. B. Shaw, William Archer,
Henry Arthur Jones, James A. Herne, and William Winter have found in
some of his plays the essential characteristics of social comedy. On the
other hand, Augustin Daly, Daniel Frohman, and Augustus Thomas
spoke of Howells' plays mainly in terms of farce."[57] Meserve concluded
that the wisest judgment might be "that Howells wrote both types successfully: He could write effective farce, yet some of his plays also figure
prominently in the rise of American social comedy."[58] But this does not
help with the essential generic fuzziness that now exists in the consideration of Howells's one-act plays.

One reason for the critical hedging is a traditional unwillingness to
take the farce seriously as an object of study. In the eyes of the academy,
social comedy has always been respectable; farce has not. This viewpoint
may be partly ascribed to the traditional conception of farce available to
literary critics – that described, for example, by *The Oxford Companion to
the Theatre:*

> Farce, a form of popular comedy in which laughter is raised by horse-
> play and bodily assault in contrived and highly improbable situations. It
> must, however, retain its hold on humanity, even if only in depicting
> the grosser faults of mankind, otherwise it degenerates into burlesque.[59]

It is no wonder that critics who admire Howells's farces try to rescue
them from such a description by promoting them to the class of social
comedy. The traditional notion of farce is inadequate to describe a group
of plays that, while they certainly do raise laughter through physical and
situational humor, also, as Meserve has noted, make some serious observations about Howells's society, particularly in its conception of the
morality of truth and deception.

Howells himself showed in one of his earliest essays on the drama that
what mattered to him was not the source of the laughter but its object:
"The novel of society must needs censure conditions in which odious
human traits and characters flourish when it depicts them; the play can
laugh them to scorn without a syllable of criticism on the state of things
to which they owe their existence."[60] Howells's emphasis was in keeping
with Eric Bentley's view of farce as "desecration." Bentley holds that the
fundamental impulse of farce is to damage the family, to desecrate the
household gods.[61] In Howells's case, the "family" becomes the close-
knit complex of middle-class Back Bay society that appears in most of
his farces, and the "household gods" become the seemingly sacred but
essentially baseless social assumptions on which this delicate framework

rests. Bentley remarks that "if farces are examined they will be found to contain very little 'harmless' joking and very much that is 'tendentious.' Without aggression, farce cannot function."[62] It is, of course, veiled aggression, even ambivalent aggression, but aggression directed toward societal assumptions is clearly present in the Howells farces.

This attitude, as Bentley has noted, is precisely what informs the dramatic tension in farce. The farce operates, he says, in a double dialectic, the farceur hiding, with a wink to the audience, his thought behind his joke, and at the same time hiding his seriousness from himself through his farcical form:

> The surface of farce is gay and grave at the same time. The gay antics of Harlequin are conducted with poker-faced gravity. Both the gaiety and the gravity are visible and are part of the style. If we go on to speak of a contrast in farce between mask and face, symbol and thing symbolized, appearance and reality, this will not be a contrast in styles but a contrast between either the gravity or the gaiety on the surface and whatever lies beneath. What do gaiety and gravity have in common? Orderliness and mildness. What lies beneath the surface, on the other hand, is disorderly and violent. It is a double dialectic. On the surface, the contrast of gay and grave, then, secondly, the contrast of surface and beneath-the-surface. The second is a larger and even more dynamic contrast.[63]

The first contrast becomes more and more evident in the Howells farce as it develops, the ridiculous behavior of the characters, and the even more ridiculous action of the plot, becoming less and less effectual as a mask to the serious point of the play. The point generally concerns truth and deceit, and the anomalous moral position of a social group that actually functions through deceit in various forms, chiefly the "social lie," but pretends to believe that truth is right and deception is wrong. It is most clearly evident in *The Unexpected Guests* (1893), the action of which consists entirely of a hostess's trying to deceive some unexpected guests into believing they were expected, and convincing everyone else that they "are not a bit late" when they know perfectly well that they are, all while a phonograph in the background is squeaking out a quotation from William Cullen Bryant: "Truth crushed to earth will rise again." The question of truth and deceit also informs *The Garroters* (1885), *The Albany Depot* (1892), *A Letter of Introduction* (1892), and *A Masterpiece of Diplomacy* (1894), each with its variation on the theme that this society, which professes to admire truth, could not function without falsehood and deceit.

A viewer who sat through a production of each of the twelve farces about the Roberts and Campbell families, or even someone who read each one as it appeared in print between 1892 and 1898, could not miss the serious point about deceit veiled by the surface gaiety of the Howells farce. The second contrast in the double dialectic is naturally more complex because it involves an almost unconscious action on the part of the author, an unmasking of the "disorderly and violent" feelings that lie beneath the surface of his conscious artistic management of gaiety and gravity. In Howells's plays, these unconscious feelings come out not in physical violence or some other form of veiled aggression, as they do in most farces, but in the characterization of two of the members of his little societal group, Edward Roberts and Willis Campbell, exaggerated but recognizable portraits of William Dean Howells and Mark Twain.

Roberts and Campbell clearly represent two types as old as farce itself, gull and coney, or fool and knave. Neither Roberts nor Campbell is actually a part of the social framework within which they move, Roberts because he is too innocent, and Campbell because he is too wise. Roberts is incapable of deceit, and this weakness renders him incapable of performing the simplest function, such as engaging a doctor for his sick child (*A Masterpiece of Diplomacy*) or hiring a cook for his wife (*The Albany Depot*), and also easy prey for Campbell's practical jokes. Howells evokes ambivalent feelings of contempt and empathy toward Roberts. He mouths sentiments, such as social justice, that we generally subscribe to but do not realistically expect to act on, and he openly exhibits that human mixture of moral cowardice and the desire to be thought well of that is universal but normally well hidden. Roberts, in short, embodies some universal human qualities we would much rather laugh at than identify or sympathize with. This is one side of Howells's deeper dialectic. One means of relieving these ambivalent feelings is to attack, and in his farces Howells attacks both the innocence that cannot cope with society and the societal structure that necessarily excludes the innocent from its deceitful workings.

Campbell's knowledge is the antithesis of Roberts's innocence. Like Roberts, he is outside the pale of the social framework, not because he cannot play the games of society but because he sees through social pretense only too well. He knows the way things work in society; he knows his own strengths and weaknesses; and he doesn't pretend to any belief or value that doesn't work out in reality. This is also the position of Dr. Lawton, the representative of humanistic good sense in Howells's farces. When Campbell asks him what his idea of truth is, he replies, "Mine? I have none! I have been a general practitioner for forty years" (420). Campbell, however, has characteristics that Dr. Lawton lacks. The good doctor is quite willing to use deceit, but only when he sees it as contributing to the welfare of his patients or to the general comfort of another human being. Campbell's position is closer to "Never tell the truth when a lie is just as good." His motive is pure mischief, to cause society, which moves along smoothly on a modicum of deceit, to come up short, by deceiving the deceivers. Campbell's mischief is far from harmless in its Back Bay Boston setting. In his capacity as a Western "outsider" to the societal group, he disturbs its delicate balance and thus points out the precarious foundation underlying it.

When Howells allowed a measure of bitterness to creep into his social criticism in the farces, they became something else. His one-act plays of the early twentieth century no longer employ the Robertses and Campbells; they concern an older, more serious couple called the Fountains. The plays no longer embody the tension of the farce dialectic, but instead move into other forms that embody the more critical worldview Howells was expressing. Thus in 1910 he wrote *The Night Before Christmas*, a disquisition on the hypocrisy and materialism of Christmas, and *The Impossible: A Mystery Play*, a satiric modern version of the biblical parable about the wedding guests. In 1911 he published the satiric *Self-Sacrifice: A Farce Tragedy*, which through burlesque, not the dialectic of farce, exposes the stupidity of giving up one's lover because someone else is in love with him.

No longer needing to mask this thought in a complex dialectical form, Howells moved toward greater simplicity, less action, and a clearer connection between thought and structure in his comedies. In other words, he made them more realistic. It is important to remember, however, that at their most superficial and at their deepest points, the farces exhibit the impulse of realism as well. The witty dialogue, the typical social events and settings, the careful realism of the surface that the characters present, and the mundane situations that provide the occasions for the humorous antics of the farce – all are typical attributes of early realism. The critical attitude the farces express toward contemporary society gives a realistic dimension to their thought and points out one direction Howells was to take in his development as a dramatist.

A second direction was toward the comedy of character, in which the action is propelled by a psychological dilemma. In the earliest of these, *A Counterfeit Presentment* (1877), Howells made the stock comic convention of mistaken identity into a serious problem. After Bartlett, a young painter, has been taken for the man by whom Constance believes she has been jilted, he falls in love with her but is anguished because he never knows at what level she is responding to him and at what level to her former lover. The "situation" of the play arises from this dilemma, and Bartlett's discussion of it with his friend Cummings gives an interesting insight into the psychological dilemma as it works on his character:

> From the very first she interpreted *me* by what she knew of *him*. She expected me to be this and not to be that; to have one habit and not another; and I could see that every time the fact was different, it was a miserable disappointment to her, a sort of shock. Every little difference

> between me and that other rascal gave her a start; and whenever I
> looked up I found her wistful eyes on me as if they were trying to puzzle
> me out; they used to follow me round the room like the eyes of a family
> portrait. . . . When she's with me a while she comes to see that I am not
> a mere *doppelgänger*. She respites me to that extent. But I have still some
> small rags of self-esteem dangling about me; and now suppose I should
> presume to set up for somebody on my own account; the first hint of
> my caring for her as I do, if she could conceive of anything so atrocious,
> would tear open all the old sorrows. Ah! I can't think of it. (101)

The natural language and the natural feelings this speech conveys are
far from the melodramatic sentiment of Howard's *Banker's Daughter* and
Mackaye's *Hazel Kirke,* yet Howells's play preceded both by two years
and received a fair trial on the road with Lawrence Barrett. The problem
theatrically was that it was about forty years ahead of its time. Audiences
did not have the patience for it, although it received substantial critical
approval.[64] With this play's depth of characterization, subdued treatment
of a psychological dilemma, and straightforward presentation of a problem, Howells was pointing the way for the American theater. On the
other hand, *A Counterfeit Presentment* is neither a finished discussion play
nor a psychological comedy. Although its conflict arises directly from
Bartlett's problem, it is resolved not through resolution of the psychological dilemma but arbitrarily through structural manipulation of the
action. In 1877, Howells hadn't yet solved the problem of integrating a
serious psychological dilemma with comic structure.

In the later one-act comedy *A Previous Engagement* (1895), Howells
manages a much more successful integration of the study of character,
the use of comic structure, and the resolution of a problem in human
relations. The problem here is an aspect of the Victorian overindulgence
in idealism for its own sake, the notion that an engaged couple should be
blank slates for each other, and that the previous engagement of one of
them therefore presents a serious impediment to their marriage. Howells
combines the discussion of this issue with a study of the romantically
idealistic young girl who typically entertained such notions. When Philippa is putting herself and her lover, Mr. Camp, through the emotional
wringer over this issue, her aunt puts her finger on the quality of character that brings about such actions as she explains Philippa to her bewildered uncle:

> You never can understand that women can't go about things as men do,
> and you think if they use a little finesse with themselves, they are doing
> something criminal and false. . . . Women not only have to hoodwink
> men; they have to hoodwink themselves too. A girl – such a girl as
> Philippa – enjoys putting herself through her paces before a man; she
> likes to exploit her emotions, and see how he takes it; though she may
> not know it! (458)

The union of Philippa and her lover takes place only when Philippa herself removes the impediment to their happiness by resolving the issue. Pressed to the point of having to give him up, she admits that she never cared at all for Camp's having been engaged before, and thus relinquishes the pretense of her idealism. Through the action of his little comedy, Howells exposes the absurdity of the notion he attacks, makes a convincing analysis of the character who holds it, and suggests that realistic deflation of inflated romantic ideals will bring about the harmony and integration that the comic ending celebrates. Here he is anticipating the thrust of the popular theater by about twenty years, and again he is pointing the way.

Although *A Previous Engagement* is the most finished example of Howells's psychological comedy, the adaptation he did of his novel *The Rise of Silas Lapham* with Paul Kester in 1895 is the most fully developed. The playwrights kept the novel's basic structure as well as its central theme and most of its dialogue. The important thing about the play as comedy is that the happy integration of the ending is achieved *through* Lapham's moral rise, not imposed on it. The business failure that produces the "falling action" of Acts II and III in the play is not reversed miraculously to produce the comic resolution in Act IV. In terms of external action, the upward thrust in Act IV is very modest. Lapham the former millionaire is taken on as a minor partner in the firm he had sought to take over. His feeling at the end is chiefly relief at having behaved morally in a difficult moment when he could have saved his fortune by behaving immorally, and at having discharged his debts honorably: "The transfer will lift the last load of debt off, and when the papers are signed I won't owe any man a cent. You don't know what that means, young man – you never want to" (515).

The romantic plot involving Tom Corey and Lapham's daughter Penelope, which parallels the business story, is also well integrated both with the study of the question that informs it – whether Penelope should give Tom up because her sister was in love with him first – and with the psychological development of the characters. It is her sister's good sense that saves Penelope from the foolish self-sacrifice she is about to inflict on herself and on her lover: "Penelope Lapham, have you been such a ninny as to send that man away on my account? If you have, I'll thank you to bring him back again. I'm not going to have him thinking that I'm dying for one that never cared for me. It's insulting, and I'm not going to stand it. Now you just stop it!" (515). The common sense underlying this plea brings about Penelope's union with Tom and the integration of the family that ends the comedy.

Despite his success in integrating structure with content and in character development, Howells did not completely succeed in making *Silas Lapham* into a play. As the managers to whom he offered it remarked, the play is not very dramatic, and this is not just because of its large amount of dialogue. In Howells's successful plays the dialogue *is* action, of a very interesting sort – the confrontation of two minds or of two wills that leads to some result, either in action or in conviction. In *Silas Lapham,* he devotes nearly all of Act I to conversations that narrate exposition. The combination of this narrative use of dialogue with sharp climaxes of crisis brought about by coincidence does not add up to drama. In the process of adaptation, Howells and Kester did not thoroughly transform the story from one medium to the other – the play is novelistic.

Howells's most interesting experiment with dramatic structure was his independent development of the discussion play in 1877, fourteen years before Shaw's *Quintessence of Ibsenism* was published, and two years before the first production of *A Doll's House.* Howells's *Out of the Question* was serialized in the *Atlantic Monthly,* February–April 1877. In a letter to John Hay on February 22, Howells wrote of his "joy in your liking my comedy," and continued, "The play is too short to have any strong effect, I suppose, but it seems to me to prove that there is a middle form between narrative and drama, which may be developed into something very pleasant to the reader, and convenient to the fictionist. At any rate my story wouldn't take any other shape."[65]

The shape was that of a drama of discussion in six scenes, in which the action grows out of, depends on, and in large measure consists of, the discussion of an issue. The structure is simple and linear. The action takes place at a resort hotel. In the first scene it becomes evident that Blake, a Western man belonging to no class whatever, has been helpful to the Bellingham family, a collection of socially particular Boston Brahmins. When her aunt insults Blake by treating him like a servant, Leslie Bellingham makes a point of acknowledging his acquaintance formally, although she knows he is "out of the question" as far as any permanent social connection goes. Blake subsequently gives up his room for the aunt, and in every way shows himself the soul of courtesy and tact. He and Leslie fall in love after he saves her from being molested by two tramps in the woods, and she keeps him company while he recovers from the broken wrist he has suffered during the fight. Most of the play consists of discussions about social position, marriage, and Blake's qualifications for the title of gentleman. It ends with a confrontation between Blake and Leslie's snobbish brother Charles, and although Blake's marriage to Leslie is secured by the good fortune of his having saved Charles's life in the war, Charles's final line leaves the issue clearly in the laps of the audience as he queries, "if Blake were merely a gentleman somewhat at odds with his history, associations, and occupation, and not also our benefactor and preserver in so many ways, – whether we should be ready to – ah –" (68).

In 1926, G. B. Shaw wrote a short retrospective description of the discussion play's development after *A Doll's House:*

> The discussion, though at first it appears as a regularly placed feature at the end of the last act, and is initiated by the woman, as in *A Doll's House* and *Candida,* soon spreads itself over the whole play. Both authors and audience realise more and more that the incidents and situations in a play are only pretences, and that what is interesting is the way we should feel and argue about them if they were real. . . . In *A Doll's House* and *Candida* you have action producing discussion; in *The Doctor's Dilemma* you have discussion producing action, and that action being finally discussed. In other plays you have discussion all over the shop. Sometimes the discussion interpenetrates the action from beginning to end. Sometimes, as in *Getting Married* and *Misalliance,* the whole play, though full of incident, is a discussion and nothing else.[66]

In *Out of the Question,* Howells had obviously written a play in which the incidents and situations were only pretenses for the discussion of the issue, which takes place "all over the shop." Like many of Shaw's plays, it has a comic plot that is nearly banal in its conventionality, but it has a structure most carefully constructed to contain and emphasize the discussion.

The issue is introduced in the first two scenes as Leslie counteracts the social slight her aunt gives Blake and Blake discusses the definition of a gentleman with the tramps. Scene 3 depicts both Leslie's falling in love with Blake and a faux pas that she is led into by her background and upbringing. Scenes 4 and 5 consist entirely of discussion – a conversation in which Mrs. Bellingham tries to convince Leslie that the social considerations make the marriage impossible and a conversation in which Blake points out Leslie's true feelings and convictions to her, and persuades her to change her mind. Finally, the discussion reaches its climax in Scene 6 as Charles and Blake have their confrontation. As is often true of Shaw, Howells makes no attempt to integrate the resolution of the issue with the outcome of the action, and in fact calls attention to the disparity between the comic assumption that the young couple will live happily ever after within the family circle now joined around them and the obvious answer to Charles's open-ended question. The comic ending here is a way of providing ironic closure to a discussion that doesn't admit of a simple resolution. The play's ending does not provide a satisfactory integration of structure and meaning for its audience. Instead the discussion provides commentary on the structure. By foregrounding the fairy-tale unreality of Blake and Leslie Bellingham's union, Howells emphasizes his thematic statement that class distinction is disruptive to a democratic society.

Howells integrates the discussion with the love story as well as with the characterization in the play, and builds the argument so that the climax of the action coincides with the heat of the argument. The discussion involves two basic issues, the definition of a gentleman and the extent to which social class should be considered in marriage. Howells handles the first deftly, engaging the audience's sympathy with Blake before the issue ever becomes a part of the action. When Blake first meets the tramps in the woods, he gives them some tobacco, and one of them responds, "Thank you, mister, You're a gentleman!" (43). Blake, fresh from his first meeting with the snobbish Bellinghams, asks why he called him a gentleman, and the tramp answers, "Well, you didn't ask us why we didn't go to work; and you didn't say that men who hadn't any money to buy breakfast had better not smoke; and you gave us this tobacco. I'll call any man a gentleman that'll do that" (43). When Blake is getting acquainted with Leslie, he mentions the incident to her, and muses:

> It made me think of the notion of a gentleman I once heard from a very nice fellow years ago: he believed that you couldn't be a gentleman unless you began with your grandfather. I was younger then, and I remember shivering over it, for it left *me* quite out in the cold, though I couldn't help liking the man; he was a gentleman in spite of what he said, – a splendid fellow, if you made allowance for him. You have to make allowance for everybody, especially for men who have had all the advantages. It's apt to put them wrong for life; they get to thinking that the start is the race. (49)

Neither the audience nor Leslie knows at this point that Blake is talking about Leslie's brother, but Howells has clearly ranged his audience on Blake's side by the time of Blake's confrontation with the Bellinghams.

Howells is more manipulative in his approach to the second issue, for he uses all the sympathies and expectations the comic structure arouses to enlist the audience's approval of the match between Leslie and Blake before he has Mrs. Bellingham try to persuade Leslie, and Charles persuade Blake, that it is "out of the question" because it will provoke society's disapproval. Despite the arguments, there is no denying that the marriage will turn the two into social pariahs on Beacon Hill, and that the alternatives are not very attractive for a girl raised as Leslie has been. The love-conquers-all solution evokes audience approval as much through the universal impulse of comedy as through the particular case of Blake and Leslie Bellingham.

Howells's blending of comedy and discussion in *Out of the Question* is both sophisticated and effective. Unfortunately, after a disappointing attempt to get the play produced at the Boston Museum,[67] he abandoned the discussion play until well after Shaw had made it a respected dramatic genre. His later one-act plays *The Night Before Christmas* (1910) and *A True Hero: Melodrama* (1909) are discussion plays that make use of conventional dramatic structure to highlight their themes. In *The Night Before Christmas,* the Fountains' indictment of Christmas as a pagan saturnalia celebrating hypocrisy and commercialism is not entirely mitigated by the picture of their child's innocent joy in the holiday with which Howells ends the piece. The same irony that undercuts the ending of *Out of the Question* undercuts the picture of family bliss that is brought about in this play by the child's innocent belief in the Christmas myth.

In *A True Hero,* Howells's dramatic structure supports rather than counterpoints the discussion. The play is an attack on the romantic notion of self-sacrifice in the form of a young man's wanting to confess to a crime he saw committed by a woman because "I am a man, and she is a woman. She is a wife, and it will break her husband's heart; she is a mother, and her motherhood makes her sacred. . . . The man who sees a woman in the toils of her own error, and doesn't feel it is his duty, his right, his God-granted privilege to save her at any cost to himself, is a traitor to every tie that binds him to his mother, his sister, and – any one who is more precious than either" (596–7). The young man's friends disabuse him of this nonsense and get him back to his fiancée by exposing the reality of the woman he pictures so romantically, and thereby sticking a pin in his inflated ideals. When the young man laments at the end of the play that he has fallen below his "ideal," the play's truth teller ends with the coda of the discussion: "The ideal of a man who thinks such a woman does such things once in a way, and may be redeemed by a good round lying piece of self-sacrifice? But such a woman always does such things in every way, and she can only be shielded, never saved. No, no! Never regret that in this case you've looked out for yourself. You've shown yourself a true hero! Some day I hope we shall have you in the novels and the plays" (601). In this case, Howells's perennial plea for realism and truth informs the action, and the comic ending is its triumph over the nonsense of inflated idealism.

HAMLIN GARLAND AND JAMES A. HERNE

Howells was clearly the most successful of the realistic fiction writers at creating a drama that embodied his aesthetic principles, expressed his ideas, and also made a positive impact on the theater. But the most immediate connection between realism and the theater came in the relationship between James A. Herne and Hamlin Garland. As a zealous young realist and disciple of Howells's, Garland was the direct link between the literary realists and Herne. By his own account, Garland was so impressed with the production of Herne's *Drifting Apart* that he sought out Herne and his wife, actress Katherine Corcoran. A deep friendship developed, and Garland became an "unpaid, self-appointed press agent"[68] for *Drifting Apart* in 1889. Garland's enthusiasm about the possibilities for realism in the theater is evident in a piece he wrote for the *Literary World* in September of that year. Advocating a realistic spirit in drama criticism, he echoed Howells and foreshadowed Herne:

> Above all, I plead for truth as a criterion. Is the play true, does it express American life? Does the plan unfold from the characters, and is the author looking at life, special definite facts of life, as the subject of his American drama? If any writer shall do this, he should be sure of our aid always, whether known or unknown, successful or a failure. We demand no set form for a drama, but insist simply on truth and a certain gravity of intent.[69]

In 1890 this realistic fervor produced two consciously realistic plays, Garland's *Under the Wheel* and Herne's *Margaret Fleming*. Garland's play was published in *Arena* but was never produced, although he did give it an "author's reading" in Boston. *Under the Wheel* is far from dramatic. As Herne noted, Garland's idea of a play was "a scene in which two people discuss, for instance, the purchase of a ton of coal. One says, 'I think we are running short of coal.' The other replies, 'We have enough to last until next week.' To him, this is realism. To me, it is not drama."[70] Nevertheless, as an indication of the kinds of changes the realists hoped to make in the drama, Garland's play is a useful text. It is a thought-centered piece with a simple linear structure that expresses its theme both explicitly through set pieces of dialogue and implicitly through action. Because it directs its thought presentationally toward the audience rather than containing it in the conflict on the stage, the play tends almost as much toward the didactic as the mimetic mode, although it does maintain a tenuous hold on the fourth-wall illusion and the representational frame.

Each of *Under the Wheel*'s six scenes is built around a social statement. In Scene 1 the Edwards family faces urban poverty as it is forced out of its tenement by "rents goin' up and wages goin' down."[71] Garland presents his thematic statement thinly disguised as the musings of the progressive newspaper editor Walter Reeves, addressed to his fiancée, Alice Edwards:

> I stood on the Brooklyn bridge the other day and looked down on New York. Over me soared and sung those stupendous cables, the marvel of man's skill, etched on the sky, delicate as a spider's web. I stood there looking down at the sea of grimy roofs, a lava-like hideous flood of brick and mortar, cracked, and seamed, and monstrous for its lack of line or touch of beauty, a modern city. I saw men running to and fro like ants, lost in the tumult of life and death struggle. I saw pale girls sewing there in dens reeking with pestilence. I saw myriads of homes where the children could play only in the street or on the sooty roof, colonies of hopeless settlers sixty feet from their mother earth. And over me soared the bridge to testify to the inventive genius of man. And

I said then what I say now, that men have invented a thousand ways of
producing wealth, but not one for properly distributing it. I don't know
where the trouble is. If we once knew the trouble, somebody'd find a
cure. Abolition of poverty. (*He muses a moment, then starts.*) Well, good-
bye, I'll write this up in a leader. (189)

As the scene ends, the Edwards family has taken the Western myth –
"Everybody is happy and successful that goes west – it's the refuge for
all like us" (194) – as the solution to their poverty, and the scene closes
with their enthusiastic singing of "O'er the Hill in Legions." The rest of
the play is Garland's typical deflation of the Western myth by exposing
the evil forces of Capitalism and Nature at work on the Western farmer.
The Edwardses are ruined by the foreclosure of their mortgage, following on three bad seasons, a drought, and a hailstorm. "We're in the jaws
of a machine," says Edwards (215). Garland's ending is a compromise
between hope and despair. Alice is about to marry Reeves, who has
embraced the cause of the Western farmer with the hope that "spring
will come again." He tells Edwards, "You can't help believing it, as you
live the next five years, the air is already electrical with inquiry. Over us
the shadow still hangs, but far in the west a faint, ever-widening crescent
of light tells of clear skies beyond. Live for that time, it's worth living
for. Strike hands with me. Let me carry your knapsack. Believe in the
future" (227). But Reeves's optimism is undercut by the paralytic stroke
that Edwards suffers, presumably as a result of his unrelenting battle
with the system. The last line of the play is spoken by Edwards's young
daughter Linnie, symbol of the rising generation: "And now we'll go
back to Boston, won't we, Allie?" (228).

The denatured comic ending was advanced for 1890, as was the realism in setting and costume that Garland used, emphasizing the typical
rather than the unusual as the local colorists did. He was less advanced in
dialogue and character. His dialogue tends to mix slang and broad dialect
with stilted stage English and set pieces like Reeves's lecture on poverty
quoted above. The characters also are closer to the conventional types
with local-color touches used by Mark Twain and Harte than the psychologically realized individuals Howells created. On the whole,
Garland's artistic conception was far more realistic than his talent for
writing drama would allow him to render.

Garland's influence on Herne was more productive than his own play-
writing efforts. Herne's *Margaret Fleming* was a cause célèbre for literary
Boston when it was produced in 1890. Considered much too daring to be
worth any manager's risk, it was finally put on, after considerable pub-
licity effort by Garland, Howells, and *Arena* editor Benjamin O. Flower,
in Chickering Hall, a recital hall seating five hundred that Herne had
rented and remodeled. Most of literary Boston and Cambridge attended

the opening performance in 1890, but the play didn't get far beyond that circle. When Herne attempted a regular run in 1891, the play closed in three weeks. It played only one matinee performance at Palmer's in New York in 1891, and closed after twelve performances in Chicago in 1892. After that it was dropped regretfully from the Hernes' repertoire as too expensive an artistic luxury, and Herne went on to fame and financial success with his less controversial if less artistically satisfying vehicle *Shore Acres*.

The manuscripts of *Margaret Fleming* were destroyed by a fire in 1909, but the play was reconstructed from memory by Garland and Katherine Corcoran Herne, who had played Margaret, in 1914. Mrs. Herne also rewrote parts of Act I and standardized the dialect of the original, but Julie Herne, who had played Margaret in a 1907 revival, said that the reconstructed manuscript was "substantially as written by my father."[72] Herne himself had cut the play from five acts to four, eliminating some rather sensational events connected with a subplot and focusing the final act completely on his thematic issue. In the text as it is now, Act I shows the love between Philip and Margaret in the context of their middle-class domestic life, and exposes as well Philip's thoughtless treatment of his young mistress, Lena Schmidt, who has just given birth to his child. In Act II the depiction of the Flemings' family life continues while the action reveals that Lena's sister is employed as the Flemings' nursemaid and that Margaret has glaucoma, which according to the doctor, will result in blindness if she is upset. In Act III, Margaret is persuaded to visit Lena, who dies after revealing that Philip Fleming is the father of her child. Margaret, of course, goes blind from the shock. Act III ends with the scene that caused the most heated controversy in 1890, as Margaret sits down and tries to comfort the newborn infant: "*scarcely conscious of what she is doing, suddenly with an impatient swift movement she unbuttons her dress to give nourishment to the child, when the picture fades into darkness.*"[73] Act IV consists of the meeting between Philip and Margaret nine days later, their discussion of the situation, and their partial reconciliation.

The discussion also sparked considerable controversy, for it treated the touchy subject of the sexual double standard. When Philip asks Margaret to forgive him, and expects to be welcomed with open arms in the wifely spirit of sentimental domestic comedy, Margaret balks: "The wife-heart has gone out of me," she says (311). Failing to make Philip understand her, she suggests, "Suppose – I – had been unfaithful to you? . . . You are a man, and you have your ideals of – the – sanctity – of – the thing you love. Well, I am a woman – and perhaps – I, too, have the same ideals. I don't know. But I, too, cry pollution." Philip responds, "I did not know. I never realized before the iniquity – of my – behavior. Oh, if I only had my life to live over again. Men, as a rule, do not consider others when urged on by their desires" (311). Philip's realization helps toward a reconciliation, but Margaret does not suggest that her loss of faith in him will be restored by good intentions. "I will help you – we will fight this together," she says (312), but she makes it clear that the full restoration of their marriage is a long way off.

Herne's play suffers by being too "theatrical" from the literary point of view to the same extent that Garland's suffers by being too "literary" from the theatrical point of view. Howells and other realist critics deplored the coincidence and the "big moments" in the play, as they did those in the plays of dramatists like Ibsen and Hermann Sudermann. They applauded the play's honest look at sexual relations. Stating the case as bluntly as one could in 1890, *The Woman's Journal* asked the reader to imagine the case reversed: "Would anyone blame the husband if, while forgiving her and consenting to be friends with her, he declined to live with her again?"[74] The other side was equally vocal. Margaret was called a "monster of morality" for not forgetting as well as forgiving, and Herne's mild statement was seen as dangerous and subversive by conservative critics. On the other hand, the play's "commonplace" quality was condemned as trivial and boring. William Winter, for example, complained that "several babies are introduced, and at one time the stage is replete with bathtub and sponges, baby pins and diapers, scented soap and powder puff, towels and carminative; and this paraphernalia of the nursery is exploited with abundance of that soft nonsense of prattle which always sounds well beside the cradle and always makes people sick in public."[75]

In short, conservative critics objected to all of Herne's efforts to create what he called "art for truth's sake" in the play. Despite its short theater life, *Margaret Fleming* had thus accomplished what none of Howells's more literary efforts had succeeded in doing. It had raised the issues of realism as they applied to the drama, and made them subjects of widespread popular discussion, even creating a fad. "To admit that you have not seen 'Margaret Fleming,'" declared the *Boston Herald,* "is to acknowledge that you are 'not in the swim.'"[76] In this sense, *Margaret Fleming* achieved the "epoch-making" effect Howells had predicted for it.[77] It made realism a force for the theater to contend with. It alerted playwrights, critics, and public alike to the change that was on the horizon. In 1890 the American popular theater began slowly to change, and along with the Norwegian Ibsen, whose work was first produced in America in 1889, the native James A. Herne was a catalyst for that change. Before 1890 the realistic ideas were coming from novelists who hadn't fully learned the language of the theater. Now that the theater people were faced with one of their own, they began to consider fundamental changes in the way they wrote and produced plays.

4

The Transition: American Realistic Drama in the Commercial Theater, 1890–1915

The years between 1890 and 1915 were crucial for the establishment of realistic principles in American drama. During this period the conceptions of setting, dialogue, thought, character, and structure that realists like Howells and James, Garland and Herne had devoted such thought and energy to developing began to take shape in the commercial theater. The turn-of-the-century playwrights who had ambitions toward writing drama that was good literature as well as good theater were the generation who grew up with the sense of realism as avant-garde. Whether they acknowledged its theoretical influence directly as Herne, Augustus Thomas, Clyde Fitch, and William Gillette did, reacted against it as the neoromanticists Percy Mackaye, Stephen Phillips, and William Vaughn Moody did, or simply displayed it in their writing as Edward Sheldon, Rachel Crothers, and Langdon Mitchell did, there is no question that they were aware of realism as the driving force for literary development in American drama.

The new realistic playwrights were literary people. All but Herne and Thomas had some college education. They knew the literature of the day, and they were aware of its new principles. They also knew the theater. They were popular playwrights, and their plays show the reality of compromise – the sense of just how much realism, and how much literature, would "go" with their audience. In reviewing their plays over this 25-year period, it becomes clear that these playwrights managed to educate their audience. The gradual evolution from the limited local-color realism of setting, costume, and dialogue in the early nineties to a self-conscious realism that had begun to touch every aspect of the representation in the teens is a phenomenon that can be read in the texts of their plays. Our study naturally follows realism's development from the outside in, from setting and dialogue to thought, character, and structure.

86

SETTING

During the nineties, the use of setting to add a touch of local color to the popular play, which was usually formulaic melodrama or comedy, underwent a subtle change. Following upon the efforts of Bret Harte, Mark Twain, and Joaquin Miller, as well as Herne, local-color plays of the nineties such as *Blue Jeans* (1890), *Arizona* (1899), and *The Cowboy and the Lady* (1899) were slowly moving beyond local colorism and toward regionalism. These plays tended to focus on local customs, people, and peculiarities as part of their subject matter, rather than simply to use them as window dressing. Nevertheless, they still tended to exploit them as outré or sensational. One reviewer complained in 1893:

> There is a great danger that this public will be wearied by an over-production of American "dramas of character" as Augustus Thomas calls them. We are already getting too much, for variety's sake, of the eccentric traits of inhabitants of town and village on the stage. We have had "In Mizzoura," two of Mr. Harrigan's plays, "Peaceful Valley" and "The Corncracker," all within a few weeks, and "Shore Acres" and "In Old Kentucky" are still pending. . . . These rustics may be exactly like the Hoosiers and the Corncrackers, but if they are Indiana and Kentucky are pretty badly off for sane inhabitants. I doubt their verity.[1]

Whether the plays were veracious or not, the new trend toward making the setting and the supposed characteristics of a local group of people their central interest was fairly well set by 1900, and plays about American regions had become a fad. The period between 1898 and 1907 saw productions of the Western plays *Arizona, The Cowboy and the Lady, The Virginian, The Girl of the Golden West, The Three of Us,* and *The Round Up;* the North-country plays *Up York State, York State Folks, New England Folks, Lover's Lane,* and *Eben Holden;* and the Southern and Midwestern plays *Under Southern Skies, Alice of Old Vincennes, The Wilderness,* and *Jim Bludso of the Prairie Bell.* Although the overt aim of the playwrights was to analyze and represent on the stage a particular region's way of life, the settings in these plays tend to be divorced from the plots. Even the plays built around a historical event, such as Fitch's *Nathan Hale* (1898) and *Barbara Frietchie* (1899) and Gillette's Civil War plays, *Secret Service* (1895) and *Held by the Enemy* (1886), were manipulated into conventional love plots so they would "work" on the stage. Their conflicts are essentially the conventional conflicts of stage love.

After the turn of the century, the dramatic conflict began to grow at least partly out of the setting, the milieu in which the characters lived. In Langdon Mitchell's *New York Idea* (1906), the cynical view of marriage that causes problems for the characters proceeds directly from the New

York "smart-set" environment they inhabit. Eugene Walter's *Easiest Way* (1908) suggests environmental determinism in the milieu of New York show girls. One of the girls expresses the connection between the life and the worldview explicitly:

> Don't you realize that you and me, and all the girls that are shoved into this life, are practically the common prey of any man who happens to come along? Don't you know that they've got about as much consideration for us as they have for any pet animal around the house, and the only way that we've got it on the animal is that we've got brains. . . . All this talk about love and loyalty and constancy is fine and dandy in a book, but when a girl has to look out for herself, take it from me, whenever you've got that trump card up your sleeve just play it and rake in the pot.[2]

Clyde Fitch suggested the opposite view on environmental determinism in *The City* (1909), but took just as much interest in the relationship between his characters and their environment:

> Don't blame the City. It's not her fault! It's our own! What the City does is to bring out what's strongest in us. If at heart we're good, the good in us will win! If the bad is strongest, God help us! Don't blame the City! *She* gives the man his opportunity; it is up to *him* what he makes of it![3]

It was Edward Sheldon, in *Salvation Nell* (1908), who took the greatest step toward integrating setting with character and action to create the forceful sense of character-determining milieu that realist critics demanded. His stage directions move beyond representational fidelity to suggest a way of life, a combination of forces that has made his characters what they are and that opposes the young barmaid Nell's fight to attain "respectability." The play's opening stage directions are an extensive but central document in the development of realistic setting:

> *A bitterly cold Christmas Eve at Sid J. McGovern's Empire Bar in New York. To the right front is a door leading to Timmy Watson's poolrooms. It is half open; the sound of men's talk, the click of balls, laughter, and an occasional shout are heard. To the right, from front to back, is the bar itself. Behind is an arrangement of mirrors, with bottles of whiskey, glasses, etc. A telephone at the nearest end. In front of the bar is an irregular line of spittoons. There are brilliant Welsbach gas lights hung above, shedding a hard white light. . . . Back to left of entrance is a large, rather deep show window. It is brilliantly lighted; the audience can see the backs of the pictures (beer and whiskey advertisements and loose theatrical posters) which face the street outside. A streetlamp gives a dim idea of the exterior. Just to the left of the window, there stretches to the immediate foreground a slight partition, about eight feet high. It is ornamented on both sides with lithographic malt advertisements, highly colored. Toward the foreground end is a pair of swinging doors, connecting the two rooms. The space to the left is the ladies' buffet. There are two small windows*

I. A scene from Edward Sheldon's *Salvation Nell*, 1908. (Photo by Byron)

on left, but very high to left front is a door leading directly to the alley. When it is opened, the sign "Family Entrance" can be seen stuck out above it. . . . There are Welsbach chandeliers in both rooms; the light is white and glaring – bare tables and kitchen chairs are scattered about the ladies' buffet. In the bar proper, against the partition, is a long, narrow table, covered by a solid, ragged, white cloth; on it are the various articles which make up a "free lunch" – sausages, cheese, pickles, crackers, etc. There are one or two chairs in the barroom, but not many.[4]

As the curtain rises, the scene has what Sheldon calls a *"kaleidoscope"* effect. At the bar, the cash register rings continually as the two bartenders serve the *"shabby, ill-dressed, poor-looking men,"* already *"jovial with liquor,"* who come and go throughout the act. A trio of ragged Italians plays a popular song out of tune, and four women are in the "ladies' buffet" – *"a sodden, wretched hag, already drunk,"* huddled in her chair; *"a fat old Irish woman with her shawl over her head"*; and two *"shabby, painted streetwalkers,"* one of whom secures a customer. Sheldon notes that *"the first scenes are to be played easily and swiftly, for a purely atmospheric effect."*[5] It is the bar itself, the milieu in which Nell exists, that is her antagonist.

II. William Gillette (left) in *Secret Service*, 1895. (Photo by Pach)

The setting is a concrete scenic image of the limits life has imposed on her spirit, and of the forces she will be fighting throughout the play.

Sheldon's is an extreme case, but he, along with Mitchell and Walter, was making a sociological statement about his characters through his setting and the conflict it engendered. By the first decade of the twentieth century, the emphasis in setting had clearly shifted for the serious realistic playwright, from superficial local-color details for their own sake to use of detail to create a representation of the environment's influence on the character and conflict that generate action.

Sheldon's meticulous attention to detail grew naturally from a new awareness of the set's importance, which had evolved during the nineties. Contributing to the sense of environment, playwrights such as Sheldon, Gillette, and Herne had an underlying aesthetic assumption that the audience will share with the dramatist a common vision of the reality being represented, to the extent that they are given the details of that reality as the dramatist envisions it. These playwrights maintained absolute control over their sets, with a degree of detail that Ibsen and Shaw never thought of. Gillette's telegraph room in *Secret Service* is a perfect example of the attempt to re-create exactly the image of a room that the playwright has in his mind:

> *Plain and somewhat battered and grimy room on the second floor of a public building. Moldings and stuccowork broken and discolored. Stained and smoky*

*walls. Large windows, the glass covered with grime and cobwebs. Plaster fallen
or knocked from walls and ceiling in some places. All this from neglect – not
from bombardment. The building was once a handsome one, but has been put to
war purposes. . . . Three wide French windows up left and left center obliqued
a little and opening down to floor, with balcony outside extending right and left
and showing several massive white columns, bases at balcony and extending up
out of sight as if for several stories above. . . . Large disused fireplace with
elaborate marble mantel in bad repair and very dirty on right side behind
telegraph tables. Door up center opening to cupboard with shelves on which are
battery jars and telegraph office truck of various kinds.*[6]

Herne's directions for *Shore Acres* (1893) are not quite so exhaustive,
but they show a similar attention to detail in his scenic image of domestic
bliss. In the kitchen, for example: *"There is a worktable, right, below the
sink, covered with material for making bread, and on it are several loaves of bread
fresh from the oven. Below the worktable is a door leading outside. To the right,
between the door and the sink, is an alcove where stands a large old-fashioned
dresser, holding dishes, pans, and various kitchen furnishings, also several large
pies."*[7] Playwrights who were not so fastidious about the details in stage
directions still maintained the assumption that attention to detail in the
stage representation was essential to the realism of the piece. Clyde Fitch,
for example, sprinkled his New England plays with vignettes of pas-
sersby, children's games, and the details of the schoolhouse and the
tavern.

A more interesting, and more important, development in the use of
the set was the synthesis of concern for detail with a new concern for
depth of character, producing a new means of characterization. The
connection between set and character began as a rather quaint piece of
sentiment in *The New York Idea* when Mitchell expressed John Karslake's
undiminished love for his former wife, Cynthia, through the set. The
fact that John has kept her portrait on the wall and her hat, gloves, and
sewing basket where she left them on the day she walked out lets both
Cynthia and the audience know that he still cares for her. In the following year, Augustus Thomas used his set in *The Witching Hour* (1907) to
express aspects of his hero's character that are significant for the plot. His
modern paintings depict his modern frame of mind. The other works of
art in his room suggest his interest in poetry and the occult:

*Above the center door is a marble bust of Minerva, surmounted by a bronze
raven, lacquered black, evidently illustrating Poe's poem. The Antomarchi
death-mask of Napoleon in bronze hangs on the dark wood fire-place. A bronze
mask of Beethoven is on one of the bookcases and on another is a bust of Dante.
A bronze Sphinx is on another bookcase.*[8]

Other playwrights quickly moved beyond this simple use of set for
exposition of character, and attempted to capture the fuller relation of .

character to environment by depicting the dynamics of their reciprocal influence. In *Salvation Nell,* for example, Sheldon uses the set at the opening of Act II to show how far Nell has come from the saloon and how much she has been influenced by the Salvation Army: *"To the right, door leading to the bedroom with a framed text hanging over it. . . . To front, left, a table with one or two books, a copy of the* War Cry, *a workbasket . . . Various texts, colored lithographs of General and Miss Booth in uniform on the walls. . . . Everything is neat and clean, homely but comfortable."*[9] The inner change in Nell has spurred the change in her environment, but before the inner change could begin, she first had to escape the saloon.

Combining the expressive and the dynamic functions, the later sets of Sheldon and Gillette, and those of Rachel Crothers, reinforce the plays' conflicts. In Crothers's *Man's World* (1909), Frank Ware's Bohemian apartment helps to emphasize her conflict with conventional social attitudes. In *Electricity* (1913), Gillette emphasizes debutante Emeline Twimbly's starry-eyed idealism in wanting to marry Bill Brockway, a "man of the people," through the incongruous juxtaposition of the Twimblys' Manhattan townhouse in Act I and the Brockways' Bronx walk-up in Act II.

During the years between 1890 and 1916, costume underwent a development similar to that of setting. In the nineties, it was naturally used in local-color and historical pieces as an aid in the representation of a particular place and period. In the later plays, however, costume was often used as a means of characterization and as an indication, sometimes to a fine degree, of differences in class, taste, and experience, as well as personality. In *The Boss* (1911), Sheldon's nouveau riche Mike Regan, for example, appears *"elaborately dressed in a morning coat, with a gardenia in his button-hole. He wears a diamond scarfpin, and is very conscious of his clothes."*[10] By contrast, the socially established James Griswold is *"carefully and soberly dressed"* (851), and his daughter Emily is *"dressed very simply for the street, wearing furs"* (852). Ever careful about the details of characterization, Gillette specifies that the locomotive engineer in *Electricity* *"wears an old house coat and slippers and has a handkerchief tied around his neck loosely – but not in any fancy way – in place of a collar."*[11]

Special staging effects continued throughout the period to serve their main purpose of adding interest, excitement, and emotional engagement to the play, but they tended to become less sensational and more integral to the play's action and setting. The local-color plays exploited the features of their locales unashamedly. Herne wrote into *Shore Acres* a lighthouse, a storm, and a turkey dinner that was to become legendary. Thomas exploited a backwoods cabin and a blacksmith shop in *In Mizzoura*. Gillette got tremendous mileage from his telegraph office and his battle scenes in *Secret Service* and *Held by the Enemy*. Fitch used the

Western gunfight and the dance hall in *The Cowboy and the Lady*. When the locale began to assume serious importance for the theme, however, the playwrights began to look more closely at such features. Low-life scenes, for example, had been the stock-in-trade of Harrigan's comedies as well as sensational melodramas like Boucicault's *Poor of New York* and Daly's *Under the Gaslight*. These vignettes of street life began to take on serious thematic significance as early as 1899, when Gillette punctuated the acts of his *Sherlock Holmes* with scenes of street musicians, dope-dealing sailors, and a hurdy-gurdy man. His juxtaposition of these street scenes with the little drama of the wealthy being enacted within doors was not the major thematic emphasis of the play, but it did make a serious point about the two ways of life. Ten years later, Sheldon took the major step of integrating these scenes of street life into the characterization and conflict of *Salvation Nell*.

DIALOGUE

The transition that dialogue underwent during the period epitomizes the development of the drama as a whole. During the eighties, standard stage dialogue was the stilted "literary" English we have seen in *Hazel Kirke* and *The Banker's Daughter* for the upper and middle classes and a very broad dialect for low-life or regional characters. A few notable exceptions among the playwrights, such as Howells and, to a lesser extent, Harrigan and Herne, paved the way for a slow development toward colloquial English, the representation of normal speech patterns, and the use of dialogue for characterization and the dramatization of social conflict. During the nineties, even such attempts at realism as *Margaret Fleming, Secret Service, In Mizzoura,* and *The Cowboy and the Lady* employed an unbelievable stilted English for the main characters and an equally unbelievable dialect – New England, Southern, German, Pike County, or Western – for the minor ones. With the exception of Augustus Thomas's *Oliver Goldsmith* (1900), the period pieces reflect a complete lack of concern for historical accuracy in the representation of speech. The only step popular playwrights took toward realistic dialogue in this decade was to follow Howells's lead in the repartee of society comedy. In Fitch's *Moth and the Flame* (1898) and Gillette's *Too Much Johnson* (1894) the characters speak colloquial, if unrealistically clever, American talk.

In the first decade of the twentieth century, playwrights began to show more interest in the dialogic realism that H. A. Kennedy had described in 1891, where "only the clever people say clever things" and "no rhetorical flourishes are required." In Thomas's *Other Girl* (1903), the society talk is played off against the street slang of the boxer Kid Garvey for thematic as well as humorous effect. In *The New York Idea*, Mitchell not only represents society people talking as they would normally talk, though with more than usual cleverness, he also attempts to use speech appropriate to class, personality, experience, and social point of view, thus helping to dramatize the conflicts among his characters. The clash between the viewpoints of "Old New York" and the new "smart set" generation is clear in the opening scene, for example, as the curtain rises on the older generation in the midst of a discussion about the precise wording of a divorcée's wedding invitation and the persons "to whom the announcement should not be sent." Cynthia enters with a racing form in front of her, muttering "Belmont favorite – six to one – Rockaway – Rosebud, and Flying Cloud. Slow track – raw wind – hm, hm, hm."[12]

Sheldon attempted to make a similar point in *Salvation Nell* with the juxtaposition of lower-class speech and the proper English of the Salvation Army's few upper-class members, but his dialogue is not very convincing. His upper-class characters say things like: "I'm going to fight for you and stand by you, and drive away all these – these ghosts of suffering and sin and darkness!"[13] The lower-class characters say things like: "Mebbe yous t'ink I'm green. They give me a pink stockin' over to the Mission 'cause I ain't ben late t' Sunday school once, an' it had an orange 'n a bag o' candy, an' a dime, but Pa pinched the dime's soon's I got home, an' I et the orange already so Ma couldn't give it to the kid'n–."[14] He was more successful in *The Boss* (1911) at contrasting the upper-class characters with the Irish dock workers, and he even managed a piece of characterization with Mike Regan's dialogue, having him consciously shift his way of talking to suit the class of his listener. To Emily, the upper-class woman who has married him to keep him from destroying her father's reputation, he says, "I tell ye my kids are goin' to be born 'cause I loved their mother with all me body an' mind an' soul, an' 'cause she loved me back with all o' hers! And if such things as that can't be, why then, so help me Gawd, I'll have no kids at all!" (880). To his old street-fighting buddy Porky, he says, "D'ye remember one night in the old bar on Lake Street? Gee, it's fifteen years ago now! . . . We got behind the bar, an' ye grabbed the bung-starter, an' I broke four bottles o' Canadian rye over Kelley's head before I laid him out. Gee, that was a swell scrap!" (887).

Augustus Thomas took another step toward realism when he introduced broken rhythms and colloquial syntax to his dialogue. In *As a Man Thinks* (1911), two characters discuss Christmas:

Clayton. . . . Ha! "Glad tidings of great joy."
Seelig. Comes only once a year.
Clayton. You any respect for the whole business – that Christ fabrication?
Seelig. (*Going to fireplace.*) You mean the Church idea – the creeds?[15]

Thomas sometimes loses control of his natural conversational rhythm when his characters speechify, but in general it heightens the illusion of everyday life in his plays.

In short, none of the dramatists who wrote between 1890 and 1916 produced thorough dialogic realism, but many of them contributed to its development. During this period, capturing the rhythm of colloquial speech became as important to realistic playwrights as recognizing the social and regional differences in dialect. The use of dialogue for the characters' individuation and psychological development was not yet as important as its use for the dramatization of the social conflicts they were involved in, but it was beginning to be a consideration. All of these effects contributed to the realism of the more fundamental dramatic elements of thought, character, and structure.

THOUGHT

Of these fundamental elements, thought underwent the greatest change during the period, from generally the least considered element in the play to often the most considered. The general trend was a development away from simple formulaic comedies and melodramas *set* in a given milieu to dramas *about* a given milieu or about a social or psychological problem that it produced. A simple example of this development is the political play, which began as a fad in the nineties with humorous local-color plays about country politicians, like *The Senator* (1894) and *The Governor of Kentucky* (1895), and developed into a representation of serious political problems in Sheldon's *Nigger* (1909), which examines the difficult decision of a Southern politician who wants to do something for blacks, and *The Boss* (1911), a serious, though sensational, treatment of corruption in big business and city political machines.

Through Mike Regan, the "Boss of the Fourth Ward" in a Midwestern city and a self-proclaimed "grafter an' a thief" (857), Sheldon demonstrates how a man could control the whole city's politicoeconomic system because he owns the grain contracts that are the base of its economy, the graneries where the people work, the saloons where he forces them to drink, and the banks that hold the mortgages on their houses. Intertwined with the story of the Regans' marriage is the story of Mike's defeat in business, through the combined forces of a union and the Catholic church, to the great relief of the entire city. Of course the realism falters when Mike is saved from prison by a stroke of good fortune and is morally regenerated through his wife's well-bred efforts to civilize him, but Sheldon manages along the way to expose his techniques of graft, extortion, blackmail, mob killings, and strikebreaking.

The most common social subject during the period was the perennial one of the relations between the sexes – more specifically, marriage and divorce, the double standard, and the topical issues of the emancipated "new woman" and women's rights. The Ibsenesque treatment the double standard had received in *Margaret Fleming* was not to be seen again for fifteen years, when the formal discussion play came into its own in America. There was, however, a sprinkling of discussion about the topic in many plays – comedies, melodramas, and dramas of pathos – that indicated the playwrights were willing to "wrestle with problems" as Howells had challenged them to do. Fitch, in *The Cowboy and the Lady* and *The Frisky Mrs. Johnson,* and Thomas, in *Mrs. Leffingwell's Boots* and *The Other Girl,* flirted with the problem before it received full-fledged discussion in Crothers's *Three of Us* (1906), *A Man's World* (1909), and *Ourselves* (1913), Sheldon's *Salvation Nell,* Walter's *Easiest Way* (1908), Thomas's *As a Man Thinks* (1911), and Sheldon's *Romance* (1913). The attitudes expressed on this much discussed topic are as varied as the viewpoints of the playwrights and the forms they chose for their expression. Sheldon, like Herne, insists that sexual infidelity is wrong for both men and women, and that those who fail their partners must be saved through expiation. Fitch indicates that it's both wrong and risky for the woman, but not particularly so for the man. Thomas suggests that because either might fall, the other should be forgiving, but at bottom, it's a woman's nature and social duty to be "better" than a man. Walter suggests that women are by nature weak and will succumb to the sexual importunities of men, who have a right to despise them for it. Crothers insists that whatever happens between a man and a woman ought to happen equally. This issue was clearly the most debated aspect of the relations between the sexes right through the thirties, and it became more and more the central issue out of which the action of the plays developed. The earlier treatments are comedies or melodramas with a scene or two devoted to discussion of the issue, but later treatments like Crothers's *Man's World* (1909) and Thomas's answer, *As a Man Thinks* (1911), have action that grows out of the problem and attains closure only through its resolution.

In *A Man's World,* Frank Ware, a young female writer, is raising a friend's illegitimate son in a Greenwich Village milieu of writers, painters, and musicians. During the course of the play, she finds out that the father of the boy is Malcolm Gaskell, the man she is planning to marry. His unrepentant attitude toward his treatment of the boy's mother, whom he deserted, so changes Frank's feeling for him that she tells him finally, "The future doesn't seem possible for us together."[16] The ensuing discussion shows the operation of the double standard, and Frank's despair of ever getting Malcolm to see its injustice. He steadfastly maintains that, in sexual matters, "Man sets the standard for woman. He knows she's better than he is and he demands that she be – and if she isn't, she's got to suffer for it" (40). "Since the beginning of time one thing has been accepted for a man and another for a woman," he says, and he asks Frank, "Why on earth do you beat your head against a stone wall? Why do you try to put your ideals up against the facts?" (111).

Frank pleads with him to show her that he understands his own responsibility toward his son and the boy's mother: "Oh, I want to forgive you. If you could only see. If your soul could only see. Oh, dear God! Malcolm, tell me, tell me you know it was wrong – that you'd give your life to make it right. Say that you know this thing was a crime" (112). Malcolm responds, "No! Don't try to hold me to account by a standard that doesn't exist. Don't measure me by your theories. If you love me you'll stand on that and forget everything else" (112). By ending the play with Frank's refusal to "forget everything else" and Malcolm's departure, Crothers was clearly identifying the play's issue with its action. The audience was left to resolve the question of the debate rather than to accept a closure arbitrarily provided by the action, as in comedy or melodrama.

As a Man Thinks is a less unified work, for it discusses anti-Semitism as well as the double standard, but it is the latter that informs its basic structure. This part of the plot turns around Elinor Clayton, who, finding out that her husband, Frank, is involved in yet another affair, decides she will pay him back in kind, and goes to the hotel of a man she had been engaged to nine years previously. Frank finds out about the visit and sues for divorce. The play's plot is complicated, but it mainly involves the efforts of Dr. Seelig to convince Frank that his action is unjust and wrongheaded.

Thomas hedges on the issue by making Elinor guilty only of the indiscretion of going to a man's room, not of adultery, and by having the doctor argue both sides of the case. To Elinor, he claims that it is not, as "that woman dramatist with her play" said, a "man's world" but a woman's world, moved by "the mainspring of man's faith in woman – man's *faith*."[17] As he puts it: "Every father believes he is a father only by his faith in the woman. Let him be however virtuous, no power on earth can strengthen in him a conviction greater than that faith. There is a double standard of morality because upon the golden basis of woman's virtue rests the welfare of the world" (66–7). In other words, he argues that a woman must be faithful so that a man can be sure of the paternity of his children. To Frank, he objects to the extremes of the double standard: "Your position is that of a thief – a confessed embezzler – complaining in his hypocrisy of what? – that his partner's books appear inaccurate. That is the proportion. . . . For God's sake, Frank Clayton, cleanse your mind of its masculine conceit, prejudice, selfishness and partiality" (75). In Act IV, Seelig manages to reconcile the Claytons by convincing Frank of his male prejudice, but he can persuade him to return to his family only by proving his paternity. Thomas's happy ending affirms the family and rejects infidelity, but it also promotes the double standard. Elinor accepts her husband back with open arms after he has demonstrated his lack of faith in her and his lack of responsibility toward their marriage vows. In this wedding of comic structure to the resolution of the issue, Thomas makes his answer to Crothers's plea for equal responsibility abundantly clear – No! in thunder.

At the turn of the century, the institutions of marriage and divorce were almost as popular topics for discussion as the double standard. Marriage is discussed seriously in Fitch's parable about the bad effects of jealousy, *The Girl with the Green Eyes* (1902), and in Bronson Howard's *Kate: A Comedy* (1906). The more common treatment, however, took the humorous, almost cynical tone of Fitch's *Moth and the Flame* and *The Climbers* and Thomas's *Other Girl*. In 1906, Mitchell's *New York Idea* began a fad and set the prevailing tone for the discussions of divorce that would follow. The Karslakes are presented as a case of "premature divorce" in a New York society that has made the pattern of "marriage, divorce, remarriage, redivorce" all too common. In his celebration of the Karslakes' reunion, Mitchell suggests that divorce had become too easy an answer to problems that could be worked out within the context of a marriage if people had more incentive to do so. Many permutations on the marriage-divorce theme appeared during the first two decades of the twentieth century, in plays with such daring titles as *Is Matrimony a Failure?* (1909), *A Modern Marriage* (1911), and *The Trial Marriage* (1912), but the subject didn't receive serious treatment until Jesse Lynch Williams presented the issues without coy evasions or titillating suggestions in his watershed discussion play *Why Marry?* (1917). As in the treatment of the double standard, the general trend in these plays, whether humorous or serious in tone, was toward a clearer focus on the social issue as central to the play's conflict.

A similar trend appeared in the discussion of the new woman and women's rights. The emancipated woman is present in Charles Barnard's *Mary Lincoln, M.D.* (1890) and in Herne's *Shore Acres* (1893), whose young heroine, Helen Berry, has read such daring books as *Descent of Man* and Howells's *Hazard of New Fortunes* and rebels against her father's objection to anyone's "a-learnin' my daughter a pack o' lies, about me an' my parents a-comin' from monkeys."[18] Helen's escape from the patriarchal domination of her father to marriage with a free-thinking young doctor constitutes the play's comic action, and Herne's comic ending affirms the place of the new woman in the new order. The struggle of the new woman to achieve freedom and independence is also a dominant theme in Crothers's early plays *The Three of Us* and *A Man's World,* both of which have strong female protagonists who are single-handedly raising orphaned children, and who accept offers of marriage and help from men only if they are assured of equality in the relationships being proposed.

In the later play *He and She* (1912), Crothers modified this view. *He and She* is a serious investigation of the decisions the new woman faced in 1912. Each of its three female characters faces the dichotomy of marriage and career. Ruth is a writer engaged to Keith, a sculptor. When she is offered the editorship of a woman's magazine, Keith balks at the idea of her continuing to work after their marriage, for "What in the name of heaven does loving a girl amount to if you don't want to take care of her from start to finish?"[19] Ruth suggests the compromise of letting her try both marriage and career for a while: "What you ask of me is to cut off one half of my life and throw it away. What I ask of you is only an experiment – to let me try and see if I can't make things comfortable and smooth and happy for us – and still take this big thing that has come as a result of all my years of hard work and fighting for it" (914). When Keith cannot agree to the compromise, Ruth chooses the career rather than the marriage, agreeing with him that she couldn't be happy without her work. Ruth's opposite is Daisy, a young woman who works in the "man's world" because she has to earn a living, but who would much rather be supported and taken care of as someone's wife. As she tells Keith, "There are lots and lots and lots of women taking care of themselves – putting up the bluff of being independent and happy – who would be so glad to live in a little flat and do their own work – just to be the nicest thing in the world to some man" (916). In the end, Daisy marries Keith, as happy in her dependence, presumably, as Ruth is in her independence.

These two characters exist primarily to emphasize the conflict of the play's protagonist, Ann, a sculptor who has just won a competition for a major commission. She must decide between taking the decisive step of accepting the job, and thus launching a full-fledged professional career, and fulfilling her ideal notion of her duty as a wife and mother. Ann's husband, Tom, also a sculptor, is dismayed that she has beaten him in the competition and fears the loss of her love. Ann at first resists giving up the commission. Then, learning that their sixteen-year-old daughter is romantically involved with the chauffeur at her boarding school, Ann decides she must give up the commission in order to be closer to her child. In the end, Tom offers to give in, but Ann has decided that her prior obligations as wife and mother preclude her ambitions as a sculptor, and she asks Tom to take the commission and execute her design. Through each of these cases, Crothers states that a woman's life is compromise. Marriage *and* career means inadequacy in both; marriage *or* career means giving up an entire sphere of life.

The inevitable concern that changing class distinctions, the disruption of settled notions about "society," and the intermixture of the "well bred" and the "vulgar" provoked among such typically conservative Americans as the patrons of the theater fostered another thematic trend. The issue of social class informs *The Climbers, The Other Girl, The Woman in the Case* (1905), *The Boss, Electricity,* and *Romance* (1913), and functions in many other plays of the period. These plays are overwhelmingly conservative. Except for Sheldon, who suggests that there is a possibility for happiness in the union of Mike Regan and Emily Griswold, "a guy born in a back room over a bar an' a lady like yerself" (890) – once he accepts her values – the playwrights depict a complacent social order that is impervious to inroads from the vulgar.

Edward Sheldon's *Nigger* (1909), which exposes the evil of racism, expresses a more progressive attitude toward the social order. It concerns Philip Morrow's realization that he has Negro blood, and the difficult process that he, as governor of a Southern state, goes through in deciding to reveal it. His first problem is that he has been raised in an atmosphere of race prejudice, and he considers black people dirty, oversexed, drunken, ignorant, and idle. He cannot see how he could be one of them, or how they could be worthy of his efforts on their behalf. In his struggle to comprehend his predicament, he enlists the aid of Senator Long, a liberal who has been his political enemy. The Senator takes a line of argument that apparently was progressive in 1909: "Try an' like the niggahs. That don't mean sayin' theyah's good as you – it's one to a million they ain't! But hatin's the ol'way o' gettin' roun' the folks that bothah ye – likin's up-to-date! So crack a smile, sonny, an' stick out yo' han's, an' all pull t'gethah – top an' bottom –rich an' po' – black an' white!"[20]

Philip is convinced eventually that he should "wo'k fo' the niggahs – shouldah t' shouldah – b'cause I'm a niggah myself, an' b'cause they need me awful bad!" (254). He tells his fiancée, Georgie, who is willing to stand by him if he will go north and try to take up his life there, that he must stay in the South and fight the system. He decides that he must suffer as a scapegoat for the collective guilt the institution of slavery has incurred, but that through his suffering will come expiation and salvation for the whole country: "My gran'fathah did somethin' wrong, an' it's resultin' in mighty seveah pain fo' ev'ry one conce'ned. But aftah this pain's been used – fo' it *has* a use, an' a good one too! – why, we'll get the fruits o' the whole experience, an' I reckon they'll make up for ev'rythin'" (259). The play closes with Philip about to make the speech exposing his racial identity and beginning his fight to help the "niggahs." Sheldon's call for reform is temperate, to say the least, but in its time, even its suggestion that the new order is dependent on social change and the breaking down of class and race barriers instead of their preservation was unusual.

On the whole, although the discussion of social issues became a standard feature of the drama during these early years of the twentieth century, it was a fundamentally conservative discussion. Although it might point out flaws in the reigning social order and suggest that action was needed to remedy them, this drama did not advocate fundamental change. The beginnings of a more radical attitude can be discerned toward the end of the period. New theater groups like the Provincetown Players and the Washington Square Players tended to foster radical thinking about a play's subject as well as its production. Though little noticed at the time, such plays as Theodore Dreiser's *Girl in the Coffin* (1915), a naturalistic treatment of the labor movement, helped to pave the way for the more radical thematic developments that began in the twenties and mushroomed in the thirties.

CHARACTER

Like thought and structure, character underwent a fundamental transformation between 1890 and 1915. Characters at the beginning of this period were what Howells called the "immemorial puppets of the stage," the stereotypes of comedy or melodrama, sometimes with local-color characteristics laid on for humor or added interest, in the spirit of Mark Twain and Bret Harte. At the end of it, the typical character was the social type, who often attained some individuality through the pscyhological conflicts engendered by social issues or problems, that Howells applauded. During the nineties, characterization was limited by the plays' rigid structures. The characters were the heroes, heroines, and villains of melodrama or the eirons and alazons of comedy first, and the types of local-color literature second. In Gillette's melodrama *Held by the Enemy* (1886), for example, Colonel Brant is the dashing hero of melodrama, and also the cool Yankee officer; Eunice McCreery is the beleaguered young heroine, and the Southern belle; Surgeon Fielding is the villainous sexual threat to Eunice, and the Southern army officer. Young Beene and Susan McCreery are the juvenile lovers who provide some relief to the heavy emotion of melodrama, and they are also a young Yankee boy and a young Southern girl. Here character, in the Aristotelian sense of the moral traits that impel the play's action, is clearly derived from melodrama; the regional differences have been laid on to intensify the emotional effect and add interest to the stock melodramatic situation. Gillette, a Northerner himself, chose a Northern hero to save an innocent young Southern maiden from a Southern villain, and a love relationship uniting the North and the South as the restoration of order in society. The universal types of melodrama were thus made more immediate to the audience's experience, but they were still universal types.

The master at this kind of combination was Augustus Thomas, whose characters in three local-color melodramas, *In Mizzoura* (1893), *Alabama* (1898), and *Arizona* (1899), were conscious manipulations of melodramatic and regional types, as he described them in his prefaces.[21] In each case the characters' regional qualities were used to intensify the audience's feelings toward them as melodramatic types, as well as to heighten the production's immediacy. The characterization in such local-color comedies as Herne's *Shore Acres* (1893) and Fitch's *Lover's Lane* (1901) had a similar dynamic, though the playwrights tended to exaggerate and stress the regional characteristics in order to exploit them for humorous effect. Herne's Uncle Nat, one of the most famous local-color characters in the history of the American theater, was the last incarnation of the "Jonathan" character, the hayseed whose countrified exterior masks the time-honored Yankee virtues of shrewdness and practicality as well as kindness:

> Uncle Nat is a man of sixty, and his large sturdy frame shows signs of toil. His eyes, of a faded blue-gray, have the far-seeing look common to sailors. He wears his yellow-white hair rather long, and he is clean-shaven save for the tippet of straw-white beard that seems to grow up from his chest and to form a sort of frame for his benevolent, weather-beaten old face. Uncle Nat is of the soil, yet there is an inherent poise and dignity about him that are typical of the men who have mastered their environment. He has great cheerfulness and much sly, quiet humor. He wears overalls of a faded blue, a blue checked jumper, beneath which one glimpses a red flannel shirt, and on his head is a farmer's much-battered wide straw hat. His sleeves are rolled back, and he carries a pitchfork in his hand. (673–4)

It was some time before realistic playwrights became interested in psychological characterization. The major development along these lines during the nineties was the introduction of new types for the theater, characters who were not the psychologically complete personalities that Howells was calling for, but who were more particularized than the types preceding them. This development thus marked a transition between the notion of characterization solely by means of dramatic type and the notion of characterization by personality. Gillette invented the calm, cool man of the world who came to be known as the "Gillette hero," whether in the shape of Sherlock Holmes or the Civil War spy. The gay divorcée and the wild young Western girl appeared during the nineties along with the emancipated new woman. Augustus Thomas introduced the streetwise young boxer Kid Garvey, and his tough but good-hearted girl, Myrtle Morrison. The introduction of such types was a fad at the turn of the century, but it was also a step toward the individuation of dramatic characters.

Fuller psychological individuation occurred, as Howells had suggested it would, when the playwright had to "struggle with motives," when a specific social issue generated conflict that demanded a personal response from the character. A good example is Bronson Howard's *Kate* (1906). It begins as a lightly satirical society comedy, poking fun at an international marriage between American money and a British title, and at the light way marriage was regarded among the wealthy on both sides of the Atlantic. Its plot concerns Kate Hardenbeck, an American millionaire's daughter who is engaged to Archibald Pengure, Earl Cathurst. Archie's sister Dorothy is engaged to the Reverend Lord John Vernor, a younger son educated for the ministry who has been persuaded after twelve years of fairly loose bachelor life to take over the living at the family seat. Although Jack knows that Dorothy will make an excellent minister's wife, he is in love with Kate. Kate is in love with him, but considers marriage to Archie a more prudent connection. Archie, meanwhile, has impregnated Bianca Dunn, a very young girl of vaguely Mediterranean origin who has been adopted by a local sea captain and loves Archie passionately and completely. In form, the play is a comedy–melodrama. The main outline of its complicated plot is that Bianca attempts suicide, and Kate, after learning that Bianca loves Archie and carries his child, gives up and marries Jack; Dorothy is matched up with Edward Lyell, who becomes rector of the parish when Jack resigns. Thus the comic new order, represented by the appropriate pairings of the couples, is established only after Bianca has risked her life for it with melodramatic seriousness.

The new twist in the play's characterization is that Howard takes a step beyond comic convention in the characters' consideration and discussion of marriage. When they confront their attitudes about marriage and act on their new self-knowledge, they break out of their comic or melodramatic stereotypes. Jack's doctrine is so rusty that he has someone else write his sermons, but he writes the one on *Marriage and the Marriage Ceremony* himself because, as he says, "there isn't another clergyman in England that knows more about social morality than I do. The rest of them take a bird's eye view of it and twitter; I have had a closer view and I can screech."[22] In the sermon he says: "*The Holy Church has no authority to sanctify a marriage based on mere worldly interest or social ambition. In such a case even the church service cannot make a man and a woman husband and wife in the eyes of God. Their cohabitation is sin!*" (21–2). Bianca, a sort of nature-child who is sanctified by her innocent amorality, adds the idea that only love can raise the institution of marriage above the animal level. Without sexual attraction, she says, it is below the animals; with sexual attraction, it is on the same level; with full human love, it is above them. When Jack is forced to take his own views seriously, and when Kate is forced to see her proposed marriage through Bianca's eyes, a psychological conflict arises in the play, and the characters' resolution of the conflict is what impels the actions they take.

The difference between this play and the typical comedy-melodrama of the *Banker's Daughter* variety is precisely the difference that Howells had called for from American playwrights: The audience is privy to the characters' wrestling with the conflict, and is aware of the specific individual motivations behind their responses and their actions. The characterization is overt and rather crude, but the conflict can be seen working in a speech like Kate's to Bianca: "Most of us young women in society get married as a matter of course; and it strikes one as odd to – to think much about it – except the trousseau of course. But to-day – to-day! – I *have* been thinking about it – another side of marriage. Go on! Marriage is love! – to a *real* girl. Go on!" (81). This is not the sort of speech the heroine of nineteenth-century American comedy makes. Kate goes on to perform the action that comic structure dictates by marrying Jack, but the audience has seen that her conflict is personal and individual, and thus that she is a "real girl" herself, and not just the conventional prize for the hero at the end of a typical comedy.

A similar individuation occurs with John and Cynthia Karslake in *The New York Idea*. Although they are the natural hero and heroine of comedy and young New York "smart set" millionaires, they are also in some degree individuals who realize that their precipitous divorce was a mistake and that something wrong in their milieu has promoted such capricious actions. Their coming together in the end is not *merely* the necessity of the comic form, it is also an action the audience can understand in terms of individual motives in the context of a particular class in a particular time and place.

After 1908 the trend is toward the development of just such social types, types who achieve some individuality through their responses to the conflicts they face, whether internal or external, emotional or social. Examples are numerous. Sheldon's Nell is a stereotypical "fallen woman," saved from her pernicious environment and nurtured into bloom by the Salvation Army, but she also has moments that suggest the real woman caught in the emotional conflict between love for "her man" Jim on the one hand and desire for middle-class respectability and "salvation" on the other. Sheldon's attempt to make the audience see Nell's conflict saves the character from complete stereotyping. He creates a similar balance between type and individual with Phil Morrow in *The Nigger* and Mike Regan in *The Boss,* but his most successful attempt at a character with psychological depth is Tom Armstrong in *Romance*

(1913). This treatment of a young minister who, in order to reconcile his morals with his passions, tries desperately to "save" the amoral opera star he loves, is emotional rather than intellectual, but it focuses on the character's psychological dilemma nearly as much as on the love story's outcome.

Discussion plays like Crothers's *Man's World* and *He and She* tend to achieve the greatest individuality in characterization. Frank Ware is not simply the bohemian writer, but also a young woman with affection for, and a sense of responsibility toward, her adopted child that makes personal and passionate what her fiancé calls her "ideals" and "theories" about the double standard. Each character in *He and She* takes a stand on marriage that proceeds from a unique personal perspective, and the actions they take are significant only when one considers that perspective. When the dramatic action involves specific ideas or issues, the conflicts that produce it are specific and deeply felt. In plays that don't develop this kind of social conflict and that rely on the traditional forms for action and structure, the characters remain typical as well. In terms of characterization, plays like Thomas's *Witching Hour* (1907) and *The Harvest Moon* (1909) and Fitch's *City* (1909) were old-fashioned when they were produced. Although each playwright tried to capitalize on an "issue" – Thomas on the uses of parapsychology and Fitch on the corrupting influence of the city – his characters remained types, rendering the arbitrary resolution of the issue neither particularly believable nor particularly interesting. The "new drama" was successful only when a playwright was able to integrate his new depth of thought with a corresponding depth of character.

STRUCTURE

It was dramatic structure that underwent the most important development between 1890 and 1915. The attempt to represent reality mimetically was now extended, as Howells had hoped it would be, to the play's structure as well as its other elements. Playwrights tried to create incidents that could and would occur in real life and to achieve closer interdependence among plot, character, and thought. Their major achievement, however, was the full development of a discussion–play structure similar to those used by Howells, Ibsen, Herne, and Shaw, but adapted to the demands of the American commercial theater.

Except for Howells's *Out of the Question* and Herne's *Margaret Fleming*, American plays before 1906 were simple comedies, melodramas, comedy-melodramas, or dramas of pathos. Each of these traditional forms has a conventional structure that grows out of the attitude it expresses toward human experience. In comedy, the playwright depicts some flaw or corruption in the social order, represented usually by the members of the middle-aged generation that controls it. The hope for the future lies in those of the younger generation who see the flaw and eliminate it from the society by displacing their elders and, through their coming of age, establish a new order that remains, as Northrop Frye has described it, free and undefined. The worldview of comedy is optimistic. It expresses confidence in the younger generation's ability to purge the society's corruption, and through the sexual union that nearly always both symbolizes the hero's coming-of-age and gives the play formal closure, it affirms the natural cycle of the generations. The comic playwright inevitably conveys two thematic implications through his comic form: that the older generation is corrupt and should be overthrown and that the new order that must "crystallize around the hero" and his bride[23] will be harmonious, integrated, and better than the old. The comic playwright may focus satirically on the old order or romantically on the new, but if one uses the comic form, one must accept the general worldview it implies.

Melodrama implies a similar worldview, but its tone is different. Comedy, of course, is humorous – it pokes fun at the old order and celebrates the new. Melodrama is deadly serious. Its worldview envisions a battle between good and evil, personified clearly by the hero and the villain, with the heroine as the battleground. The villain seeks to destroy the heroine, usually by killing, raping, or seducing her. The hero seeks to save her from the villain, and usually to marry her.[24] Thus melodrama embodies the same assault on corruption and the same triumphant emergence of the hero and his bride as comedy, does, but its new order represents conquest and revenge rather than harmony and integration. Melodrama moves to destroy the evil one; comedy, to convert him. Comedy represents a triumph of the natural and the free; melodrama, a triumph of the moral order. Comedy thus tends to subvert the reigning social order; melodrama, to support it. The melodramatic playwright accepts the assumption that the reigning order's morality is just, that it is threatened by evil, which must be destroyed, and that this threat is deadly serious. But the playwright also accepts the assumption that society will be saved when the evil is routed from it.

Comedy-melodrama resulted from the attempt to write comedy "with a message" or melodrama that was not unremittingly dreary. It usually involved mixing two plots, a comic love story and a melodramatic battle against evil. The most common mixture in the late nineteenth century was the addition of a juvenile love story to an otherwise serious plot, as in Gillette's *Secret Service* and *Held by the Enemy*. In this form, the overall worldview is still clearly that of melodrama. A more complicated version arose at the turn of the century, when the comic and melodramatic plots were combined into an action in which the natural comic union of the young lovers was blocked by an irretrievably evil person or social force, and the eventual union was accomplished only after the evil was destroyed.

Tragedy was much less common than either comedy or melodrama as a vehicle for late-nineteenth-century playwrights. Without speculating on the cultural values involved, it is safe to say that the fated defeat of the hero and his subsequent transcendence through suffering was not the reigning American myth at the time. Nevertheless, a few attempts were made to translate American experience into this form and to suit the form to American experience. Fitch's *Nathan Hale* (1898) and *Barbara Frietchie* (1899) were attempts to couch national legends in tragic form. In structuring the action of each around a love plot and emphasizing the individuality of his characters, however, Fitch ended up with an emphasis on emotion, and his final effect was pathos rather than catharsis or transcendence.

With Howells's *Out of the Question* and Herne's *Margaret Fleming* came the inroads that the experimental drama of discussion made into this group of conventional forms. Similar discussions of social problems began to crop up in the commercial theater after the turn of the century. Fitch's *Climbers* (1901), Thomas's *Other Girl* (1903), and Crothers's *Three of Us* (1906) all have scenes in which the characters sit down to discuss a social issue with immediate bearing on their lives. In *The Other Girl* the issue of the double standard becomes the subject of general discussion and is resolved when Reggie forgives his fiancée, Catherine, for "going around" with the boxer Kid Garvey because he has behaved worse than she in having an affair with the Kid's girlfriend. A similar discussion occurs in *The Three of Us* when the innocent Rhy is caught by her fiancé, Steve, in the room of the villain Beresford, who has tried and failed to seduce her. A discussion of Rhy's social reputation ensues, and is resolved when Steve shows that he believes in her despite appearances.

In these two plays, the discussion's function is to give the outcome dictated by the comic structure a plausible and intellectually satisfying reason for happening. *The Climbers* is less satisfying, for its action is at odds with its discussion. Blanche Sterling's husband is a confessed embezzler who has deserted her. She must decide whether to let him return, in order to restore social appearances and her son's "good name," or to marry the devoted man who loves her. She is convinced through the discussion that she must sacrifice herself for her son and her social duty, but her husband commits suicide, leaving her conveniently free to marry the man Fitch makes us feel she should have had all along. By bowing to his society's norms in the discussion, yet confirming the natural comic "urge to merge" in the action, Fitch is trying to have it both ways, and the play ultimately fails. The discussion undercuts the comic resolution; the comedy mitigates the noble self-sacrifice of the discussion.

Sheldon's *Nigger* provides the most interesting structural use of discussion in these early experiments. The discussion in which Philip is convinced to change his mind and work against racial prejudice explains and provides thematic justification for an ending that would otherwise be a structural disruption and a dramatically unsatisfying forced closure. Through the discussion, the audience, which has been expecting the comic union of Philip and Georgie and a happy resolution to Philip's problem, is educated to accept Philip's giving her up and taking on the enormous task of fighting for social change. The discussion supports the open-ended action and prepares the way for this departure from the conventional structure of comedy-melodrama.

In such plays as *A Man's World, He and She,* and *As a Man Thinks,* Crothers and Thomas abandoned the structure of comedy-melodrama entirely, and changed the whole notion of dramatic action. When the action of the play became synonymous with the discussion of the issue – and the conflict of the play, with the conflict over the issue – then the structure of the play became the structure of the discussion's resolution. Thus, instead of imposing a pattern of events on reality to make it conform to an a priori worldview, these playwrights attempted to take from their experience a common pattern of everyday life, the process of considering and arguing about an issue, and allow it to give the play its structure. Because the action in these plays is predicated on the discussion, there is no forced closure, no "happy ending," unless the issue is resolved happily.

When Frank Ware and Malcolm Gaskell are unable to come to an understanding in *A Man's World,* the issue remains unresolved, and the action open-ended. Like Nora in *A Doll's House,* Malcolm simply walks out of the room, leaving the audience to speculate about the future actions of the characters and, more important, to reconsider the positions argued in the debate. By refusing the audience its expected happy-ever-after union for Frank and Malcolm, Crothers is suggesting that no such union is possible in this "man's world," thus questioning the basic assumption of the comic worldview. By subverting her comedy, she is asking, in the realistic spirit, that her audience look at "the truth," at their common experience, and see that the comic version of happy union is impossible as long as the relations between men and women continue to be unequal. The realistic structure and the realistic theme are thus inseparable and mutually supportive.

He and She is a more complex illustration of the same principle. Here the traditional comic action is present in the union of Keith and Daisy, the traditional husband and wife. But Ruth's decision to give up the man she loves in order to maintain her independence and pursue her career is antithetical to the comic spirit of harmony and integration, which seeks to encompass all members of the new order in some sort of union. Ruth subverts the comic spirit and disrupts the closure of the comic structure by walking away from the comic society. Ruth is a minor character, of course, so her disruption is not enough to change the overall comic form, but the provisional decision that Ann makes is also problematic. Here we have considered acceptance of the traditional balance in the family, with Tom resuming the role of major breadwinner and major artist. Ann is returning to her family responsibilities with a renewed sense of how much her daughter needs her and how much her family's welfare means to her, but the resolution is not entirely comic. There is an unmistakable sense of loss as well as gain in Ann's choice, which carries over to the choices of the other women as well.

The spirit here is not the happy-ever-after spirit of a new "free and undefined" order, but the spirit of realistic compromise, made with a clear understanding of one's limited options in the world as one finds it. The action does not end with the play but suggests a future life full of such compromises and their consequences. It was this lack of closure more than anything else that characterized realistic structure as it began to develop in American drama. More and more, the task for the realistic playwright became not the representation of *an* action, but the representation of the action of life; not one clearly defined rhythm, but a short time in which many rhythms come together, producing the impression of life as it is lived and felt. The full accomplishment of this sense of drama was still a few years away, but it was made possible by these early rejections of the prescribed traditional structures for dramatic action.

The emergence of the discussion play did not *necessarily* mean the rejection of conventional structures. The comic resolution could be maintained by allowing it to grow out of the discussion, by making the discussion the turning point in the action. This is what Thomas did with *As a Man Thinks*. The Claytons' reconciliation is not simply the arbitrary end to the action that is demanded by the comic structure. It is a conscious and willed action on the part of the characters, brought about by their consideration of the alternatives and the resulting conviction that, despite their mutual distrust of each other and their unequal relationship, their imperfect union is best available option for all concerned. The spirit of this comic resolution is not the youthful joy of sexual union and ingenuous hope for the future; it is a more adult sense of the limitations imposed by reality on these youthful dreams, and the will to sacrifice one's personal good, even one's personal integrity, in order to live in harmony and to maintain the social order for the next generation. It is a resolution that comes of the characters' acting on an explicitly stated realistic worldview.

The effect of these early steps toward a realistic dramatic structure was to make the play seem more like a natural flow of events and less like an arbitrary manipulation of dramatic action – in other words, to make the action more mimetic. This achievement, more than any other, contributed to the solution of the apparent paradox in the phrase "realistic drama." The drama of discussion allowed for reproducing the conflicts and the sequences of events that the human consciousness perceives in reality without creating an expectation about their resolution or closure. In good drama of discussion there is no "expected" resolution to the conflict, as there is none to the conflict in life. The open ending of the drama of discussion does not allow the observer to impose a pattern of expectation on its representation of reality, because there is no convention for its closure, as there is none in life.

It was a long transition period from Herne's *Margaret Fleming* in 1890 to the first realistic efforts of the Provincetown Players in 1915. But this was the time it took for the commercial theater to absorb the new realistic principles and put them to use in commercially successful plays. In terms of the drama's general development, the change was tremendous. During these twenty-five years, the typical notion of setting for playwrights whose conscious aim was realism went from mere window dressing to the representation of a regional way of life, a character-determining milieu, or an interior expressive of its inhabitants, through carefully chosen detail. The dialogue went from stilted stage English or broad dialect to dialogue that captured the rhythms of normal speech and was appropriate to the class, personality, experience, and social perspective of the character who spoke it. Thought became central to the serious realistic play, as the social issues of marriage, divorce, the double standard, the new woman and women's rights, and anti-Semitism and racial prejudice became the objects of serious discussion. The new centrality of thought helped to change the structures of the plays from formula comedy and melodrama to more flexible comedy-melodrama and to the full dramas of discussion that Shaw and Howells had described. Finally, the notion of character went from the stereotypical puppet of comedy or melodrama to the social type that approached some individuation through psychological conflict.

In short, most of the changes the realists had been calling for in the eighties and nineties began to take hold during the next twenty-five years. Realism's development during this period was chiefly a matter of refinement – greater depth and sophistication in the thought; more individuation and greater psychological depth in the characters; more meaningful and integrated representation of the milieu. The one element of realistic drama that still had far to go in 1915 was structure. If structured carefully, the discussion play was one way of representing action that created the illusion of depicting the rhythm of life. The great development over the next decades was the experimentation with structures that deepened this illusion and that integrated the realism of the other elements.

5

The Cutting Edge: Eugene O'Neill's Realism, 1913–1933

Eugene O'Neill's literary influences have been thoroughly studied and well documented. Although Strindberg's influence has received the most attention by far, scholars have also demonstrated the important effects that Ibsen and Shaw had on his work.[1] O'Neill's suggestion that Theodore Dreiser should have been given the Pulitzer Prize in 1936 and his chance mentions of such writers as Stephen Crane, Jack London, and Edith Wharton also shed significant light on his realistic development.[2] He was clearly familiar with realistic fiction and with the important documents of dramatic realism in Europe. For our purpose, though, it is more important that his ideas be situated in the context of dramatic realism as it developed in the American theater.

When he started writing plays in 1913, O'Neill was well aware of what had been happening in the American theater. As the son of a prominent actor, he had grown up with intimate knowledge not only of his father's perennial *Count of Monte Cristo* but also of the whole range of Broadway to which the privilege of free passes entitled him. O'Neill made a number of statements that reveal the positive influence of realism, as well as the negative influence of his father's romantic melodrama. In 1926 he wrote to Edward Sheldon, "Your *Salvation Nell* . . . was what first opened my eyes to the existence of a real theatre as opposed to the unreal – and to me, then, hateful – theatre of my father in whose atmosphere I had been brought up."[3] Although he was perhaps exaggerating his debt to the older playwright, the statement shows his awareness that some of his earliest realistic influences had come directly through the American theater. His first acquaintance with European influences had also tended to come through Broadway. It was the scandal surrounding Arnold Daly's production of *Mrs. Warren's Profession* that first interested O'Neill in Shaw and prompted him to buy *The Quintessence of Ibsenism* in 1905, at the age of seventeen. Louis Sheaffer noted that he "marked in red ink everything he agreed with and ended with a book in which every page

112

was aflame with color."[4] In his youthful enthusiasm for Ibsen's realistic art, he attended ten performances of Nazimova's *Hedda Gabler* in 1907. As he later saw it, however, it was the 1911 American tour of Dublin's Abbey Players that brought the possibilities of dramatic realism home to him. In 1923 he said,

> As a boy I saw so much of the old, ranting artificial romantic stage stuff that I always had a sort of contempt for the theater. It was seeing the Irish players for the first time that gave me a glimpse of my opportunity. . . . I thought then and I still think that they demonstrated the possibilities of naturalistic acting better than any other company.[5]

Whatever the greatest source of influence, O'Neill's broad exposure to the turn-of-the-century theater, from the most theatrical melodrama to the most avant-garde realism, is clear in the amazing array of dramatic compositions he turned out when he started writing plays. In 1913–14 alone, he wrote eleven plays that reflect a wide range of the dramatic types in the American theater of the time, from *A Wife for a Life,* a brief Western sketch intended for vaudeville, to *Bound East for Cardiff,* the experimental "slice of life" that eventually won him the support of the Provincetown Players. At the beginning, his father's influence was as evident as Ibsen's, Shaw's, Strindberg's, or Sheldon's, for several of the plays are aimed directly at the popular audience. These include the society melodrama *Recklessness;* a farcical satire of the movie industry called *The Movie Man;* and *Abortion,* a one-act melodrama about a college baseball hero whose girlfriend dies after the abortion he persuades her to have. The realism O'Neill had encountered in Ibsen and Strindberg is evident in the more ambitiously literary efforts: *The Web,* a study of the social and economic forces that promote prostitution; *Warnings,* a play in which environmental and social forces lead inexorably to the protagonist's suicide; *Fog,* a fusion of philosophical discussion and the supernatural; and *Servitude,* a fully developed three-act drama of discussion in which O'Neill uses Ibsen's dramatic structure to argue against Ibsenist self-actualization for women and in favor of romantic self-sacrifice in love.

Calling on a play-writing imagination that resembled a catalog of American drama in 1913, O'Neill appears to have been trying out the current dramatic types until, in *Bound East,* he discovered one that suited his own perspective on life. Unfortunately, the situation wasn't as simple as that, for O'Neill went on experimenting, with both successful and unsuccessful artistic results, for the rest of his career. But he did keep returning to the successful forms, and the interest he took in his realistic studies of sailors was appropriate to his success with their structure. The sea plays he valued least, *Ile* and *In the Zone,* were those that went back to prerealistic dramatic structures. Whereas these two plays build to moments of climax – Mrs. Keeney's mad scene and the crew's frenzied attack on Smitty – the others emphasize the ongoing cycles of life that undercut their conventionally dramatic "big moments," such as Yank's death in *Bound East* or the fight in *The Moon of the Caribees*. O'Neill wrote that he considered *"In the Zone* a conventional construction of the theater as it is, and *The Moon* an attempt to achieve a higher plane of bigger, finer values."[6] His early conception of realism emerges from his contrast of the two plays:

> Smitty in the stuffy, grease-paint atmosphere of *In the Zone* is magnified into a hero who attracts our sentimental sympathy. In *The Moon,* posed against a background of that beauty, sad because it is eternal, which is one of the revealing moods of the sea's truth, his silhouetted gestures of self-pity are reduced to their proper insignificance, his thin whine of weakness is lost in the silence which it was mean enough to disturb, we get the perspective to judge him – and the others – and we find his sentimental posing much more out of harmony with truth, much less in tune with beauty, than the honest vulgarity of his mates. To me *The Moon* works with truth . . . while *In the Zone* substitutes theatrical sentimentalism.[7]

This statement is a good summary of realism's aesthetic ideals in revolt against dramatic conventions. Whereas the traditional forms of tragedy, comedy, and melodrama tend to emphasize, to exaggerate, to inflate the piece of human experience being represented, the impulse of realism is to deflate it by emphasizing its context, the larger rhythms of human life within which it occurs. This notion of realistic form was to become a preoccupation of O'Neill's as he persistently tried to find more effective ways of setting the action of the play into the larger rhythms of life. A second preoccupation, the dramatization of character, is also evident in this early statement, for Smitty's character is O'Neill's central consideration in both plays. From the realist's perspective, his whole career was a development of these two early impulses: the search for a dramatic structure that would give an appropriate shape to the illusion of reality in his dramatic action, and the search for theatrical ways to depict the deepest reality of his characters within the dramatic structures he discovered. He was to find the fulfillment of the two impulses in the fully developed realism of his masterpieces, *The Iceman Cometh* (1939) and *A Long Day's Journey into Night* (1940).

O'Neill's direction during the intervening twenty-five years was by no means an unwavering pursuit of the real. His experiments with presentational, expressionistic drama, and with such devices as masks, dramatic asides, chanting choruses and drumbeats that represent heartbeats could not have been more consciously antirealistic. But in many of his experiments there is an underlying consistency with the original impulse to pursue realistic structure and deeply psychological characterization, as well as a slow evolution toward his considered acceptance of mimetic realism as the appropriate dramatic medium in which to express his notion of truth. Both shed a great deal of light on the impulse of realism in O'Neill's work and, consequently, on the development of American drama, for during fifteen of those twenty-five years, the American theater tended to follow in the wake of its daring self-appointed icebreaker.

In the first of his full-length plays, *Beyond the Horizon* (1918), O'Neill waved the banner of innovation with unmistakable fervor. The play is a New England tragedy, the story of three mistaken lives. Robert Mayo, a poetic soul who yearns for the sea, falls in love with his brother Andy's natural mate, Ruth, on the eve of his departure for a voyage with his uncle, Captain Scott. He gives up his dream of the sea to marry Ruth and manage the family farm while Andy, the natural farmer, goes to sea in his place. The result is three desperately unhappy lives and Robert's eventual death from tuberculosis caused by overwork. *Beyond the Horizon*'s mixture of realistic stage technique, deterministic philosophy, and tragic structure was a first on the American stage. Its setting, its dialogue, and its characters were the now familiar standbys of local-color drama, but they had an unfamiliar depth. O'Neill's stage directions are a fulfillment of the theater's development toward representing character and milieu in the setting. In Act II, Scene 1, for example, he describes the change in the Mayo farm after Robert and Ruth have been married for three years:

> The room has changed, not so much in its outward appearance as in its general atmosphere. Little significant details give evidence of carelessness, of inefficiency, of an industry gone to seed. The chairs appear shabby from lack of paint; the table cover is spotted and askew; holes show in the curtains; a child's doll, with one arm gone, lies under the table; a hoe stands in a corner; a man's coat is flung on the couch in the rear; the desk is cluttered up with odds and ends; a number of books are piled carelessly on the sideboard. The noon enervation of the sultry, scorching day seems to have penetrated indoors, causing even inanimate objects to wear an aspect of despondent exhaustion.[8]

This room is an eloquent representation of Robert's failure on the farm and the state of disillusionment he and Ruth have reached in their married life.

O'Neill achieves similar depth in his characterization, so that even the minor figure of Captain Scott is psychologically believable as an aging and lonely man eager to take his young nephew under his wing and pass on his sailing lore. But O'Neill's conception of Robert, Andy, and Ruth is also rooted in a programmatic notion of the forces that control them. Each of them makes a wrong choice, a choice that leads inevitably to the play's tragic outcome. Robert chooses his love for Ruth over the poet's dream of the horizon; Andy chooses the sea over the farm, his natural element; and in Robert, Ruth chooses a romantic love of the moment over her natural mate, Andy. But the choices are no freer than the characters who make them. O'Neill once described Robert's "fate" in terms of deterministic forces. Like the Norwegian sailor on whom the character was modeled, Robert would have an

> . . . inborn craving for the sea's unrest, only in him it would be conscious, too conscious, intellectually diluted into a vague, intangible wanderlust. His powers of resistance, both moral and physical, would also probably be correspondingly watered. He would throw away his instinctive dream and accept the thralldom of the farm for – why, for almost any nice little poetical craving – the romance of sex, say.[9]

This does not keep the choice he makes from having tragic consequences for him, or the play itself from being a tragedy. O'Neill simply indicates that those mysterious forces dignified by the concept "fate" in older times might be better understood in the modern terms of psychology and sociology.

On the other hand, our ability to name these forces does not mean that we can escape them or escape the consequences of the actions they cause us to take. O'Neill was quite emphatic about the tragic nature of *Beyond the Horizon*. Robert's dying speech clearly signifies that his death is transcendence: "Don't you see I'm happy at last – free – free – freed from the farm – free to wander on and on – eternally! . . . I've won to [*sic*] my trip – the right of release – beyond the horizon!" (167–8). O'Neill wrote that "the one eternal tragedy of Man in his glorious, self-destructive struggle to make the Force express him instead of being, as an animal is, an infinitesimal incident in its expression" was the only subject worth writing about, and that "it is possible – or can be! – to develop a tragic expression in terms of transfigured modern values and symbols in the theatre which may to some degree bring home to members of a modern audience their ennobling identity with the tragic figures on the stage."[10]

In part, his translation of the ancient tragic spirit into modern terms was the translation of fate into the forces of environment and psychology. Its counterpart was the reworking of the traditional tragic form into a more flexible and more modern one. Beneath the familiar tragic form in *Beyond the Horizon* is another structuring of experience, what O'Neill called "a deliberate departure in form in search of a greater flexibility."[11] He was referring to the subliminal rhythm he created in the play through the constant alternation of scenes inside the farmhouse with scenes on the hilltop. As he described it:

> One scene is out of doors, showing the horizon, suggesting the man's desire and dreams. The other is indoors, the horizon gone, suggesting what has come between him and his dreams. In that way, I tried to get

> rhythm, the alternation of longing and loss . . . rhythm is a powerful
> factor in making anything expressive. People do not know how sen-
> sitive they are to rhythm. You can actually produce and control emo-
> tions by that means alone.[12]

This notion of rhythm was to become the fundamental structural principle in O'Neill's great realistic plays. In *Beyond the Horizon* it was just a
faint suggestion of the larger cycles of life underlying a traditional tragic
structure, but the fact that it was there, and placed there consciously by a
playwright who was in search of a flexible form in which to express
truth, suggested that a new sophistication and a new artistry were being
brought to bear on realistic drama.

The four plays that followed *Beyond the Horizon* – *The Straw* (1919),
"Anna Christie" (1920), *Diff'rent* (1920), and *The First Man* (1921) – are
unsuccessful experimental mixtures of structure and tone. *The Straw,* a
pathetic love story set in a tuberculosis sanitorium, combines a representation of the environmental and psychological causes of a girl's illness
with the romantic story of a young man's awakening to the meaning of
self-sacrificing love. Eileen Carmody, a girl of eighteen who has been
taking care of her four brothers and sisters since her mother's death, is
sent to a tuberculosis sanatorium, over her miserly father's objections
that he will have to pay for her treatment and hire a housekeeper. At the
sanatorium she meets Stephen Murray, a cynical young newspaper reporter, and while helping him with his writing, falls in love with him.
The night he leaves the sanatorium, she tells him that she loves him and
has broken her engagement to her childhood sweetheart.

Over the next few months, Eileen's condition deteriorates, mainly
because of the depression that her family's and Stephen's neglect brings
on. As she is about to be sent to the state farm by her father and her new
stepmother, Stephen comes to visit, finds out about her condition from a
sympathetic nurse, and agrees to tell her that he loves her, just to make
the short time remaining to her a little less miserable. In an emotional
final scene, he discovers that he really does love her and wants to marry
her, but also that it is too late because she is now too weak to recover.

Obviously, it is not the play's action or its treatment that is realistic.
The realism lies chiefly in the minute attention to the characters' psychological states and the careful representation of milieu – the Carmody's
Irish-American working-class home and the sanatorium are both depicted in detail. O'Neill's stage directions are specific about the way to
express the effect each event has on Stephen and Eileen. When Eileen has
been living with her unrequited love for about three months at the sanatorium, for example:

> She has grown stouter, her face has more of a healthy, out-of-door color, but
> there is still about her the suggestion of being worn down by a burden too
> oppressive for her strength. . . . She is evidently in a state of nervous depres-

> *sion; she twists her fingers together in her lap; her eyes stare sadly before her; she clenches her upper lip with her teeth to prevent its trembling.* (III, 367)

"Anna Christie" exhibits a more interesting tension between the influences of realism and theatrical convention that O'Neill was juggling early in his career. O'Neill is careful to have Anna explain the influences that have made her into a prostitute who hates men. Ill-treated and seduced on the Minnesota farm where she was left while her father was at sea, "caged in" and harassed sexually when she tried to make a living as a "nurse girl," she explains, "at last I got the chance – to get into that house. And you bet your life I took it!" (III, 18). But Anna succumbs finally to deeper, less easily explainable forces when she is reunited with her father Chris's "old davil," the sea. On the sea, which has claimed all her ancestors, male and female, for generations, Anna feels "like I'd found something I'd missed and been looking for – 's if this was the right place for me to fit in . . . I seem to have forgot – everything that's happened – like it didn't matter no more. . . . And I feel happy for once – yes, honest! – happier than I ever have been anywhere before!" (28–9). The play's ending with Anna's marriage to Burke the sailor affirms the deeper force that is the Christophersons' fate and negates the typical destiny of the Minnesota farm girl gone wrong. This deeper force is what O'Neill called "supernatural," his rejection of the "banality of surfaces"[13] that bothered him in the nascent realism of his contemporaries.

The most controversial realistic innovation in *"Anna Christie"* was its structure. O'Neill found it necessary to defend himself against critics who complained about the play's seemingly facile happy ending. Why end the play with the union of Burke and Anna when its tone and subject – the inexorable force that the sea represents in the lives of the Christophersons – would be so much better suited to tragedy? O'Neill defended the ending's realism in terms of both structure and character. In a letter to the *New York Times* he wrote: "Not even the most adversely prejudiced could call this a 'happy ending.' Meaning that I wish it understood as unhappy? Meaning nothing of the kind. Meaning what I have said before, that the play has no ending. Three characters have been revealed in all their intrinsic verity, under the acid test of a fateful crisis in their lives. They have solved this crisis for the moment as best they may, in accordance with the will that is in each of them. The curtain falls. Behind it their lives go on."[14] In a letter to George Jean Nathan, he confessed that the ending was problematic for the play's realistic structure, but defended it in terms of consistency with his realistic characters:

> From the middle of that third act I feel the play ought to be dominated by the woman's psychology. And I have a conviction that with dumb

people of her sort, unable to voice strong, strange feelings, the emotions can find outlet only through the language and gestures of the heroics in the novels and movies they are familiar with – that is, that in moments of great stress life copies melodrama. Anna forced herself on me, middle of third act, at her most theatric. In real life I felt she would unconsciously be compelled, through sheer inarticulateness, to the usual 'big scene' and wait hopefully for her happy ending.[15]

O'Neill's problem was to balance this sense of his character with the statement he wanted to make through the structure: "The sea outside – life – waits. The happy ending is merely the comma at the end of a gaudy introductory clause, with the body of the sentence still unwritten."[16] In *"Anna Christie,"* the emphasis was off. O'Neill had not yet found a way to take his audience beyond the introductory clause and into the larger rhythm of the sentence. Despite its author's protests, the play's structure is comic. The ending clearly suggests a return, though only a temporary one, to the "golden age" before Chris tried to interfere with his and Anna's destiny by separating them both from the sea. Via his belief in Anna's regeneration through the sea, Burke participates in the new order. And by accepting their "supernatural" destiny, the characters transcend their deterministic environment. As O'Neill admitted, the play did not finally succeed in expressing the perspective he had hoped for. He had meant to leave the ending open, and to let these various forces lie, maintaining their existence, but there is too much residual convention in his structure to allow for that. The determinism, "supernaturalism," and comedy remain separate, without coming together in the realistic synthesis he was hoping for.

Diff'rent carries out a study of the psychological grotesque that moves too far beyond the normal to fit the standards for realism articulated by Howells, James, and the other nineteenth-century critics. The play begins in a New England fishing village in 1890. Its protagonist is Emma Crosby, a woman who thinks of herself as set apart, "diff'rent" from her neighbors. In Act I, she breaks her engagement with Caleb Williams when she finds out that he has slept with a native girl on a voyage to the South Sea Islands, thus proving that he was like all the other men in the village, and not diff'rent enough to be worthy of Emma. Act II takes place thirty years later. Emma, having lived her life as an "old maid," goes through a midlife crisis, falls in love with Caleb's good-for-nothing nephew Benny, and tries to make herself and her house over for the flapper era. In order to avoid some trouble, Benny asks Emma to marry him. When Caleb returns from his voyage and grasps the situation, he asks Emma one final time to marry him, is refused, and then hangs himself in the barn. Meanwhile, Benny's callous attitude has finally brought Emma to her senses. She begs him to go away, and starts to get

III. A scene from Act I of the Provincetown Players' production of Eugene O'Neill's *Diff'rent,* showing Emma Crosby's parlor in 1890. (Photo by Van Damm)

rid of the new furnishings. When she hears about Caleb's suicide, she too heads for the barn, determined to follow him.

This play is far from O'Neill's best, and its study of regional eccentricity and psychological disorder was not the subject for realism, but he developed some realistic techniques to set his eccentrics in a believable context, which he was to put to much better use in *The Emperor Jones* (1919) and *The Hairy Ape* (1922). The two acts of the play are divisions in tone as well as time. O'Neill uses the realistic staging and the commonplace action of Act I both for characterization – to dramatize the change that Emma will undergo in the same way he used the farmhouse in *Beyond the Horizon* – and to anchor the improbable action of Act II in reality, to bring his unusual story within the mimetic illusion. The Crosby home in Act I is a familiar New England local-color set, distinguished mainly by its specific detail. It is scrupulously neat, and contains a horsehair sofa, an old mahogany chest, an old-fashioned piano, a marble-topped table, an old china lamp, and other typical furnishings of its time and place. It also contains, significantly, *"several books that look suspiciously like cheap novels,"* a clue to the sources for Emma's romantic notions about being "diff'rent."

In Act II, thirty years later, *"the scene is the same but not the same"*:

> The room has a grotesque aspect of old age turned flighty and masquerading as the most empty-headed youth. There is an obstreperous newness about everything. Orange curtains are at the windows. The carpet has given way to a

IV. A scene from Act II of the Provincetown Players' production of
Eugene O'Neill's *Diff'rent*, showing the change in Emma Crosby
through the change in the set from Act I. (Photo by Van Damm)

> *varnished hardwood floor, its glassy surface set off by three small, garish-colored*
> *rugs, placed with precision in front of the two doors and under the table. . . .*
> *The horsehair sofa has been relegated to the attic. A cane-bottomed affair with*
> *fancy cushions serves in its stead. A Victrola is where the old mahogany chest*
> *had been. . . . Only the old Bible, which still preserves its place of honor on the*
> *table, and the marble clock on the mantel, have survived the renovation and*
> *serve to emphasize it all the more by contrast.* (II, 519)

The room's incongruous newness serves mainly to intensify the change
in Emma:

> *The thirty years have transformed* EMMA *into a withered, scrawny woman.*
> *But there is something revoltingly incongruous about her, a pitiable sham, a too-*
> *apparent effort to cheat the years by appearance. The white dress she wears is*
> *too frilly, too youthful for her; so are the high-heeled pumps and clocked silk*
> *stockings. There is an absurd suggestion of rouge on her tight cheeks and thin*
> *lips, of penciled make-up about her eyes. The black of her hair is brazenly*
> *untruthful. Above all there is shown in her simpering, self-consciously coquet-*
> *tish manner that laughable – and at the same time irritating and disgusting –*
> *mockery of undignified age snatching greedily at the empty simulacra of youth.*
> (520)

The scenic image of the room and Emma's appearance tell a great deal of
the play's story before either she or Benny utters a line in Act II. O'Neill
perfected a technique for dramatizing his character's psychology here
that had been evolving in the American theater from its roots in Ibsen
and Herne through Sheldon, Thomas, Mitchell, Susan Glaspell, and
others. The play, however, doesn't get much beyond this characterization. There is no real explanation for the particular change that Emma

undergoes in the play, a circumstance that left puzzled reviewers to trot out their amateur Freudian psychology and speculate about the effects of repression and regression.[17] Nevertheless, the play reflects some deep thought about the realistic depiction of character that was to stand O'Neill in good stead later on.

The next play, *The First Man* (1921), is an intense Strindbergian marriage play relieved by some Langdon Mitchell–type discussion of current mores. Although it is written in a realistic mode, its realism is not remarkable. At the same time that he was working at realistic techniques for representing the psychological forces in characters like Anna Christie and Emma Crosby, however, O'Neill was working at new ways to dramatize character that would be of use to him in later realistic plays. In *Where the Cross Is Made* (1918), he said he wanted to "see whether it's possible to make an audience go mad"[18] by actually putting the ghosts that the four mad characters see on stage. This single and deliberate violation of the mimetic illusion brought him into the realm of expressionism. His use of expressionism reached its full development when he employed it to dramatize the character's psychological state against the realistic stage picture in *The Emperor Jones* and *The Hairy Ape*.

The Emperor Jones begins in mimetic realism, with Jones and Smithers having a credible conversation in a realistic set. The play's structure is an innovative attempt to suggest realistic action. As Timo Tiusanen describes it, the structure is O'Neill's prototypical circle: "The play consists of a realistic exposition scene, a rapid series of six scenic images, all expressionistically shaped, and a return to realism: a familiar circular structure."[19] It might be better figured as a downward spiral, however, for Jones does not return to the same place in reality. His journey is also a journey within. Each scene, taking him deeper into his own memory, then finally into racial memory, presents a different reality to him and to the audience as well. As in *Where the Cross Is Made,* O'Neill's audience is led to "go mad" with Jones while it experiences the phenomena of Jones's mind against the established mimetic background of reality. The famous expressionistic device of the quickening drumbeats, which represent the audience's heartbeats as well as Jones's, was the most dramatic instance of this technique, but it occurs throughout the entire representation. The forest, for example, is always recognizable as a forest, but it is wrought by Jones's mind into other things as well. In Scene 2, "*the forest is a wall of darkness dividing the world,*" the trees "*enormous pillars of deeper blackness*" (III, 187). In Scene 3, "*a dense low wall of underbrush and creepers is in the nearer foreground, fencing in a small triangular clearing. Beyond this is the massed blackness of the forest like an encompassing barrier*" (190). In Scene 4, as Jones's hysteria rises, the forest is personified and the road takes on increased importance: "*The moon is now up. Under its light the road glim-*

mers ghastly and unreal. It is as if the forest had stood aside momentarily to let the road pass through and accomplish its veiled purpose" (192).

With the completion of Jones's circle through the forest comes the completion of his journey within. O'Neill's structure implies that reality runs in cycles – cycles of life, cycles of race, cycles of good fortune and bad – supporting the theme that Jones's rise and fall as emperor, the appropriate subject for Greek tragedy, is only one small incident in the larger cycles that encompass all reality. O'Neill's structure provides the tension that impels the play forward through a manipulation of rhythm similar to that in *Beyond the Horizon.* Tiusanen calls *Emperor Jones* "a special kind of multicellular play in which the scenes are, as it were, minor cells within a similar major one."[20] Within each of the first seven scenes, Jones's fear and his memory produce a similar, almost ritual pattern of tension, which rises to a climax, ends in a quick, violent deflation, and results in Jones's moving on. This multicellular string of conflicts, similar to Edward Harrigan's "continuity of incidents," was an important step toward the realistic structure O'Neill was to develop for his later plays.

The structural innovation was one way O'Neill's later realism profited from his experiments with expressionism. Another and deeper consequence of this experimentation was the achievement of a greater depth of psychological realism, much as Henry James's novels achieve a greater depth of realism by representing his character's consciousness against a background of "objective" reality. In one sense, O'Neill violated the fourth-wall illusion in order to attain a deeper realism than he had been able to reach within the limits of mimetic representation. Much of his experimentation during the next fifteen years led toward the technique that eventually allowed him to retain his psychological depth while re-instating the fourth-wall illusion.

The Hairy Ape, written after O'Neill had seen Georg Kaiser's *From Morn to Midnight,* exhibits a more straightforward and less interesting use of expressionism to dramatize his protagonist's inner reality than *The Emperor Jones* does. His stage directions for the first scene make it clear that *"the treatment of this scene, or of any other scene in the play, should by no means be naturalistic"* (III, 207). Nonetheless, the play's expressionistic elements – the cage motif, the hell motif, the automatons of the Fifth Avenue scene – are played against the realistic elements of dialogue, character, and action. O'Neill gives the characters recognizable idiom to speak, though the rhythm in the ship and jail scenes and the repetition of motifs like "it don't belong" give the dialogue poetic resonance as well.

In characterization O'Neill is careful to provide social and psychological motivation for the characters in order to give them greater depth and sympathy for the audience. In one sense, Yank is simply the victim of a "deprived childhood," which has produced his skewed view of the world as well as his alienation from everything except the ship: "Home! T'hell wit home! Where d'yu get dat tripe? Dis is home, see? What d'yuh want wit home? (*Proudly*) I runned away from mine when I was a kid. On'y too glad to beat it, dat was me. Home was lickings for me, dat's all. But yuh can bet your shoit no one ain't never licked me since!" (211). Mildred Douglas, the steel heiress who sets off Yank's identity crisis by calling him a "filthy beast," is a student of sociology, and she provides the audience with an objective view of her own character:

> I would like to be sincere, to touch life somewhere. (*With weary bitterness.*) But I'm afraid I have neither the vitality nor integrity. All that was burnt out in our stock before I was born. Grandfather's blast furnaces, flaming to the sky, melting steel, making millions – then father keeping those home fires burning, making more millions – and little me at the tail-end of it all. I'm a waste product in the Bessemer process – like the millions. Or rather, I inherit the acquired trait of the by-product, wealth, but none of the energy, none of the strength of the steel that made it. I am sired by gold and damned by it, as they say at the race track. (219)

Just as the characters are explicable in the realistic terms of psychology and social environment, the action is plausible given the characters, even when, driven to distraction by his constant rejection from human society, Yank tries to join the gorillas. The cyclical, multicellular structure in which the action takes place is similar to *The Emperor Jones*'s, except that the cycle is suggested symbolically rather than contained in time and space. Yank begins in the hold of the ship, "*a cramped space in the bowels of a ship, imprisoned by white steel. The lines of bunks, the uprights supporting them, cross each other like the steel framework of a cage*" (207). He ends in the cage at the zoo. Like the psychological scenes in *Jones*, Yank's cages suggest a downward movement, from ship to jail to zoo, impelled inexorably by the rhythm of his rejections – first by Mildred, then by the Fifth Avenue crowd, by the jailer, by the IWW, and finally by the gorilla. *The Hairy Ape*, like *The Emperor Jones*, is a drama of pathos. But whereas *Jones*'s movement is a cycle downward, toward the ultimate deflation of pathos through the offhand cynicism with which Smithers and the natives treat Brutus Jones's offstage death, *The Hairy Ape* ends in the climactic moment of its pathos, with Yank's on-stage death in the gorilla's cage. Although O'Neill employed his symbolic cycle and his multicellular structure as underpinnings for the action, the structure of *The Hairy Ape* is that usually associated with expressionism, a building of tension through a series of alienating incidents, ending in an emotional climax of the individual's agonized defeat by forces beyond his control that proceed largely from his social milieu. Yank's death gives the play definite closure and conveys a typical expressionistic message.[21]

O'Neill's next play, *Welded* (1922), was a conscious attempt to attain this deeper realism of psychodrama but still maintain the mimetic illusion. As he put it, "I want to write a play that is truly realistic. . . . That term is used loosely on the stage, where most of the so-called realistic plays deal only with the appearance of things, while a truly realistic play deals with what might be called the soul of the character. It deals with a thing which makes the character that person and no other."[22] *Welded* ended up having very little of that "surface realism." It is an intense study of the forces of jealousy, possessiveness, and revenge that operate in Eleanor and Michael Cape's marriage, a marriage they have determined to make "a consummation demanding and combining the best in each of us! Hard, difficult, guarded from the commonplace, kept sacred as the outward form of our inner harmony!" (II, 448). With the exception of a prostitute Michael encounters, the characters all talk in this stilted, stylized way, and simply amount to mouthpieces for O'Neill's views on the love-hate relationship in marriage.

He did, however, develop some new ways of conveying the "soul of the character" while maintaining a tenuous hold on the fourth-wall illusion. Within the frame of the realistic set, for example, *"two circles of light, like' auras of egoism, emphasize and intensify* ELEANOR *and* MICHAEL *throughout the play. There is no other lighting"* (443). And the play's final meaning is conveyed not through words but through a scenic image: *"He moves close to her and his hands reach out for hers. For a moment as their hands touch they form together one cross. Then their arms go about each other and their lips meet"* (489). This use of the image to suggest the marriage to which the characters have bound themselves was a structural as well as a thematic statement. Ending with the characters in the same position on the stairs as in the first scene – when Eleanor interrupted a passionate moment to answer the door, in order to escape Michael's possession of her – completes the cycle that is the pattern of their marriage as well as the structure of the play. The suggestion of a cyclical pattern undercuts the note of reconciliation and union that the last scene would otherwise evoke as the denouement of a well-made problem play. The quarrel, separation, and reconciliation of the couple has a neat construction – à la Pinero, as O'Neill would say. But in the subtle retreat from closure accomplished in that final scenic image, he managed a more realistic treatment of even this unrealistic dramatic structure.

A more interesting innovation in *Welded* is O'Neill's use of dialogue for deeper characterization. As early as *Bound East for Cardiff*, he had made use of a device that Tiusanen has named the "modified monologue," a speech "spoken in spite of another character, out of inner compulsion, not in reaction to a previous speech, nor aside, as an interpolation of the playwright."[23] In *Welded* the modified monologues are carried on simultaneously and used to dramatize both the characters' inner thoughts, not otherwise accessible within the limits of mimetic realism, and the isolation each feels from the other when it comes to his or her deepest sense of self: "*Their chairs are side by side, each facing front, so near that by a slight movement each could touch the other, but during the following scene they stare straight ahead and remain motionless. They speak, ostensibly to the other, but showing by their tone it is a thinking aloud to oneself, and neither appears to hear what the other has said*" (452). Using the premise behind the modified monologue, that under the circumstances the characters neither listen to what the other is saying nor take any notice of whether the other pays attention to them, O'Neill is able to reveal the deepest of conjugal emotions without disrupting the mimetic illusion:

Cape.   I've grown inward into our life. But you keep trying to escape as if it were a prison. You feel the need of what is outside. I'm not enough for you.

Eleanor.   Why is it I can never know you? I try to know you and I can't. I desire to take all of you into my heart, but there's a great alien force – I hate that unknown power in you which would destroy me. (453)

The modified monologues supply the basic knowledge of the characters that brings a fuller meaning to the surface realism of Eleanor's scene with her would-be lover John and Michael's scene with the prostitute. The ultimate effect of both the modified monologues and the cyclical structure was a slight movement toward the "real realism" that O'Neill was looking for. By deconventionalizing realism, he sought to get beneath what he saw as the banal realism of surfaces to which his fellow dramatists had confined themselves, and to reveal the unplumbed depths still open to realistic representation.

All God's Chillun Got Wings (1923) is similar to *The Emperor Jones* and *The Hairy Ape* in its mixture of realism and expressionism. Its opening scene, with black and white children from contiguous neighborhoods playing street games together, could have come from any example of early-twentieth-century scenic realism, such as *Salvation Nell*. The play gets progressively more expressionistic, however, for as the children grow up and learn to hate each other, the menace in the environment grows. Finally, at the end of Act I, the scene in front of the church is fully expressionistic as the white girl Ella marries the black boy Jim. The people are formed into "*two racial lines on each side of the gate, rigid and unyielding, staring across at each other with bitter hostile eyes*" (II, 319), and the church doors "*slam behind them like wooden lips of an idol that has spat them out*" (319–20). In their apartment the scene is realistic, expressing the personalities of the people who live there in a manner familiar since *Beyond the Horizon*, except for the reflexive device of the Congo mask, which becomes the central symbolic presence in the room: "*A grotesque face, inspiring obscure, dim connotations in one's mind, but beautifully done, conceived in a true religious spirit. In this room, however, the mask acquires an arbitrary accentuation. It dominates by a diabolical quality that contrast imposes on it"* (322). The mask carries the heavy symbolic weight of Jim's blackness, the unseen presence in the house that drives Ella mad.

O'Neill's innovation in *All God's Chillun* is that Ella's madness is portrayed not expressionistically, with a device like the little "formless fears" of *The Emperor Jones,* but realistically, through the modified monologues brought within the fourth-wall illusion by the premise that she is raving. In the speech that reveals her psyche in greatest depth, Ella addresses the Congo mask, for her the personification of Jim's blackness:

> This is the first time he's dared to leave me alone for months and months. I've been wanting to talk to you every day but this is the only chance – (*With sudden violence – flourishing her knife.*) What're you grinning about, you dirty nigger, you? How dare you grin at me? I guess you forget what you are! That's always the way. Be kind to you, treat you decent, and in a second you've got a swelled head, you think you're somebody, you're all over the place putting on airs; why, it's got so I can't even walk down the street without seeing niggers, niggers everywhere. . . . What have I ever done wrong to you? What have you got against me? I married you, didn't I? Why don't you let Jim alone? Why don't you let him be happy as he is – with me? Why don't you let me be happy? He's white, isn't he – the whitest man that ever lived? Where do you come in to interfere? Black! Black! Black as dirt! You've poisoned me! I can't wash myself clean! Oh, I hate you! I hate you! Why don't you let Jim and me be happy? (338–9)

Using the assumption that Ella is mad, O'Neill is able to reveal her obsession and its causes without violating the mimetic illusion. Ella's madness is thus objectified rather than represented expressionistically as Brutus Jones's is. Judging from the portrayals of madness and emotional distress in *Strange Interlude, The Great God Brown, Days Without End,* and *Long Day's Journey into Night,* O'Neill found the objectifying treatment more effective. *All God's Chillun* thus marks a transition for O'Neill from the expressionistic dramatization of the psyche to its dramatization within the conventions of mimetic realism. In this play he had found the means of objectifying psychic experience, and a way to let a real, commonplace object – the mask, in this play – carry as intense symbolic significance as the expressionistic setting in *The Hairy Ape.* The new objectified psychological drama led in one direction, toward *The Great God Brown* and *Strange Interlude,* and the symbolic realism in another, toward *Desire Under the Elms.*

O'Neill infused the realism of *Desire Under the Elms* (1924) with the new expressive techniques he had discovered in the experimental plays, but its symbolic elements are inherent in its realistic stage picture. Like the mask in *All God's Chillun,* the elms become the symbolic center of the play, as O'Neill indicated in his description of the farm:

> *Two enormous elms are on each side of the house. They bend their trailing branches down over the roof. They appear to protect and at the same time subdue. There is a sinister maternity in their aspect, a crushing, jealous absorption. They have developed from their intimate contact with the life of man in the house an appalling humaneness. They brood oppressively over the house. They are like exhausted women resting their sagging breasts and hands and hair on its roof, and when it rains their tears trickle down monotonously and rot on the shingles.* (I, 202)

Although the elms dominate, nearly every element of the realistic stage picture takes on symbolic significance as well – the stone wall, the "gold" in the western sky, even the single decorative object in the farmhouse kitchen, the advertising poster of California. The dialogue is in the well-developed and by now familiar New England idiom first employed during the nineties in plays like Herne's *Shore Acres.* Without violating the mimetic illusion, O'Neill lifts the dialogue from its banal simplicity at the denotative level to a more poetic way of meaning through the repetition of phrases and motifs, and the rhythm of the language, and thus conveys the play's theme with an articulateness that the characters don't possess. Like the recurring motifs of *The Hairy Ape,* the repetition of nearly meaningless clichés and simplistic observations – such as "they's gold in the West," "like his Paw," "dog'll eat dog," and "the cows knows us" – conveys meaning in a way that no character's statement does or could. Similarly, the rhythm of dialogue like "I air hungry! / I smells bacon! / Bacon's good! / Bacon's bacon!" (205–6) portrays the oxlike nature of Peter and Sim and the effect of their life on the farm as effectively as any speech they could make.

The characters bear a similar multilevel significance. As in the earlier plays, O'Neill suggests their motives in sociological and psychological terms. Abbie offers an explanation for her marriage to Cabot that is reminiscent of Anna Christie's analysis of how she "went wrong": "Waal – I've had a hard life, too – oceans o' trouble an' nuthin' but wuk fur reward. I was a orphan early an' had t' wuk fur others in other folks' hums. Then I married an' he turned out a drunken spreer an' so he had to wuk fur others an' me too agen in other folks' hums, an' the baby died, an' my husband got sick an' died too, an I was glad sayin' now I'm free fur once, on'y I diskivered right away all I was free fur was t' wuk agen in other folks' hums, doin' other folks' wuk till I'd most give up hope o' ever doin' my own wuk in my own hum, an' then your Paw come" (226). It is consistent with her history that Abbie be obsessed with the desire to possess the farm. Similar apologies for Ephraim's "hardness," his own desire for the farm, and his "loneliness" are conveyed in his long modified monologue in Part II, Scene 2. Like the objects in the scene, however, the concrete images in the dialogue become symbolic entities representing the thematic concepts of hardness, the land, and the many forms of desire – lust, greed, possessiveness, desire for freedom, for home, for power and control. In the entire scenic representation as well as the characters, O'Neill thus created a realistic whole charged with symbolism.[24] In developing this mode of dramatic representation, he opened a new level of meaning and a new way of meaning to the local-color realism traditionally associated with rural simplicity.

The play's structure also profited from the innovative experiments that preceded it. Like *Beyond the Horizon, Desire Under the Elms* is a carefully structured tragedy, with the attempt at transcendence made very clear as the meanings conveyed by all the elements of the representation converge into a final scenic image. After Eben decides that "I got t' pay fur my part o' the sin! . . . I want t' share with ye, Abbie – prison 'r death 'r hell 'r anythin'!" (267), O'Neill completes his statement with a scenic allusion to Milton's Adam and Eve and the hope that their freedom from the "garden" now brings them:

Abbie. Wait. (*Turns to* EBEN.) I love ye, Eben.
Eben. I love ye, Abbie. (*They kiss. The three men grin and shuffle embarrassedly.* EBEN *takes* ABBIE's *hand. They go out the door in rear, the men following, and come from the house, walking hand in hand to the gate.* EBEN *stops there and points to the sunrise sky.*) Sun's a-rizin'. Purty hain't it?
Abbie. Ay-eh. (*They both stand for a moment looking up raptly in attitudes strangely aloof and devout.*) (269)

Although it is much more understated than Robert Mayo's rhapsodic hymn to the horizon, the ending's symbolic import is equally transcendent. But the ending contains a formal element that works against the tragedy. Encompassing the tragic action is a circular pattern of experience, beginning with Peter and Sim's freedom and the sunset gold in the west, and ending with Abbie and Eben's freedom and the sunrise gold in the east. Similarly, Ephraim's failure to leave the farm and the play's final line, the sheriff's comment "It's a jim-dandy farm, no denyin'. Wished I owned it!" (269), drive home the circularity of human experience through the cycle of desire. It is the suggestion of the life around and beyond the tragic action that keeps O'Neill's tragedies within the realm of realistic structure. They suggest that tragic experience is one reality in human life, not that reality is tragic.

Each of the experimental plays that followed – *The Great God Brown* (1924), *Strange Interlude* (1927), and *Mourning Becomes Electra* (1931) – marks a stage in O'Neill's attempt to dramatize the psyche. Taking off from *All God's Chillun,* the major step in *Brown* and *Strange Interlude* is the notion of dramatizing the character's thought in the *context* of the realistic stage picture through stream-of-consciousness – objectifying it – rather than putting the audience into the mind of the character and having it experience what the character experiences – subjectifying it. The device of the mask in *Brown* gives the audience an easy way to distinguish between what a character is saying and what he is thinking, thus viewing two levels of reality simultaneously and, of course, dispensing with the fourth-wall illusion. The psychodrama here is in the tension between two consciously articulated feelings or ideas, such as Dion Anthony's inner vulnerability and his outer callousness. O'Neill was most insistent that neither level of reality should usurp the other. In a letter to the *New York Evening Post* he wrote:

> It was far from my idea in writing *Brown* that this background pattern of conflicting tides in the soul of Man should ever overshadow and thus throw out of proportion the living drama of the recognizable human beings Dion, Brown, Margaret and Cybel. I meant it always to be mystically within and behind them, giving them a significance beyond themselves, forcing itself through them to expression in mysterious words, symbols, actions they do not themselves comprehend.[25]

The trend in his psychodramas is constantly to make the division between the two levels of reality less distinct, to make the internal drama and the external drama one. In *Strange Interlude,* dispensing with the actual prop of the mask makes the the division between internal and external reality less emphatic. The secret thoughts of the characters in *Strange Interlude* are masked only by a protective social decorum. The physical shifts between internal and external reality on the stage are faster, smoother, and thus less reflexive as a theatrical device. Although there are still two distinct levels of reality in the play – the mimetic "common" reality and the inner reality behind it – the dropping of the masks is a step toward re-creating the fourth-wall illusion.

In *Strange Interlude,* O'Neill discarded the masks; in *Mourning Becomes Electra,* he discarded the asides. Although there are modified monologues in *Electra,* they exist within what O'Neill called the "unreal realism" of the representation. *Electra* is a dramatization of the psyche as it is a dramatization of the myth, but couched within the fourth-wall illusion. The Mannons' faces may give a "mask impression in repose," but the impression is nonetheless "lifelike" (II, 10). With the strange Mannons placed within the otherwise realistic milieu, O'Neill's effect is precisely "unreal realism." Similarly, although in *Days Without End* (1933) he reverts to the mask as a device for figuring the two "selves" of John Loving, the play is otherwise mimetically realistic, and everything the evil cynic "Loving" says is actually articulated by the character John in the "objective reality" figured by the theatrical representation.

The psychodramas are experiments for O'Neill, in structure as well as in characterization. *The Great God Brown* is tragic, both Dion Anthony and Bill Brown achieving transcendence through their suffering and death. *Strange Interlude* is a *drame bourgeois* with a rather complicated but well-made structure. *Mourning Becomes Electra,* of course, is a tragedy on the Greek model. *Days Without End* is the most original of the experiments, a combination of Shavian discussion play and melodrama. On the one hand, the characters discuss belief in God along with the more familiar subjects of love, marriage, and adultery. On the other, the evil Loving attempts to defeat the combined forces of good represented by his better side, John, and his uncle Father Baird by killing the one person he still loves, his wife, Elsa. The twist is that the melodrama is also psychodrama. The battle is fought and won on psychological ground. Fusing the drama of discussion with the melodrama, however, O'Neill sees to it that the resolution of the discussion is clearly in action, not simply in conviction. As John and Loving fight out the last battle in a church, Loving's dying words express the defeat of his spirit of hatred: "Thou has conquered, Lord. Thou art – the End. Forgive – the damned soul – of John Loving!" (III, 566). The ending, melodramatic in the extreme, is a scenic image of crucifixion, much more elaborate than the one that ends *Welded:*

> *He slumps forward to the floor and rolls over on his back, dead, his head beneath the foot of the Cross, his arms outflung so that his body forms another cross.* JOHN *rises from his knees and stands with arms stretched up and out, so that he, too, is like a cross. While this is happening the light of the dawn on the stained-glass windows swiftly rises to a brilliant intensity of crimson and green and gold, as if the sun had risen. The gray walls of the church, particularly the wall where the Cross is, and the face of the Christ shine with this radiance.*
>
> JOHN LOVING – *he, who had been only* JOHN – *remains standing with his arms stretched up to the Cross, an expression of mystic exaltation on his face. The corpse of* LOVING *lies at the foot of the Cross, like a cured cripple's testimonial offering in a shrine.* (566)

Like that of the earlier *Dynamo* (1929), the ending of *Days Without End* is emotionally climactic, and thus antirealistic, perhaps the most sensationally so of O'Neill's experiments. In his development toward a new realism, he was to achieve his innovative realistic structure only when his two earlier lines of development, symbolic realism and dramatizing psychological reality within traditional mimetic representation, came together in his great realistic plays *The Iceman Cometh* and *Long Day's Journey into Night.* Meanwhile, other American playwrights had capitalized on his daring efforts to produce a deeper realism in the American theater at large.

6

Place and Personality: Innovations in Realistic Setting and Character, 1916–1940

After World War I, realistic playwrights had to accommodate a faster-changing philosophical and social perspective within the limits of what had become traditional realistic aesthetics. With the severe disillusionment that followed the war, they had to adapt to the general philosophical shift away from positivism and pragmatism and toward phenomenology. And they had to respond to their audiences' new awareness of Freudian psychology and changing social norms. Obviously many mid-nineteenth-century philosophical assumptions that had served as underpinnings for realistic aesthetic theory were no longer operating in the postwar artistic milieu of phenomenology, modernism, expressionism, and Freudianism. The full development of realism in American drama occurred at the same time that the importation of expressionist drama from Germany and symbolist drama from France was stimulating experimentation with nonmimetic forms, and modernist stage design was developing under the influence of Edward Gordon Craig, Max Reinhardt, and such Americans as Norman Bel Geddes and Robert Edmond Jones. As seen in O'Neill's work, the attempt to achieve an artistic synthesis of these new twentieth-century developments with the now established realistic mode of representation resulted in some of the most imaginative play writing of the innovative twenties.

Nevertheless, out of the chaotic juxtaposition of philosophies, styles, modes, and forms that is the dramatic history of the years between the wars, there does emerge a clear line of development impelled by the artistic desire to achieve realism in dramatic representation. As in O'Neill's career, there were false starts and blind alleys in the general development of realism, but there were also productive discoveries and genuine achievements. The period between the wars, particularly the years between 1918 and 1929, was the most productive in the history of American drama. The 1927–8 season was the peak year, with 264 new productions on Broadway, compared with 87 in 1899–1900 and 69 in

1966–7.[1] There probably were more playwrights at work in New York during the twenties and thirties than at any time before or since.

It would be ridiculous to suggest that these creative minds were marching in lockstep behind Eugene O'Neill, or indeed that they completely shared a common line of aesthetic development with him or with each other. Although realism was by far the reigning mode of dramatic representation by the mid-twenties, for example, the socioeconomic conditions of the thirties fostered the growth of two new lines of development as well. On the one hand, a new presentational didacticism arose when conditions in America became so immediately oppressive that there seemed no choice but to break through the fourth wall and demand action instead of discussion. On the other, an audience seeking to escape rather than to engage contemporary reality took a new interest in the distancing modes of historical costume drama, verse tragedy, and "screwball comedy." These developments have no place in this discussion, though. The innovations that brought realism to full maturity on the American stage served to strengthen the mimetic illusion, not to break it, and they took place in every aspect of realistic drama, from setting to structure. They provide the direction for an investigation of realism's final evolution.

SETTING: A SENSE OF PLACE

O'Neill's earliest plays at the Provincetown had helped to spark a new interest in setting that became a major concern for American dramatists during the twenties. The sense of place evident in such early realistic studies as *The Moon of the Caribees* and *Where the Cross is Made,* as well as in more ambitious realistic pieces like *Beyond the Horizon* and *Desire Under the Elms,* assumes a central role in Susan Glaspell's early plays *Trifles* (1916) and *The Outside* (1917). Both of these one-act plays are similar to O'Neill's in structure. They are slices of life whose structures emerge from a series of commonplace events without apparent closure. Like that of O'Neill's *Fog, The Outside*'s realistic setting grounds its mystical discussion of life and afterlife in a recognizable frame of realistic action. But in its complete integration of the sense of place with the theme and form of the play, the small masterpiece *Trifles* is more like the sea plays. Its setting is "*the kitchen in the now abandoned farmhouse of* JOHN WRIGHT, *a gloomy kitchen, and left without having been put in order – unwashed pans under the sink, a loaf of bread outside the bread-box, a dish-towel on the table – other signs of incompleted work.*"[2] The setting comes to be central in the play, both because of what it reveals about Mrs. Wright, the main character, who never appears onstage, and because of the thematic statement it makes.

The plot is simple. The sheriff of a small New England village has

V. A scene from the Provincetown Players' production of Susan Glaspell's *Trifles*, 1916.

come with the district attorney and a neighbor, along with their wives, to investigate John Wright's murder. Because she has "acted peculiar," Mrs. Wright has been taken into custody, but the sheriff and the district attorney find no evidence in the house to convict her and no evidence of a motive for the murder. Meanwhile the women sit in the kitchen concerning themselves with what the men dismiss scornfully as "trifles." From the details of her housekeeping and a dead canary they find in her workbasket, the women conclude that Mrs. Wright strangled her husband because he broke the neck of her canary – the one thing in her childless, isolated life that gave her joy. Knowing the dreary hopelessness of her life, they easily put the story together from their own experience and tacitly exonerate her among themselves, while allowing the men to laugh at their concern with trifles and conclude from the evidence of the woman's home merely that she was a sloppy housekeeper. The whole meaning of the play is invested in that kitchen where the action takes place – the bleakness of Mrs. Wright's life, the "trifles" of which that life is composed, and the extent to which a woman's existence depends on understanding that the trifles of daily life become the "grand passions" in the outside world that men consider worthy of their concern. Glaspell's setting in *Trifles* anticipates O'Neill's use of the farmhouse in *Beyond the Horizon* and *Desire Under the Elms,* because it is employed not only for characterization but to determine the play's mood and action.

Because its eclectic nature reflects several lines of development, the dramatic regionalism that followed upon these early efforts by the Provincetown playwrights requires some contextual explanation. One line led directly from O'Neill, whose *Beyond the Horizon* and *Desire Under the Elms* proved that American regionalist or "folk" plays could also be serious drama. In turn, two important influences were at work on O'Neill. One was the Abbey Theatre, and in particular J. M. Synge, whose plays were considered to have a "primitivist" or "folk" style when they were seen in America in 1911. The other was the sense of place, a particular interest of the Provincetown group that was derived, as O'Neill saw it, from Edward Sheldon as well as from Ibsen. These two strands – the folk and the regional – tended to merge so that, as both Felix Sper and John Wentz have noted, the terms came to be used interchangeably during the twenties.[3] Wentz maintains that a regional or folk play in the twenties could be any "dramatic composition, in which essential elements of plot, theme, tone, characterization, motivation, or conflict are at least partially determined by strongly emphasized local peculiarities of a specific nonurban geographical setting. Such local peculiarities include those of speech, music, custom, occupation, religion, climate, topography, ethnology, social structure and the like."[4]

Actually, despite the more ambitious artistry of early practitioners like Glaspell and O'Neill, and the influence of such academic programs as Frederick Koch's at the University of North Carolina and Thomas Dickinson's at Wisconsin, the regional drama of the early twenties was similar to the local-color drama of the 1890s. Whereas urban "low-life" plays had moved toward fuller integration of milieu with structure and the representation of environmental forces that formed characters and motivated conflicts, most rural plays remained essentially what they had been in the hands of Harte, Mark Twain, and their imitators: conventional melodramatic or comic structures with an overlay of realistic detail in staging, costuming, and dialogue calculated to produce a sense of verisimilitude for an audience unfamiliar with the locale. Only through the efforts of serious dramatists like O'Neill, Paul Green, DuBose and Dorothy Heyward, and Owen Davis was rural regional drama affected by realistic innovations.

Two plays from 1923, Hatcher Hughes's Pulitzer Prize winner, *Hellbent fer Heaven,* and Lula Vollmer's *Sun-up,* epitomize regional drama at the beginning of the twenties. Both plays capitalize on the immediacy of their subject, the effect World War I had on the people of the North Carolina mountains. Each has a setting replete with detail. Hughes specifies that the Hunts' house should have walls and ceiling of "*rough boards, smoked and stained with age,*"[5] and that a "Red Rambler" rose should hang on a trellis over the door. *Sun-up* features "*a rough table, covered with oilcloth,*"[6] a bench, three straight-backed chairs, an old cupboard, and some cooking utensils near the fireplace, all of which get a good deal of use during the play.

The characters are built on a local-color model as well. They are eccentric but genial mountain types with specific accoutrements like pipes and shotguns, and they speak in carefully wrought dialect. *Sun-up* begins this way:

MRS. CAGLE *is seated before the fireplace, smoking her pipe. Her thoughts seem far away. The door opens, and* PAP TODD *enters.*
Todd.   Thought I'd come and set with yer awhile, Mis' Cagle.
Mrs. Cagle. (*Not looking up to greet her visitor.*) Pull ye up a chair.
Todd.   (*Pulling a chair toward the fireplace.*) How air yer to-day?
Mrs. Cagle. Jest tolerable.
(TODD *seats himself and takes out his pipe.*) Bring yo' own terbacker?
Todd.   Yer, I brung my own. (*He fills his pipe, and they sit for a moment without conversation.*) Shore is a fine day.
Mrs. Cagle. Shore is. (679)

Both casts of characters contain the conventional local-color elements of the North Carolina mountains in the twenties – hard-bitten old moonshiners; hot-blooded mountain boys, just spoiling for a feud; nubile young mountain girls getting ready to choose their mates; strong-willed matriarchs who hold their families together at any cost. *Hell-bent* also has a hypocrite who spouts old-time religion while he sells moonshine and finagles to get the girl on the side, and *Sun-up* has a rural local sheriff who has to choose between "the gov'ment" and the more endemic laws of mountain society.

What distinguishes these plays from their local-color predecessors may not be startlingly evident, but it is significant. While the local color is laid on pretty thick over conventional characters and dramatic structures, the playwrights are careful to indicate that the motivation for the action in these two plays comes directly from forces and attitudes peculiar to the environment they represent. *Hell-bent,* for example, has a dual plot composed of two elements that are as old as the hills themselves. The basic conflict is a melodramatic struggle between the hero, Sid, and the villain, Rufe, a smooth-talking hypocrite, for the young heroine, Jude. Complicating this struggle is the factor of the feud between the families of Sid and Jude, long forgotten but now being stirred up again by Rufe, who plies Jude's brother Andy with moonshine and convinces him that Sid is trying to kill him.

Only Shakespeare could make this stuff into significant drama, but Hughes manages to bring new life to it by connecting the hackneyed action with the environment. The feud is peculiarly a mountain feud – "It 'us at a shootin' match that the feud fust strated twixt your two gran'daddies . . . an' they 'us both fetched home on stretchers, 'long 'ith lots more o' your kin on both sides, afore it 'us patched up" (241). Whereas Andy's aggression is fired up by some twenty-year-old native moonshine, Sid's recent experience in the Big War has given him some perspective on the family feud. It has taught him that one need not always rise to the challenge of a drunk, a suggestion that the milieu might be changing with the times.

It is Rufe who most evokes the environment, however. He is specifically a fundamentalist hypocrite, constantly quoting the Bible, vocally opposed to fighting, drinking, and sex, but ready to encourage all three when it suits him. Hughes gets beyond the mere caricature of the hard-drinking, Bible-thumping revivalist con artist, though, in suggesting that Rufe might not be so much a calculating villain as a weak and bitter man deluded, by a mean-spirited quality in the religious rhetoric he has heard, into seeing God as an agent for his own revenge on the world. He has several "prayers" to speak, such as, "It bothers me, though, Lord, that You let the wicked prosper more 'n the righteous. They git the best o' everything in this world now. It wusn't so in Bible times, Lord. Then You cut the wicked down afore the congregation o' Israel" (260). Finally Rufe commits the unpardonable sin of shouting in hysterical bitterness, "Damn you, God!" (274).

Although these forces of the North Carolina mountains – family pride, feuds, alcoholism, "ole time religion," and especially the land – are evident in these early regionalist plays and in a sense determine the lives of the characters, this drama is a far cry from realism. There is a sense of place in these plays but no attempt to go beyond types in characterization or to analyze the types presented, and certainly no thought of moving beyond the conventional dramatic structures to get at the real "action" in the daily lives of the people. Regionalism's importance for realism lay primarily in its development of milieu. Keeping a sense of place before the audience was an important function in the early twenties, and these plays had a part in keeping that sense alive, but in essence they and their many imitations were commercial exploitations of regional eccentricities rather than serious studies of regional customs and mores.

The full development of both trends in regionalism – realistic attention to the sense of place and antirealistic exploitation of the eccentric – can be seen in the regional plays of the thirties. The first trend led to honest attempts to dramatize a milieu, such as Steinbeck's *Of Mice and Men* (1937) and Owen and Donald Davis's adaptation of Edith Wharton's *Ethan Frome* (1936). The extreme development of the other came in 1933 with Jack Kirkland's adaptation of Erskine Caldwell's novel *Tobacco Road*, in which the attempt to represent the humor of the eccentric degenerated to the extremes of the grotesque and the ludicrous. In this play, which, Quinn noted, "marks probably the depths of degradation into which the drama may descend,"[7] Kirkland was aware that he was depicting a form of death-in-life, his backcountry Georgia being "*a famished, desolate land, once given over to the profitable raising of tobacco, then turned into small cotton plantations, which have been so intensively and stupidly cultivated as to exhaust the soil. Poverty, want, squalor, degeneracy, pitiful helplessness and grotesque, tragic lusts have stamped a lost, outpaced people with the mark of inevitable end.*"[8] His treatment of this region exudes an irony that shades past realism into the black humor of the grotesque: "*Grim humor pervades all, stalking side by side with tragedy on the last short mile which leads to complete, eventual elimination*" (3).

Similarly, Kirkland's characters move beyond stereotype to become emblems of degeneracy with local-color trappings. The family of malnourished, simpleminded, inbred Lesters is a microcosm of this degenerate world, from Jeeter, who sells his twelve-year-old daughter for seven dollars and arranges an income of two dollars a week from her doltish husband by forcing her to sleep with him, to the terrified grandmother who creeps across the stage gathering firewood while her sixteen-year-old grandson throws baseballs at her, then crawls off in the brush to die one night, an event that evokes only passing comment from the Lesters. *Tobacco Road* represents the ultimate antirealism in the regionalist movement, the impulse to seek out the eccentric and grotesque that has more love of the sensational about it than interest in the commonplace.

The more literary line of regionalism tended toward such meaningful realistic detail as the symbolic realism of *Desire Under the Elms* and the use of set to heighten the psychological drama in plays like *The Emperor Jones*. With plays like these for models, playwrights of the twenties began to use the dynamic relationship between setting and character as a means of thematic development. Owen Davis's two early realistic plays, *The Detour* (1921) and *Icebound* (1923), are regional in the sense that the characters and their conflicts are inseparable from the milieux that produce them, but his use of setting is at the opposite pole from that in *Sun-up* or *Tobacco Road*. Rather than calling attention to itself as the subject of the play, Davis's realistic setting points indexically toward the characters and their conflicts. Thus in *The Detour*, "*the room should be as unpretentious as the play and as far away from symbolism, – just the plain home of plain people.*"[9]

Davis's program is more complicated than he would have it appear, however, for the relationship between character and setting provides a major underpinning for his theme. The Long Island truck farm where *The Detour* is set becomes the center of conflict between the play's men and its women. It has produced both the farmer's sense of rootedness and the desire to escape that the farmer's wife has nurtured in her daughter. In its cycle of milieu producing character, which reinforces milieu, *Icebound* has a more dynamic use of setting. Its theme is expressed by Ben, the black sheep of the Jordan family, who is able to describe their "icebound" New England village with some objectivity because he has served for a time as a soldier in France: "It's like that half the year, froze up, everything, most of all the people. Just a family by itself, maybe. Just a few folks, good an' bad, month after month, with nothin' to think about but just the mean little things, that really don't amount to nothin',' but get to be bigger than all the world outside. . . . Icebound, that's what we are all of us, inside and out."[10] The characters have grown "icebound" in response to the natural setting, and they have in turn created the interior setting that reflects it:

> It is late October, and through the two windows at the back one may see a bleak countryside, the grass brown and lifeless, and the bare limbs of the trees silhouetted against a gray sky. . . . The room . . . is as dull and drab as the lives of those who have lived within its walls. Here we have the cleanliness that is next to godliness, but no sign of either comfort or beauty, both of which are looked upon with suspicion as being signposts on the road to perdition. (195)

Davis's cycle was a way of accounting for the fully integrated reality he was trying to depict.

Paul Green, a product of Frederick Koch's program at North Carolina and a professor of philosophy, represents the folk tradition at its most literary. *In Abraham's Bosom* (1926) and *The Field God* (1927) owe an obvious debt to O'Neill's symbolic and psychological use of setting, but Green was much more concerned than O'Neill was with weaving the sense of place into the texture of his plays through a wealth of realistic detail. Where O'Neill employed dialogue, Green preferred the object; where O'Neill employed the scenic image, Green preferred activity. Thus, whereas O'Neill uses his symbolic elms to represent the spirit of the Cabots, Green depicts in *The Field God* some graphic details of a hog butchering to represent the active animal spirit of Hardy Gilchrist, the moving force behind his prosperous farm.

Green made more interesting use of his setting in *In Abraham's Bosom* to represent the environment that both reflects and in part effects the psychic split in Abe McCranie that is the play's subject. The setting is North Carolina in 1886, and Abe is the son of a black woman and the town's local squire, Colonel McCranie. The conflict is Abe's internal struggle, defined by his black co-workers in this way:

> Abe is bad mixed up all down inside. . . . (*Thumping on his chest.*) Nigger down heah. (*Thumping his head.*) White mens up heah. Heart say do one thing, head say 'nudder. . . . De white blood in him coming to

de top. Dat make him want-a climb up and be sump'n. Nigger gwine
hol' him down dough. Part of him take adder de Colonel, part adder his
muh, 'vision and misery inside.[11]

In seven scenes the play depicts Abe's struggle to educate himself and
his people while he constantly fights against his more primitive "natural
man." At times he makes progress, opening a school for the black children in the area, for example. But his passionate side always causes him
trouble. In an early scene he "sasses" his half brother, the Colonel's
legitimate son, and is horsewhipped for his insolence. When he opens his
school, he gets so angry with one of the students that he beats him within
an inch of his life, and in the court settlement with the boy's parents, he
loses the farm the Colonel had left him. Later he loses a factory job in
Durham because he fights the whites who insult him. Finally, after he is
beaten up by a hostile crowd while making a last plea to reestablish his
school, he comes upon his half brother in the woods and kills him in an
argument.

Abe's life is controlled by conflicting impulses: (1) the drive to improve his own and his race's condition through education and (2) the self-
destructive violence rooted in his inability to control his passionate sense
of injustice. Green's setting emphasizes that psychic conflict in much the
way O'Neill's setting does in *The Emperor Jones*. Green's play opens, for
example, in *"the turpentine woods of Eastern North Carolina,"* a scene that
Green carefully describes in terms of both realistic detail and vaguely
mythic suggestion:

> *a log lies rotting in the embrace of wild ivy. Maples, bays, dogwoods and other*
> *small trees overrun by tenacious vines raise their leafy tops to shade the spot.*
> *Through interstices in the undergrowth one can see the pine forest stretching*
> *away until the eye is lost in a colonnade of trees. The newly scraped blazes on*
> *the pines show through the brush like the downward spreading beards of old*
> *men, suggestive of the ancient gnomes of the woods, mysterious and silently*
> *watchful.* (385)

Rooting the scene in realistic detail while also suggesting the chthonic
force it can have for those who live there prepares the audience to accept
the expressionism of Abe's climactic scene in the forest after he kills his
half brother. There, driven to madness by the night's ordeal, he sees
visions of black men being lynched and of his mother with the Colonel in
the bushes, "lak two hawgs" (420).

The *Emperor Jones* influence is obvious here, but Green also uses his
setting to make it clear that his play is not *only* a study of Abe's psychology but also a study of the milieu that has produced it. While the forest
scenes represent the mythic or "primitive" forces in Abe, the indoor
scenes represent the condition of his people within the white man's society he is fighting so hard to change. These three sets – Abe's sharecrop-

per's cabin, his tenement in Durham, and his school – signify poverty through carefully selected details, such as the *"dilapidated old bureau, small pieces of wood taking the place of lost casters"* and the *"greasy, spotted oil-cloth"* on the kitchen table. Green also uses scenic images. A "We are Rising" poster dominates the cabin, while a washtub dominates the tenement, setting the predominant mood of the McCranies' lives at a given time, and piles of books are present everywhere in Abe's environment. These objects serve a dual purpose. They provide the scenic illusion of every-day things that is necessary to regionalism's evocation of the milieu, and they subliminally suggest Abe's inner state for the audience without breaking the fourth-wall illusion. Paul Green taught the American the-ater a great deal about the regional representation of character through setting, but it was in DuBose and Dorothy Heyward's *Porgy* (1927) that the wealth of detail in the regionalist sense of place was joined most fully to the aesthetic aim of realism in the representation. The Heywards sought to represent Catfish Row, the black neighborhood in Charleston, South Carolina, that becomes the world of the play, so fully that the audience is drawn unconsciously into the rhythm of its life. Rather than the intellectual recognition of a way of life alien to one's own, which is the aim of such regionalists as Hughes and Green and Vollmer, the Heywards sought a subliminal identification with this way of life, its mores and its values. To draw the audience into Catfish Row, they developed an opening that provided first the distancing shock of aliena-tion and then the gradual displacement of that alienation through engage-ment. The life depicted in the opening scene could hardly be farther from the average theater audience's experience:

> As the curtain rises, revealing Catfish Row on a summer evening, the court reechoes with African laughter and friendly banter in 'Gullah,' the language of the Charleston Negro, which still retains many African words. The audience understands none of it. Like the laughter and the movement, the twanging of a guitar from an upper window, the dancing of an urchin with a loose, shuffling step, it is part of the picture of Catfish Row as it really is – an alien scene, a people as little known to most Americans as the people of the Congo.[12]

Gradually, however, *"it seems to the audience that they are beginning to understand this foreign language. In reality, the 'Gullah' is being tempered to their ears, spoken more distinctly with the African words omitted"* (403). As the audience begins to "understand" this foreign language, it is drawn into the world of the play, and after watching a Saturday night crap game for a while, it is prepared to feel at home with *Porgy*'s "real" opening line, "Seems like dese bones don't gib me nuttin' but box cars tonight" (404).

By depicting the culture as completely alien, and then making the audience feel like privileged initiates, the Heywards avoid the condescen-sion of the local-color perspective – the outsider's view that represents

VI. Catfish Row, from the Theatre Guild production of DuBose and
Dorothy Heyward's *Porgy*, 1927. Scene design by Cleon Throckmor-
ton. (Photo by Van Damm)

characters as ignorant yokels engaged in a poor imitation of the audience's own culture and produces an effect of pathos or bathos, depending on its emphasis. Of course, *Porgy* does have its local color. Intertwined with its melodrama and its love story are the colorful incidents
peculiar to Southern Negro life in the twenties – the wake, the picnic, the
crap game, the summoning of the conjure woman. But except for the
humorous incident when Porgy buys Bess a "divorce" – a conscious
imitation by the blacks of the customs of the "white folks" – these
incidents take on integrity as parts of the whole way of life being represented. They might even alienate the audience if it weren't for the occasional reminders that its perceptual position relative to this culture is
privileged. Twice when white men arrive in the neighborhood, the audience watches the residents go into their Uncle Tom routines until the
incursion is over. Because the audience is with Catfish Row the entire
time, it sees the white men as alien and ridiculous, outsiders to the
culture in which it feels it belongs. By removing the mediating presence
of the dominant culture from between the audience and the stage, the
playwrights took a step toward a fuller illusion of reality in representing

VII. The kitchen, from Owen and Donald Davis's *Ethan Frome,* 1936. Scene design by Jo Mielziner. (Photo by Van Damm)

regional culture. In the terms of the nineteenth-century realists, *Porgy* is a "truer," because more immediate, representation of reality than the typical local-color play.

The extent of regionalism's contribution to realistic setting can best be seen in a play that reflects its full development, as in Owen and Donald Davis's adaptation of Edith Wharton's *Ethan Frome* (1936). Here all the functions of good regionalist setting are evident: the use of realistic objects for thematic signification, the use of setting to convey the dynamic relationship between character and milieu, and for the audience, the subliminal identification with the characters and their way of life. The Davises use five sets to indicate the Fromes' way of life: the exterior of their farmhouse, *"flimsy with age, a sadly cold and stark, unpainted clapboard structure"*[13]; the drab kitchen, with its "Fancy Hero" stove and its carefully enumerated accoutrements of stewpot and ladle, coffeepot, flatirons and pads, boiling kettle, and so on; the exterior of the Starkfield Congregational Church outside which Ethan stands, waiting to bring cousin Mattie home from the "church sociable"; the top of a hill where the village bobsled slide is located; and Ethan and Zeena's bedroom, *"a small bleak room cramped close under the slanting eaves of the roof"* (389) with a faded curtain stretched across it on a string for a closet, *"a plain washstand supporting a cracked pitcher and bowl,"* and a small bedside table, *"the top of which is littered with bottles and pharmaceutical boxes and stained tumblers with spoons in them and various other patented medical supplies"* (389) for Zeena's hypochondriacal illnesses.

Owen Davis had a special gift for showing the relation between character and milieu, and he does that most effectively here. Zeena, in her

VIII. Raymond Massey and Ruth Gordon in the National Theatre Production of *Ethan Frome:* Act I, Scene 3, "The crest of a hill above Starkfield." Scene design by Jo Mielziner. (Photo by Van Damm)

"shapeless nondescript calico dress, high black shoes, brown stockings and thick knitted shawl drawn close about her shoulders" (376) could have been born in that kitchen. Ethan is introduced as *"a drab part of the poverty-stricken farm which is his life, and like it, severe and hard and cold"* (377). Mattie, in her shabby but gay "other dress," provides the contrast that highlights the bleak environment of the Fromes and the dreary people it has made of them. When Ethan tells Mattie that he married Zeena because he was afraid the "loneliness" of the farm would drive him mad the way it did his mother, the audience is ready to accept his reasoning with sympathy.

The weakness in this adaptation is the quick transition from the vibrant and hopeful young Mattie, who delights in cooking a stew that will please and putting the pickles in a red glass dish so the table will be pretty, to the bitter, complaining invalid in the Epilogue, twenty years after her failed double suicide attempt with Ethan on the bobsled run. Nevertheless, the authors tried to indicate a dynamic interaction between Mattie and the Frome milieu. The house brightens a little under her influence, as do Ethan and the hired man, Jotham, although there are careful indications that she is a sloppy enough housekeeper to earn some of the constant complaints that Zeena makes against her, and there are signs that Mattie has felt the force of Zeena's presence. When she spills coffee on Zeena's bed, for example, *"(She sighs, unconsciously adopting* ZEENA's *perpetually worried manner),"* and says, "I got an awful lot needs tendin' to up here today . . . them floors to scrub and the win-

IX. Raymond Massey and Pauline Lord in the National Theatre Production of *Ethan Frome:* Act II, Scene 1, "The Frome bedroom." Scene design by Jo Mielziner. (Photo by Van Damm)

dows want washin' real bad . . . an' them blankets'll have to be washed out and I don't know how I'll ever get things to dry this weather!" (391). If the audience is willing to fill in the details of the twenty years between the Mattie who loves Ethan so much she wants to die with him and the querulous invalid of the play's Epilogue, the authors have provided the clues.

The important realistic achievements in Davis's setting is its indexical quality. Unlike those in the earlier regional plays, this setting doesn't call attention to itself but emphasizes the characters, reflecting the bleakness, the dreariness, the poverty of their existence in clear, objective detail, suggesting a social and economic context for their lives and for the people they have become. With designer Jo Mielziner's help, the Davises succeeded at merging setting and character to make a unified representation of milieu.

The depiction of urban life is not considered regionalism, but during the twenties and thirties American playwrights' interest in the New York milieu equaled and eventually exceeded their interest in other versions of

X. A scene from Act I of Elmer Rice's *Street Scene*, 1929. Scene design by Jo Mielziner. (Photo by White Studios)

American life. As early as 1921, Zoë Akins made the bohemian life-style of her Greenwich Village characters in *Daddy's Gone A-Hunting* an integral part of the play's lost-generation soul-searching. Akins makes it clear through the set that the Fields family's move from a typical lower-middle-class apartment in Harlem to a studio in Washington Square represents a significant choice of milieu:

> At the side of a rather large round table painted orange colour is an immense chair upholstered in shabby, faded stuff that was once brilliantly flowered chintz. A lamp with a crudely devised yellow shade stands on the table. Another table, square and painted black and set about with four painted chairs, stands in the right-hand corner. A stencilled cloth runs like a brilliant streak across it. Except for strips of red stuff at each side of the window there are no curtains. An incongruously handsome chandelier hangs from the ceiling in the centre – but later when the lights are turned on only two of the dozen bulbs flare.[14]

This visual image of the milieu provides a constant frame for the characters' versions of their bohemian life.

Soon afterward, Philip Dunning and George Abbott's hit *Broadway*

(1926) precipitated a fad of " 'backstage' drama,"[15] which capitalized on the setting, people, and events around New York nightclubs and theaters to suggest a definite milieu without elaborate detail by relying on scenic allusions to the many preceding plays of the type. Similar use was made of the New York apartment to suggest a chic, urban way of life. Playwrights like Philip Barry and S. N. Behrman produced an expectation of "smartness" – witty, daring dialogue, and a world-weary, slightly shocking theme – simply by setting a play in a Manhattan apartment. It was the sphere of high comedy and social satire, the realistic assumption being that only rich New Yorkers had the time and resources to devote to the life depicted in such plays.

The backstage setting and the Manhattan apartment quickly evolved into a form of scenic shorthand, and consequently lost the element of original representation that effective realism requires. But the New York milieu took on new scenic life with the imaginative use of exterior setting in Elmer Rice's *Street Scene* (1929) and Sidney Kingsley's *Dead End* (1936). These plays are particularly interesting because they reflect the general state of dramatic realism at two crucial points in its development. Like *Porgy*, both *Street Scene* and *Dead End* present an exterior scene that purports to be a microcosm. Each setting reflects the artistic perspective embodied in its structure.

Whereas *Porgy* casts the Catfish Row residents in a positive, somewhat exotic light, *Street Scene* attempts a more straightforward representation of New York working-class life. The play is set entirely in *"The exterior of a 'walk-up' apartment house, in a mean quarter of New York. It is of ugly brownstone and was built in the '90's."*[16] Rice once remarked that "the house was much more than background; it was an integral part of the play. It might almost be said that it *was* the play."[17] He did with that house precisely what Howells had been calling upon Harrigan to do in the 1880s. He constructed a play around the "fact" of the urban milieu. In his stage directions he takes great pains to re-create the details of an apartment house, which he identified as 25 West Sixty-Fifth Street,[18] surrounded by an equally detailed storage warehouse and the site of a building under demolition. As a further aid to the illusion of reality, he notes that *"throughout the play, there is constant noise,"* specifying "L" trains, sirens, boats on the river, trucks, musical instruments, a radio, dogs barking, and human voices (568). He also uses dialogue that does not move the plot along in the traditional sense but broadens out to constitute a more realistic notion of action. The characters spend a good deal of the play's first act sitting on the stoop and complaining about the heat.

Kingsley's play reflects the naturalistic slant that the Depression had brought out in many playwrights of the thirties, such as Clifford Odets,

XI. A scene from Sidney Kingsley's *Dead End,* 1936. Scene design by Norman Bel Geddes. (Photo by White Studios)

John Steinbeck, and Irwin Shaw.[19] Kingsley uses his set to suggest what the naturalist saw as the larger milieu, not only the physical conditions and the people who inhabit them, but the forces of environment, natural and social, that have made them what they are. His study of urban poverty is imbued with the belief in environmental determinism, the intense focus on human misery, and the cosmic pessimism of the naturalist. In fact, *Dead End*'s setting constitutes a naturalistic subtext, beginning with the opening of its lengthy initial stage direction: "*Dead end of a New York street, ending in a wharf over the East River. To the left are a high terrace and a white iron gate leading to the back of the exclusive East River Terrace Apartments. Hugging the terrace and filing up the street are a series of squalid tenement houses.*"[20] The juxtaposition of poverty and wealth continues as Kingsley compares the "*huge, new palatial apartments*" of the rich with "*the diseased street below, filthy, strewn with torn newspapers and garbage from the tenements,*" which are "*close, dark and crumbling*" (453). He also notes carefully that, beyond the wharf, the central focus of the stage picture, is the East River, "*covered by a swirling scum an inch thick. A brown river, mucky with floating refuse and offal. A hundred sewers vomit their guts into it*" (453). As the play opens, the gang of boys who are its main characters are *"swimming in the sewerage at the foot of the wharf, splashing about and enjoying it immensely"* (454).

The various characters in *Street Scene* complain about the heat, gossip about each other, have babies, get evicted, eat ice cream, get drunk, kiss goodnight, shoot one another, recite poetry, engage in foreplay, and waltz on the sidewalk. The characters in *Dead End* swim in the sewage, talk to gangsters and diseased prostitutes, beat up the rich kids and steal their watches, "rat" on gangsters, who get killed by G-men, and get sent to jail. The plots of the plays are actually similar, but the worlds in which they take place are different enough to suggest two disparate versions of reality. Rice's is the urban working-class milieu of 1929, in which life is not easy but the characters take the bad with the good, and there is hope for prosperity, a better life, and the leisure to indulge one's finer inclinations. Kingsley's characters might be the same people several years later, in a world of absolute, relentless poverty, a world with no future for the young except the dead end of reform school and organized crime or prostitution, a world whose inhabitants are taunted by the constant presence of extreme wealth juxtaposed to their obscene poverty.

In Rice's milieu the characters make choices. The environmental forces are there, positive and negative; the final outcome is unknown. In Kingsley's world there are no choices. Every detail of his picture suggests inevitable destruction by social and economic forces. Rice's stage picture is an attempt at realism of the commonplace in the American tradition that goes back by way of *Porgy* to Sheldon and eventually to Harrigan and Howells. Kingsley's is theatrical realism as Zola described it – realism with a program. The shift in the representation of milieu is characteristic of the general shift in aesthetic perspective between the dramas of the twenties and the dramas of the thirties.

CHARACTER AND PERSONALITY

As we've already seen in O'Neill's work, the major development for realistic characterization during the twenties was the combination of realistic methods with the burgeoning interest in Freudian personality theory. The realistic playwrights of the mid-twenties conceived of a character as a fully developed personality first, and only secondarily as a congeries of moral qualities and precipitator of dramatic action in the Aristotelian sense. The chief reason for this shift was the explosion of interest in Freudian psychology between 1910 and 1920 and its influence on the drama, as on every other aspect of American life. Freud's 1909 lectures at Clark University in Worcester, Massachusetts, precipitated the translation that year of his *Selected Papers on Hysteria* and the American publication of the Clark lectures in 1910. Quickly following were *Three Contributions to the Theory of Sex* in 1910, *The Interpreta-*

tion of Dreams in 1913, and *The Psychopathology of Everyday Life* in 1914.[21] These works had a radical effect on the conception of character available to the American playwright during the second decade of the twentieth century.

The new Freudian science offered an ostensibly objective theory of personality. In their conception of character, the realistic playwrights of the twenties and thirties used it to bring what had heretofore been considered the hidden, subjective aspects of psychic reality into the realm of realistic representation. When psychoanalytic theory became accepted as science, the unconscious became objective reality for playwright and audience alike. Of course, the danger of this new way of thinking about character was that it could become reductive, and, in fact, playwrights' descriptions occasionally read as if they were taken from an early psychology textbook. S. N. Behrman's description of the central character in *Meteor* (1929) is a classic example: "*An artist of some potentialities vitiated by suppression in early youth into a defensive egomania which by progressive steps was to destroy him as a human being.*"[22] Rice summed up one of the characters in *Street Scene* as "Shirley, with the gold teeth, a sallow virgin who masturbates."[23]

Even so, when dealing with the characters of the twenties, it's important to remember that their creators often had a complex program in mind about the way personality developed and the way familial, social, and economic conditions affected it. Even a character like Zero in the expressionistic *Adding Machine* had a full Freudian case history in Rice's eyes. In a long memo to the actor who was to play the part, Rice laid out the aspects of Zero's personality that he considered most important, and not surprisingly he began with sex: "Perhaps the keynote to Zero is repressed sexuality. Like so many people in America – I nearly said like most people in America – he is sex starved. The sex taboo imprinted upon him in early childhood has become almost the central factor in his emotional life."[24] Rice's summary of Zero is a most revealing document about the way a playwright under the Freudian influence thought about his characters:

> I hope that this sounds very complex. For I conceive Zero as a complex being. A bundle of inconsistencies and contradictions, of impulses and fears, of desires and inhibitions. His conduct in a general sense is determined by hereditary influences, childhood environment, education and the social inheritance, but more particularly it is influenced by the state of his digestion, the weather, his internal secretions and the multitudinous sensory stimuli of light and sound, touch and temperature, taste, motion and pain. Since all these elements are never present at once, nor in the same proportions, it follows that at no two moments in his life is Zero (or anyone else) in precisely identical psychological and

physical situations, and that therefore he is at no two moments precisely the same person.[25]

The playwright's artistic struggle lay in finding ways to accommodate this newly considered dimension of personality within the limits of realistic representation. As we have seen in O'Neill's case, the simplest answer was to shatter the mimetic illusion and develop expressive modes of dramatizing the unconscious. But playwrights who shared the new conception of character as personality and sought to remain within the limits of realistic drama had to devise new methods of characterization. The simple device of self-revelation under the influence of alcohol that O'Neill finally discovered for his four late realistic plays *The Iceman Cometh, Long Day's Journey into Night, A Moon for the Misbegotten*, and *A Touch of the Poet* was one method used extensively by playwrights as different as William Saroyan and S. N. Behrman. Others employed traditional methods, such as overt, discursive analysis of one character by another, as well as experimental ones like Philip Barry's use of actual therapeutic psychodrama in *Hotel Universe* (1930) and *Here Come the Clowns* (1938). One of the most interesting developments grew out of the close connection between character and setting already noted in the regionalist plays of the twenties, especially those of Paul Green, which employed setting as a direct expression of personality.

During the twenties, many realistic plays depicted the familial or social problems arising from the neurotic state of a single individual, most often the managing matron, castrating wife, and dominant mother, a character who lent herself perfectly to the notion of setting as an extension of characterization. The use of interior setting for characterization, of course, goes back as far as Mitchell's *New York Idea* (1906). It had developed into the comic convention of reflecting a character's personal humor in his, or usually her, notion of interior decorating. The best example is George S. Kaufman and Marc Connelly's *Dulcy* (1921), the humorous treatment of an ignorant suburban housewife who "*has a way of speaking an age-old platitude as though it were a wise and original thought – a little thing casually tossed off in the course of conversation.*"[26] Kaufman and Connelly are not subtle about their use of interior setting for characterization: "*In a word, the room is Dulcy*" (535). Because their aim is satire, their setting is a room of glaring and tasteless modernity – "*a room that is splashing rather than merely striking*" (535) – a reflexive comic device that shows its hand with a humor half directed at its own exaggeration.

The writers of psychological plays sought a more indexical effect, using the setting to focus the audience's attention on specific qualities in the character. O'Neill employed interior setting in *Diff'rent* (1920), mirroring the heroine's regression to psychological and sexual adolescence in

XII. Chrystal Herne (left) dominates her living room as Harriet Craig in the Morosco Theatre production of George Kelly's *Craig's Wife*, 1925. Scene design by Sheldon K. Viele. (Photo by White Studios)

the youthful redecoration of her living room. The settings in the psychological studies that followed – such as Lewis Beach's *Square Peg* (1923), George Kelly's *Craig's Wife* (1925), and Sidney Howard's *Silver Cord* (1926) – played more or less striking variations on O'Neill's theme. Kelly used the device most aggressively, in keeping with a generally vitriolic treatment of his subject. *Craig's Wife* takes place entirely in the Craigs' living room, which, *"like all the other rooms in the house, reflects the very excellent taste and fanatical orderliness of its mistress. It is a kind of frozen grandeur, in dark, highly polished wood – strewn with gorgeous, gold-colored rugs and draped in rich brocaded satins. . . . As* MRS. CRAIG *enters, she appears to have been dressed for this particular room."*[27] Kelly's set is an elegant pictorial representation of this frigid, mercenary wife and fanatic house worshiper at the same time that it represents the small world of her creating, her sphere of dominance. The dynamic interrelation between setting and characterization proves an effective vehicle for dramatic tension as Walter Craig vents his increasing anger and rebellion against his wife by messing up the room and smashing her most prized ornament. Ultimately, Kelly's use of the room to express character is more effective than O'Neill's because it is integrated more fully within the total representation.

Lewis Beach in *A Square Peg* uses his set most thoroughly to depict his main character, Rena Huckins. *"It is the sort of house that a woman who delights in good housekeeping but who has little feeling for beauty would much admire. . . . Artistically, it has no merit. It is as neat and clean as the notorious tack, but the furnishings are characterless and inharmonious."*[28] In the details of the set, Beach shows his acute sense both of the milieu he is representing and of the way Rena Huckins would choose to arrange her house in order to declare her place in that milieu: *"The table in the dining room is covered with a white cloth – it is not removed after a meal. . . . In the sitting room, between the two openings, is a combination bookcase and writing desk. On the bookcase, a bust of Dickens and a hand-painted vase. On the desk, a telephone. In the center of the left wall is a mantel and a gas fireplace. On the mantel, a clock, a cut-glass vase, a soapstone monkey, and a small, bright cloisonné vase"* (4). The dining room also holds a mahogany Victrola, a device for regulating the furnace dampers, and an electric lamp, advertising the Huckins family's prosperity. *"The dining room and hall are papered in a dull, blue green; the sitting room in brown. The floors and woodwork are well-polished oak with a 'natural color' finish; on the floor Wilton rugs guaranteed not to show dust"* (4), a decorating scheme that is both "safe" and practical, and utterly devoid of life or imagination. Finally, the wall decorations are icons of Rena's self-conception. They include *"a print of Whistler's 'Mother,' a short and wide pastoral etching, a colored representation of Ruth with an armful of grain, and a copy of the 'Aurora'"* (4), reminders for the family of their sainted mother, and for the audience of Beach's subject.

These settings, and many more like them in the plays of the twenties, convey the sense of a dominant neurotic personality as the psychic milieu in which the members of the family must live. Their interior settings provide not only a major means of characterization but, through their scenic images of domestic tyranny, a constant thematic statement. And because none of the women leaves her house for long, the settings provide clear definition for the play's action as well. In the best of them, the setting provides the major point of integration for the whole representation.

The burgeoning interest in personality brought new life to the traditional methods of characterization as well. The age-old methods of discursive analysis and self-revelation were more believable in the frame of realistic drama when characters saw one another and themselves as interesting subjects for amateur psychoanalysis. As character became increasingly the play's center of interest, the notion of plot as a series of incidents to represent character, which was so radical when Howells enunciated it in the 1890s, became increasingly the norm. A whole spec-

XIII. Beverly Sitgreaves as Rena Huckins in Lewis Beach's *Square Peg,*
1923. (Photo by White Studios)

trum of methods for using plot for characterization appeared during the
twenties, from the least realistic, because most reflexive, psychodrama of
Philip Barry, through the less reflexive use of dramatic action as an
exemplum, to the most realistic use of action to dramatize a personality

without calling attention to its function as plot. Finally, two new conceptions of realistic character arose because of realistic drama's evolution
during the twenties and thirties: the new, psychologically individualized
conception of the social type that appeared in the society comedies of
Barry, Behrman, and Crothers; and the new, sociologically defined
"low-life" character depicted as a creature of the socioeconomic environment in the plays of the thirties.

Discursive analysis of one character by another took on the language
of psychoanalysis. An early play like *A Square Peg* relied on the terms of
Freudian psychology for a magical explanation of behavior. Rena
Huckins's daughter explains her mother's problem to her brother with
clinical objectivity: "She was born a generation ahead of her time. She's
had the wrong job. She should have been a modern business woman. . . . She would n't [*sic*] be the person she is now if she'd been where
she belonged. Or if Father had been different. But suppression, Gene,
has ruined her" (120). As Freudian theory became the familiar and expected basis for character, this kind of clinical discussion gradually
moved into the center of the play, and its careful elaboration resulted in
long, unwieldy lectures like Christina's analysis of Mrs. Phelps in *The
Silver Cord*:

> Oh, there are normal mothers around; mothers who *want* their children
> to be men and women and take care of themselves; mothers who are
> people, too, and don't have to be afraid of loneliness after they've
> outlived their motherhood; mothers who can look on their children as
> people and enjoy them as people and not be forever holding on to them
> and pawing them and fussing about their health and singing them lul-
> labies and tucking them up as though they were everlasting babies. But
> you're not *one* of the normal ones, Mrs. Phelps! Look at your sons, if
> you don't believe me. You've destroyed Robert. You've swallowed
> him up until there's nothing left of him but an effete make-believe. And
> Dave! Poor Dave! The best he can do is dodge the more desperate kinds
> of unhappiness by pretending! . . . And what makes you doubly deadly
> and dangerous is that people admire you and your kind. They actually
> admire you! You professional mothers![29]

Such discussions were considered informative in 1926, and they still
carried the vaguely titillating aura of attacking taboo subjects. But by the
early thirties, psychological concepts had gradually been internalized, so
that a buzzword like "suppression" was no longer adequate to define a
character's personality. Once the device of overt analysis had been established as a means of characterization, it was possible to use it for the
definition of more refined and subtle nuances of individual difference.
The more personalized the device became, the more it resembled normal
conversation, and thus the less reflexive it was as a dramatic device.

There was a similar development in characterization by self-revelation. In *Craig's Wife,* George Kelly uses the scene of self-revelation as a classic recognition and reversal in the Aristotelian sense, but one charged with Freudian imagery. Like Nora's in *A Doll's House,* Walter Craig's realization about his marriage precipitates his walking away from it:

> I saw your entire plan of life, Harriet, and its relationship to me. And my instinct of self-preservation suggested the need of immediate action – the inauguration of a new régime here: so I smashed the little ornament there – as a kind of opening gun. And I was going to smash all the other little ornaments – and Gods you had set up in the temple here, and been worshipping before me. I was going to put my house in order, including my wife; and rule it with a rod of iron. . . . The rôle is not *for* me, Harriet; I can only play a romantic part. (368)

As mentioned earlier, there is a whole spectrum of realistic representation in the use of plot for characterization, from the reflexive psychodrama of Barry's *Hotel Universe* and *Here Come the Clowns* – in which the revelation of character is the overt subject of the play – to the hidden devices in plays where character, with little or no overt analysis, is gradually unfolded by means of action.

Barry's two plays barely maintain their hold on the mimetic illusion, which he anchors as firmly as he can in the setting – the terrace of the Fields' house in the one and the back room of Ma Speedy's cafe in the other – and the familiar Barry dialogue, smart, witty, and somewhat desperately flip. In both plays a powerful personality is in charge of the proceedings, serving as a maestro for conducting the action that reveals the characters' psyches to themselves, to one another, and to the audience. In *Hotel Universe* the dying Stephen Field presides over the several incidents of psychodrama that take the characters back to their lives in order to exorcise the unhappiness that weighs on them in the present. In *Here Come the Clowns* the sinister Pabst takes a group of misfits, who are managing to get along all right in the world as vaudeville performers, and destroys them by drawing out the buried secrets in their lives through the disguise of improvisations. *The Clowns* has a frame for the action in Dan Clancy's search for a God who can provide meaning to the suffering of people like them, but the central action, like that in *Hotel Universe,* is the revelation of the characters.

Next in the spectrum are plays that are essentially studies of a single character, such as Susan Glaspell's *The Verge* (1921) and *Bernice* (1919). These don't have the element of self-realization that Barry's psychodramas do, although they both call the audience's attention to the fact that the protagonists are being revealed to the other characters in the play. *Bernice* is a tour de force of characterization, for the character being revealed is dead when the play begins. The action consists of the other characters' putting together their perspectives on Bernice to form a more complete conception of her life. Its climax is her husband's realization that he never knew who she was.

Between these reflexive methods and the attempt to hide the revelation of character completely in action and dialogue is the use of action that functions as an exemplum of character, much in the way that the action in a medieval morality play functions as an exemplum of the moral. In plays like *The Silver Cord* and Behrman's *Second Man* (1927), there is constant play between hidden and overt use of action for characterization. At the center of each is a character who is gradually revealed by means of his or her behavior in various incidents, analysis by other characters, and witting or unwitting self-disclosure. The action builds inevitably toward the big moment of overt revelation, for which the audience has been prepared by hints carefully placed in the preceding action. Thus the speech of revelation becomes simply a codification of what the action has already revealed to the audience.

By the moment of Christina's accusation in *The Silver Cord*, for example, the audience has seen Mrs. Phelps ignoring her new daughter-in-law during her enthusiastic reception of her adult son, whom she calls "Dave boy"; trying to control Dave's career as an architect and belittling his wife's as a biologist; manipulating Dave to keep him in her town and away from New York, where both careers would have a chance; destroying her son Robert's engagement and calling after her sons to come back because they might catch cold when they run out to stop Robert's fiancée from drowning herself; using hypochondriacal "heart spells" to frighten her sons; and scratching at Dave's bedroom door dressed in her best negligee, and then kissing and hugging his clothes. When Christina calls Mrs. Phelps an unnatural mother, the audience is quite ready to assent, for it has made that discovery on its own. Christina's analysis follows the action in just the way the moral follows a medieval exemplum, as the point of the story, the announcement of closure through formulation. That such exempla were able to take the stage and hold it for several years shows the centrality of character in the plays of the twenties and thirties. That Freudian analysis occupied the play's climactic space shows the power of personality in realistic characterization, although its reflexiveness kept the method of exemplum from creating a completely realistic mimetic illusion.

Barry's *Animal Kingdom* (1932) is a good example of realistic technique for character-centered drama. The play approaches the exemplum, for it clearly indicates what Barry feels should be the basis for marriage and what should not be, but it doesn't state this overtly. Instead, Barry structures the action as a series of incidents to reveal the personalities, motives, and values of his three major characters – Tom Collier, a young publisher who has rejected his father's wealth and the values it implies in order to devote himself to publishing promising new writers; Daisy Sage, a budding young artist who shares Tom's values and has lived with him for five years; and Cecelia Henry, a debutante, *"twenty-eight, lovely of figure, lovely of face, beautifully cared for, beautifully presented,"*[30] who marries him and proceeds to use his sexual interest in her to get him to do what she wants, which is to turn into another version of his father and provide her with all the luxury she desires.

If the subject of the play is a little too polemical to be realistic, the characterization is neatly hidden in the action. Through a series of paired encounters between Tom and Cecelia and Tom and Daisy, the audience gradually becomes aware of Cecelia's selfishness and the deception and manipulation in her dealings with Tom. In the first scene, she is all understanding and flexibility as they make plans for the wedding, but she uses a manipulative ploy to keep him from going on a fishing trip too soon afterward. In the next two acts, her dominance becomes more and more evident in the setting, as Tom's country farmhouse, which he refers to proudly as "the house in bad taste" (351), is gradually transformed, first in Act II, *"with small, feminine touches, such as new lamps, cretonne curtains at the windows and slipcovers of the same material on chairs and sofa,"* and then in Act III, into *"CECELIA's house, which is to say, The House in Good Taste"* (396). Finally, in the last scene, when Cecelia brings out all her arts to try to get Tom to move into his father's mansion in the city, she transforms the living room into what strikes Tom as "a private room at the Florentine . . . the best twenty-guinea house in London" (412). Just as his house has gradually lost its identity in Cecelia's hands, Tom has lost whatever was unique about his own character. His old friends comment, "In his top hat, when he put it on, suddenly he looked like only anybody. . . . Domestication works fast, when it works" (382).

Barry demonstrates the relationships between Tom and Daisy and between Tom and Cecelia in four scenes after the marriage. In Act II, Scene 1, Cecelia literally seduces Tom away from attending a concert being given by one of his bohemian friends. In Act II, Scene 2, Tom and Daisy have one of their old-time encounters. Giving her some straight criticism about her one-woman show, he demonstrates both his respect for her and his understanding of what she's trying to accomplish. In Act III, Scene 1, Barry shows his audience Tom at his worst, having descended under Cecelia's control to publishing sensational bestsellers, drinking too much, and spending most of his time entertaining people he despises. In Act III, Scene 2, he gives us the final confrontation between Tom and Cecelia, when Tom finally realizes that their marriage amounts to her manipulation of him in return for sex, and he leaves her to go back to his "wife," Daisy.

There is no overt analysis of these characters, no speech of self-revelation, simply a gradual unfolding for the audience of what each woman is and of the effect she has on Tom. Barry allows the audience to accept his characters as fully realized personalities – that is, as people – without calling attention to either his method of characterization or the Freudian definition of his characters. This is realistic characterization that works, characterization producing for the audience the illusion that these are real people in the real world.

It would be hard to overemphasize the influence that Freudian theory had on realistic characterization during the twenties, but the traditional notions of character that had reached their fullest development during the prewar teens were not completely discarded after the war. As we have seen, the concept of the local-color type, consummately interesting to playwrights and audiences before the war, was alive and kicking in regionalist plays like *Hell-bent fer Heaven* and *Sun-up,* as well as in the minor characters of such playwrights as Paul Green, Owen Davis, Susan Glaspell, and Eugene O'Neill. In a well-integrated regionalist play, local-color types could be an aid to the overall illusion, and thus a realistic use of character. A more interesting development was the fusion of the local-color type with the Freudian theory of personality that produced an Abe McCranie or a Brutus Jones.

Another development was the social type that appeared in discussion plays and social comedies where the emphasis was clearly on society rather than on the individual. With the success of *Dulcy,* Zona Gale's *Miss Lulu Bett* (1921), and George Kelly's *Show-off* (1924), the social type attained new life in a new version of comedy of manners. These plays attempted in a humorous vein the same kind of social criticism that a *Craig's Wife* or a *Silver Cord* tried to do more seriously. As Kaufman and Connelly had shown up the banal middle-class housewife, Kelly exposed that typical product of twenties how-to-succeed-in-business vulgarity, the show-off. In his minute study of the manners and mores of lower-middle-class family life, he achieved a sense of character by the accretion of detail, and although the characters are too reflexively extreme to maintain the mimetic illusion, Kelly used the realistic technique of letting his characters reveal themselves through their petty concerns, and letting his audience form its judgments on the basis of these signs of what lies beneath.

A less reflexive, and thus more realistic, use of social types appeared in the upper-class comedy of such playwrights as Rachel Crothers and Philip Barry. Crothers's method was to set up a microcosm of the social world she was depicting through the selection of types that are recognizable, from a sociological point of view, the moment they appear. The characters at Mrs. Boucicault's country house in *Let Us Be Gay* (1929) are the smart-set types familiar to us through F. Scott Fitzgerald: Mrs.

Boucicault, "Boucie," the broad-minded, rich, and bored elderly woman who finances the good times of the younger people for her own amusement; Madge, the divorcée who vamps every man in sight while on the prowl for her next husband; Kitty, the "new woman" who has outgrown her former Victorian values through independence and experience; Deirdre, the young flapper who has grown up with divorced parents and no social norms and is trying to find something in life to value; Bob, the rich but lost young man in search of pleasure for lack of a better pursuit; and good old Townley, the professional visitor. These characters are recognizable as types to each other as well as to the audience. The question Crothers poses is what can the self-conscious products of this decadent society do about themselves? The characters function as human representations of social conditions. Although their personalities are often interesting, they are primarily individual instances of the psychological effects that social conditions produce.

Barry's use of character in an early social comedy like *Holiday* (1928) was similar to Crothers's. As the more serious examination of character and personality in *Hotel Universe* and *Here Come the Clowns* began to affect his attitude of social criticism, however, Barry's representation of character in social comedy took a more serious turn. Tracy Lord of *The Philadelphia Story* (1939) is as much a social type as *Holiday*'s Linda, Ned, and Julia Seton, but Barry's attack has become more serious, and he probes mercilessly at both the character and the influences that have produced her. Because of her pampered upbringing – "there's never been a blow that hasn't been softened for her. There'll never be one that won't be softened"[31] – Tracy Lord has become what her ex-husband, Dexter, calls a "virgin goddess" – frigid, detached, self-involved, convinced of her own flawless superiority and absolutely intolerant of flaws in others. Objectifying Barry's social point of view, Dexter finally sums up Tracy Lord in a phrase: "You know I think there are more of you around than people realize. You're a special class of American female now – the Married Maidens. – And of Type Philadelphiaensis, you're the absolute tops, my dear" (526).

This speech typifies both the strength and the weakness of Barry's method. As social commentary, it has the strength of epigram – a telling, incisive formulation of a complex social phenomenon. In its very concision, however, it denies the complexity in Tracy's personality and the various circumstances out of which it grew. Another trend that reached its height in the thirties attempted to account for those circumstances exhaustively. This was the portrayal of character as a creature of environment. During the Depression there was a move away from depicting both the rural people of regions that were foreign to the New York audience and the suburban upper middle class that was the favorite subject for the Freudian studies of the twenties. The dominant facts were now the economic ones, and the locus of their greatest force was the city. The realistic play of the thirties was more likely to be *Awake and Sing!* or *Dead End* than *The Silver Cord* or *The Field God.*

The concept of character in these plays was naturalistic, but it was that of a neonaturalism shot through with Freudianism. For dramatic characterization, this amounted to a union of the Aristotelian view of character as the qualities that precipitate action, the newer view of character as personality informed by Freudian theory, and the naturalistic view that character is at least partly determined by environment. In *Dead End*, for example, Baby-Face Martin's character, that of the hardened criminal who has lost all sense of the value of human life and will stop at nothing to achieve his ends, is the result of the urban poverty at the play's center: "I yain't like yew punks . . . starvin' an' freezin' . . . fuh what? Peanuts? Coffee an'? Yeah, I got mine, but I took it" (470). His personality is more complicated, involving such contradictory elements as his "whatta-hell-yuh-can't-live-faever" affect and "da jitters" underneath; his living off "da fat a da land" and his "terrific yen tuh stay put"; his pride in his "flock a dames at'd make yew guys water at da mout'" (470) and his cherished love of his first girl, Francey; his sentimental desire to see his mother and the reality of her feeling toward him: "yuh stinkin yellow dog yuh!" (493). Kingsley clearly conveys that the story of Baby-Face Martin is not simply one of urban poverty. It's also mixed up with his sexuality, his mother, and the cultural attitudes and values he has internalized despite himself. The emphasis is on environment and character, but this play, like any other play of the post-Freudian thirties, would not have seemed realistic to its audience if sufficient attention had not been paid to personality.

7

The Final Integration:
Innovations in Realistic
Thought and Structure,
1916–1940

The presentation in 1918 of the first Pulitzer Prize for drama to Jesse
Lynch Williams for his sophisticated discussion play *Why Marry?* was the
first clear sign that realism had arrived in the American theater. Williams's play combined the (by 1917) traditional subjects of the American
discussion play with the Shavian notion that serious points about serious
issues could be made through witty dialogue and comic, even farcical,
dramatic action. The production history of *Why Marry?* is a good index
to the American theater's development during World War I. Williams
had begun work on the play as early as 1910, but by his own account, it
"was written ahead of its time – *i.e.,* ahead of the public's time for such
treatment of such ideas . . . if I had treated marriage sentimentally or
salaciously, my play might have arrived earlier. But I dealt with the
matter socially and satirically, and that was still rather shocking to the
public and puzzling to the producer."[1] Used to the rather somber treatment that such dramatists as Crothers, Thomas, and Sheldon had given
social issues, the theater public was not ready for a heroine like Helen,
who delivered such lines as these: "The object of marriage is not to bring
together those who love each other, but to keep together those who do
not"[2] and "Ah, yes, my life's a failure. I haven't trapped a man into a
contract to support me" (24). It's well to keep in mind that Arnold Daly
had nearly been jailed only five years earlier for producing *Mrs. Warren's
Profession* in New York. The *reading* public, however, had long been
delighted with Shaw, and Williams managed to publish his play as *And
So They Were Married* in 1914. It was not until 1917 that a commercial
manager had the courage to produce the play, and then only after it had
been done successfully at the American Academy of Dramatic Art. That
Why Marry? was a hit in 1917–18 is a good indication that the American
theater audience had changed radically during the war.

162

THOUGHT: THE IMPACT OF SOCIAL CHANGE

Like Robert Sherwood's antiwar play *The Road to Rome* (1927), *Why Marry?* displays unashamedly the Shavian influence in treatment and style. Its discussion is based straightforwardly on two ironic twists of the normal comedy plot. Rather than blocking the marriage of the two young lovers Ernest and Helen, Helen's family is trying to get them to marry instead of going off to Europe together to pursue their scientific careers. The couple rejects marriage because they can't afford to marry on their research scientists' salaries, because Helen does not want her life taken up with domestic duties, and because neither of them believes in marriage as a legal, social, or religious institution. Meanwhile, the family is coercing Helen's sister Jean into marrying a rich boy she doesn't love, for the sake of the family's business connections and her own financial security; Helen's Uncle Everett is defending his decision to divorce his wife because they no longer love each other; and her brother John is using his economic power over his wife, Lucy, to keep her from divorcing him. After no fewer than ten different discussion scenes, the conflict is resolved by what one critic called a "Pinerotic trick":[3] Helen and Ernest are legally married in spite of themselves; Aunt Julia and Uncle Everett decide they can't live without each other because self-sacrifice has become a habit with them; and little Jean gives in to marrying Rex as the less unattractive alternative in a choice between living "on the charity of a disapproving brother or [that of] a man I can't love" (74).

The reversal of the normal comedy plot, the ironic twist in the ending, and the sparkling wit of the discussions clearly show Shaw's influence. The issues, however, are the same ones that had been argued on the New York stage for ten years and that would be argued for another twenty. Marriage, of course, was the central topic, but it was discussed within the network of issues that had grown up around it in the years since *A Man's World* and *The New York Idea*. Williams found it impossible to discuss marriage without also discussing divorce, the new woman, the role of women's economic dependency in marriage, the double standard, and sexuality as a "biological trap," hot issues throughout the twenties. And although his view of marriage was fundamentally conservative – "Bad as marriage is, it's the best we have to offer you. What are you going to do about it?" (96) – his provocatively witty attacks on the prevailing order of things helped to define the battle lines for the more radical treatments of the institution that were to follow.

Williams's attack centered mainly on the conditions that forced a young girl like Jean to "entrap a man into marriage by playing the shameless tricks of the prostitute" (70) and kept a woman like Lucy married to a man she loathed because the fact that she'd "never been trained to earn money, only to spend it," (52) gave him economic power over her. He espouses Helen as the new woman, economically independent and free to commit herself where she loves, as opposed to women who were "something to be wanted and worshipped, petted, patronized, soft things to be wooed and won, married and owned" (42). Helen's union with John, Williams suggests, is real "matrimony" in the sight of God, the union of two free people who love each other, whereas the marriage promoted by the law, the church, and the social order is a form of enslavement or prostitution based on economic necessity.

In his exhaustive study of the theme of divorce in American drama, Donald Koster suggests that *Why Marry?* "presented the first mild indication on the stage that divorce might quite possibly be a highly moral and desirable way out of an unhappy marital situation,"[4] for although he brings the divorcing couple back together, Williams also voices the criticisms of marriage that made divorce a reasonable alternative. Beginning with Williams's own positive treatment, *Why Not?* (1922), divorce became a staple topic for the domestic discussion plays of the twenties and thirties.

The extent of Williams's influence is hard to measure quantitatively, but his presence is ubiquitous in the tone and dramatic structure that American dramatists adopted in the early twenties. Before 1920, Rachel Crothers, for example, was still writing serious and rather romantic treatments of the new woman and her need for independence. Her *Little Journey* (1918) contains a discussion of essentially the same problem that Williams addressed, the need for economic independence, but it is situated in a romantic plot and setting. Julie, a useless young girl who has been forced by her genteel poverty to leave the East and go to live with her brother in Colorado, meets a young man named Jim on the train. Jim draws her out of her depression by making her believe that she can become useful if she's willing to work, and she goes off with him to his camp for reforming alcoholics, saying, "I know now that life *can* be all you said – big and sweet and wonderful – *if we make it.* I want to give all the rest of mine to you – to thank you."[5] In *39 East* (1919), a young girl is trying to earn her living in New York, but she is so impossibly naive that she must be saved from seduction at the hands of a libertine by a young man who at first is out to seduce her himself but later changes his mind when her simplicity touches him. Both plays are a far cry from Crothers's social commentaries of the twenties and thirties, whether in the form of comedies like *Nice People* (1921), *Expressing Willie* (1924), *Let Us Be Gay* (1929), and *As Husbands Go* (1931), or in discussion plays like *Mary the Third* (1923) and *When Ladies Meet* (1932).

In *Mary the Third,* Crothers took up the marriage question where Williams left off, not only discussing the biological trap, divorce, and the problem of a woman's equality in marriage, but also taking on the top-ical subjects of trial marriage and the flapper generation. Like Williams, she provides continual criticism of social institutions but makes the over-riding point that marriage seems to be "the best thing we've got."[6] The play's comic form also conveys the notion that nature is stronger than any objection the young people might make to the prevailing social institutions. In the two scenes that make up the play's Prologue, Croth-ers shows Mary's mother and grandmother succumbing in the styles of 1870 and 1897 to the importunities of their natural mates and agreeing to marry. At the fundamental sexual level where these decisions are finally made, the play suggests, Mary the Third is just like them.

The play also suggests, however, that marriage and mating are two very different undertakings. Mary is determined, as she says, to *"have my own money. I'll make it.* I shall live with a man because I love him and only as long as I love him. I shall be able to take care of myself *and* my children if necessary" (92). She will not fall into the false position that is her grandmother's notion of marriage: "Why I had my way about everything on earth. The madder your grandfather got, the more I cried and the softer I was. I just twisted him round my finger – like that. And he thought I was right under his thumb" (89). Nor will she stand for her mother's unhappy resignation to a marriage that both partners knew had failed at the end of five years, but in which they continue, "jogging along – letting out the worst side of ourselves for the other to live with" (72). Mary hopes for a marriage of equality, where the partners can look into each other's eyes, "levelly – without conditions and silly compromise because he's a man and you're a woman" (91), and that is at least what she and Lynn are planning at the end of the play.

Throughout the twenties, the clash between the generations continued to preoccupy Rachel Crothers, but the major topics for discussion plays continued to be marriage, women's equality, and divorce, with the last two closely linked. The best of the marriage-versus-divorce plays, Philip Barry's *Paris Bound* (1927) and Sidney Howard's *Half Gods* (1929), made interesting use of comic form to support the playwrights' views on social institutions. Barry's treatment is the more overtly serious, and like his other serious plays, *Hotel Universe* and *Here Come the Clowns,* it is a straightforward treatment of a single question: Does the simple fact of adultery justify ending the "higher union" of an otherwise happy mar-riage? The play opens as Mary and Jim begin their "modern" marriage, with Mary's declaration on her wedding day, "I don't expect never to see another man, and I don't expect you never to see another girl."[7] Mean-while, Jim's long estranged parents have met at the wedding and are looking back at their divorce. His father sets the stage for the discussion to come: "For following a physical impulse which I share with the rest of the animal kingdom, you destroyed a spiritual relationship which belonged only to us. For an act which in reality was of little or no importance to you, you did me out of my marriage and my home" (262).

Six years later, Mary finds that Jim has been seeing her friend Noel during his European business trips and decides to divorce him. Her father-in-law tries to persuade her that the feeling that she's "lost about everything [she] had" boils down to her "sense of possession . . . the lowest instinct you've got" (283), and that Jim's affair with another woman concerns only her physical relation to him, the least important aspect of their "uncommon marriage" (284). He fails to persuade her with his arguments, but when Mary feels a physical attraction of her own, to a man she has no respect for, the light dawns, and she greets her husband on his return as though nothing had happened. Barry presents his idea of "uncommon marriage" through their happy reunion and their talk about the children, the house, the gardener, and the relatives. They avoid talking not only about Jim's affair but also about a friend's symphony that Mary has spent the last three months helping with, and when Jim says his business went "marvelously," Mary replies, "I don't care," and he answers, smiling, "I know you don't" (292). Combining the discussion with this example, Barry represents his "higher union" of "uncommon marriage" simply and clearly. Jim and Mary's union is based on both mutual interest and well-defined limits to their intimacy. Barry's version of marriage is one in which the two partners lead essentially separate lives, coming together for the purposes of raising children, maintaining a house, and amusing each other.

Howard's *Half Gods* has less serious dialogue but treats the marital relationship more thoroughly. It concerns a young couple, Stephen and Hope, who spend most of their time fighting about the things that strained a typical upper-middle-class marriage during the twenties. Hope is the familiar flapper, trained for having fun and nothing else, who chafes at the domestic routine and expects her husband to take her out and entertain her. Stephen grumbles about not getting enough sleep and complains that he is a "cipher . . . in my own home that I pay for! God, *how* I pay!"[8] Voicing the now familiar complaint about the economic conditions in marriage, he finally explodes: "All you young wives! Do you know what your husbands are saying about you? That you're not worth the price! That's what! Not worth the price!" (23). On the other hand, Hope's position is presented to Stephen by her psychoanalyst, Dr. Mannering: "Your wife. To you she's many things. The mother of your children. The companion of your evenings. The chief advertisement of your success. Almost anything, in fact, except the person that she really is" (70). The couple separates. Hope gets a job. They both experiment with love affairs. Occasionally they meet and fight the old battles again.

Finally, Hope is about to leave for Reno to get her divorce when her children come down with the whooping cough. The children's doctor says, "Your little ideas may run away to Reno. . . . But your deep female soul will hold you with your young" (159). She stays. And she and Steve commit themselves to marriage as "one long knock down and drag out battle royal between two people who can't live without each other" (197).

The play's title is an allusion to Emerson's "Give All to Love" – "When half-gods go, / The gods arrive." The new order in its ending is based on compromise and the deflation of the unrealistic notions with which the couple started their marriage. Howard suggests that marriage fulfills fundamental human needs, which he saw even as biological necessities: the woman's instinctual nurturing of her children and the man's sex drive. In addition, the man has social needs that may or may not be biological, but that are certainly strong: "I want her back," says Stephen. "I want my children back. I need her to amuse me and keep me company and let me look after her and her children" (30). Howard's view of marriage is entirely in keeping with his deflation of such faddish notions of the twenties as the need for complete self-expression and absolute freedom from responsibility. His "Gods" turn out to be compromise, the recognition of human weakness, and mutual tolerance, as opposed to the romantic "Half Gods," the notions that marriage is a total union that makes two people one, and that life can and should be uniformly happy.

Howard and Barry both expressed the typical skepticism of the twenties toward the old assumptions underlying both the social institution of marriage and the dramatic structure of comedy. Both shed some harsh light on the meaning of "happily ever after," but, like Williams and Crothers before them, both employed the comic structure to suggest that the solution to marital misery lies not in separation and divorce but in a reformed marriage and a new kind of union, their version of the new order. It should be clear by now that the plays of the twenties expressed a fundamentally conservative attitude toward marriage and divorce. Their solutions varied greatly, but over and over again, the message was reiterated: Marriage is in a bad way, but the answer to this social problem lies in reform, not in divorce.

Rachel Crothers reversed this trend when she took up the corner of the triangle that Barry left out in *Paris Bound*. *When Ladies Meet* (1932) combines discussion and exemplum. It depicts the case of Mary, a writer in her early thirties who is in love with Rogers, her publisher. She has just written a novel with the thesis that it is possible for a "decent" woman to fall in love with a married man, for him to fall in love with her, for her to discuss the situation with his wife, and for a reasonably happy solution to emerge for all. Mary and Rogers are planning to consummate their love at a friend's country house when Rogers's wife, Claire, arrives on the scene with an ardent suitor of Mary's, who is hoping she will change her mind when she meets Claire. Thus the plot of Mary's novel is played out in the "real life" of the drama, and Mary finds the outcome somewhat different from what she had anticipated. She and Claire find that meeting "the other woman" has completely altered their views of Rogers. Neither had thought that the man she loved would treat someone he loved as he has treated her rival. Claire has put up with his affairs in the past, and she tells him: "I've always been glad to get you back before – and thankful it was over – always thinking of *you* – never of *her* – but now – I've *seen her* and something has happened *to me*. I've seen *all* of her – her whole heart and soul and self. And I know – *so well* how you made her love you like that."[9] Mary sees that it is Claire, not her, who has really loved Rogers. She tells Claire: "I'm one of the others – absolutely. *Nothing* more. . . . I didn't know what I was doing – to *you*. I didn't know anybody *could* love like that" (132).

The result is a realistic subversion of the expected comic ending, much like that of *A Man's World*. Crothers resolves the problem neither in the traditional way, by returning the husband to the wife, nor in Mary's new "modern" way, by having the three discuss the situation and the most suitable couple emerge, but in the way that these two characters would be likely to act. Claire decides to divorce Rogers, and Mary rejects him when she finds out how shallow his love for her is. In this case, Crothers suggests, divorce is the answer, not marriage. The two women do not reject Rogers because of what he does but because he has finally revealed who he is. Once they know that, neither of them can contemplate a future with him, regardless of the conditions. Crothers suggests that the problem is not in the institution of marriage but in the wider sphere of the relations between the sexes.

Although it sometimes seems so, marriage was not the only subject for American drama between the wars. In 1938, Eleanor Flexner noted a number of subjects that had arisen from the "profound sociological change which was taking place in morals and mores during the nineteen-twenties . . . prohibition, postwar disillusionment, and flight from reality, the recession of religious belief, the cult of feminine emancipation, the rising tide of Hollywood movies and tabloid journalism, and the perfecting and wide knowledge of contraceptives."[10] As economic conditions worsened, the general social problems associated with prosperity gave way to the more specific problems generated by the Great Depression. Malcolm Goldstein found that, between 1931 and 1935, "topics engaging the minds of the most talented social writers, whether independent or affiliated with institutional theaters, were the conditions endured by prison inmates, antagonism between the races, the rise of fascism, and the individual's problem of maintaining dignity and self-esteem without harming others."[11] Finally, with the increasing threat of fascism and the rising specter of war in Europe, in the years between 1935 and 1939, American playwrights took on the subjects of political freedom, democracy, patriotism, and war. As we shall see, many of these subjects lent themselves more easily to melodrama than to the discussion play, but with Robert Sherwood's witty antiwar play *The Road to Rome* as an example, playwrights like Behrman, Barry, and Maxwell Anderson demonstrated that it was possible to make serious statements in the theater without the heavy emotional effects of melodrama.

The earliest of the discussion plays about social issues other than marriage was actually Susan Glaspell's *Inheritors* (1921), a treatment of social protest on a college campus that calls to mind the 1960s. Glaspell tends to sacrifice the mimetic illusion for polemical effect, and she opens the play with the founding of the college in 1879 under the rather ostentatious banner of freedom and liberalism. The rest of the play takes place in 1920, as the founder's granddaughter Madeline, a student at the college, fights for freedom of speech for some "Hindu revolutionaries" who are also students. The discussion comes when Madeline must listen to persuasion by her uncle, the chairman of the now conservative board of trustees, her aunt, and a formerly radical professor who has been browbeaten into submission by her uncle. The play ends with Madeline's rejection of the older generation's corrupted values as she goes off to jail in the idealistic spirit of her grandfather for her refusal to give up the cause of the Hindus.

Augustus Thomas's *Still Waters* (1926) was a similarly polemical discussion of a more specific political issue. The play is an old-fashioned melodrama in form, but it contains a good many arguments against prohibition in both dialogue and action. Maxwell Anderson took up the issue of corruption in Congress with a much lighter hand in *Both Your Houses* (1933), although his play is also fundamentally a melodramatic depiction of young Senator Alan McClean's fight against corruption in Washington. McClean barely manages to escape being co-opted by the self-interested system he's trying to reform, but Anderson gives him a final speech to his fellow senators that concludes with "there are a hundred million people who are with me, a hundred million people who are disgusted enough to turn from you to something else."[12] It is corrupt old Senator Solomon Fitzmaurice, however, who gets to the heart of the matter: "The sole business of government is graft, special privilege and corruption – with a by-product of order. They have to keep order or they can't make collections" (103). On the whole, however, Anderson's dialogue, like Thomas's, barely maintains the fourth-wall illusion because his characters speechify rather than discuss the issue in the context of the action.

This tendency to strain the mimetic illusion in order to make sure the audience gets the point was typical of playwrights who tried to make a serious social statement during the thirties. In this connection, it would be a mistake to ignore the influence of the new didactic drama that sprang up in that decade, plays "created with the primary intent of teaching or persuading,"[13] and conceived of as presentational instruments rather than representational objects. These plays addressed the audience directly, demanding action rather than rational conviction, and deliberately shattering the mimetic illusion. Clifford Odets's *Waiting for Lefty* (1935) was the first didactic drama to be a popular success, but by 1933 the New York theater had already witnessed Paul and Claire Sifton's *1931——*, Rice's *We, the People,* George Sklar and Albert Maltz's *Peace on Earth,* Sklar and Paul Peters's *Stevedore,* and John Wexley's *They Shall Not Die,* all effective enough plays to influence the playwrights of the established theater.

Though none of the fundamentally realistic playwrights except Elmer Rice actually wrote didactic drama, the trend's influence on Sherwood, Behrman, Kingsley, and even Barry became clear as their plays took on more pointed social and political issues and discussed them more directly during the thirties. The plays these men wrote were a direct reflection of the world's political situation. Fascism was their major preoccupation, juxtaposed to democracy and freedom, and playwrights who had been professing pacifism and leftist politics and attacking American government as corrupt, elitist, and ineffectual during the twenties found themselves in the thirties writing patriotic plays urging their countrymen to go to war to protect democracy. This shift in thought can be traced most clearly in the work of Sherwood and Rice, but it was the general trend of American realistic drama as well.

In order to appreciate their cycle of thought, one must recall the weariness, disillusionment, and disgust with which the playwrights of the early twenties remembered World War I. Their great concern was with what the war had done to the soldiers. O'Neill's Benny Rogers in *Diff'rent,* Davis's Ben Jordan in *Icebound,* and Gilbert Emery's Oswald Lane in *The Hero* (1921) exemplified the callous, antisocial behavior expected of soldiers who had survived the horrors of trench warfare. Completely self-absorbed, fundamentally miserable, they are interested only in the quick fix of momentary pleasure and heedless of the effect their behavior has on others. These plays are primarily sympathetic toward the veteran and absolutely repelled by the war that has produced him.

The best known of the war plays, Maxwell Anderson and Laurence

Stallings's *What Price Glory?* (1921), has a more complicated attitude. When it was produced, the play caused a sensation because of its risqué scenes with the French girl Charmaine and the use of what was considered the "hard-boiled" language of soldiers: "Oh, God, Dave, but they got you. God, but they got you a beauty, the dirty swine. God DAMN them for keeping this up in this hellish town."[14] Because of this "virile," slice-of-life quality and the cynical attitude the soldiers display, the play was regarded by contemporary critics as a piece of daring realism and an attack on war. According to his biographer, "the primary purpose of the play remained for Stallings simply telling the truth about war."[15] Seventeen years after it was produced, Eleanor Flexner wrote that it was "not an antiwar play, but a highly realistic play about war as fought by professional soldiers."[16] She had to admit, however, that it was, "by the standards of 1938, precisely the evasion of reality which the authors wished to avoid."[17] In 1939, Frank O'Hara wrote that despite its attempt to capture the language and the attitudes of the soldier in World War I, in *What Price Glory?* "war, for all its sordidness and terror, still remains the romantic adventure, to which Flagg and Quirt ebulliently return as the curtain falls."[18]

In short, the perspective of time revealed that Anderson and Stallings had simply exchanged one set of romantic ideals for another. Joseph Wood Krutch, a great admirer of the play's realism, wrote that "only an audience for whom long-established ideological complexes involving patriotism, courage, and honor had completely disintegrated could have comprehended, much less accepted, the attitudes taken by the authors."[19] Perhaps only this audience could accept the "hard-boiled" attitude the authors erected in place of those old romantic ideals. Flagg and Quirt, middle-aged professional soldiers, are distinguished primarily for their ability to remain untouched by fear, by love, by loneliness, or by any human emotion that would make their life intolerable. In the course of the play they carry on a spirited adolescent rivalry over drink, sex, and fighting. This rivalry seems the only thing that matters to them, and in the end the authors call on us to admire them for practicing the very ideals they've spent the play deflating – courage, patriotism, and honor. When Quirt staggers off drunk, following Flagg back to the front line, he mutters, "What a lot of God damn fools it takes to make a war!" (89), but he exits with the line, "Hey Flagg, wait for baby!" (89). Underneath the cynicism lie the bravery and blind devotion to duty that the authors admired in spite of themselves and that make the play a romantic tribute to the soldier despite its realistic deflation of the glory of war.

When Robert Sherwood's *Road to Rome* (1927) appeared, the country had had almost a decade to recover from the emotional shock of World War I. Sherwood's play is a witty Shavian discussion of war set in Rome at the time of Hannibal's invasion. Amytis, a cultured Greek married to the Roman dictator Fabius, is entirely at odds with the Romans' bellicose view of life. In contrast to her mother-in-law, she has no interest whatever in the glory of Rome: "Now, please don't ask me to keep track of our wars, or just who our enemies happen to be at the moment. With one war after another – and sometimes two or three wars at a time – I can't follow them. The mental effort is too great."[20] Through Amytis, Sherwood wittily satirizes the mind-set of a country at war, but the underlying seriousness of his criticism emerges just enough to make his viewpoint clear. When a Roman soldier reports the outcome of the latest battle with Hannibal, Sherwood's attitude as a World War I veteran comes through:

Scipio.   They closed in on us and butchered us . . . and all through the battle their terrible African war drums kept on beating – louder – louder . . .
Amytis.   (Without enthusiasm.) It must have been thrilling!
Scipio.   Our army was a confused mass of struggling, writhing men – battling against an enemy that attacked from every side. The slaughter was unspeakably awful. . . . When it was over, at last, seventy thousand Romans lay dead on the field of Cannae.
Amytis.   (Slowly.) Seventy thousand! Why did they die? (306)

Amytis goes to Hannibal's camp in search of the answer, and ends up pleading with the great warrior on behalf of "the human equation" (323): "It's so much more beautiful than war. . . . If you could ever find it, you'd know that all your conquests – all your glory – are only whispers in the infinite stillness of time – that Rome is no more than a tiny speck on the fact of eternity – that the gods are the false images of the unimaginative" (323). After he sleeps with Amytis, Hannibal too discovers the human equation, and he turns his army away from Rome, "a conqueror who could realize the glory of submission" (329).

Sherwood's discussion play embodies a two-pronged attack, on the national psychology of imperialism and on the romanticizing of war. He deflates inflated ideals about war, uncovers the sham arguments suggesting that religious and familial values support warmongering, and reminds his audience of the grim realities behind the rhetoric. Through vague concepts like "the glory of submission" and "the human equation," he tries to replace the glory of war with the glory of pacifism, beating the patriotic phrasemongers at their own game. He also structures the action in his play to give the fullest audience support to his argument. The family discussions about war and patriotism in Act I prepare for Amytis's confrontation with Hannibal in Acts II and III, and each act ends in a climactic moment of choice between war and humanity. In Act I, will Hannibal destroy an essentially defenseless Rome? In Act II, will Hannibal choose to sleep with Amytis (love) or to put her to death (war)? In Act III, will Hannibal serve war or "the human equation"? Sherwood is careful to provide satisfaction for the audience in the discussion's coming out "right" despite the play's not having a traditional comic structure. When Hannibal marches off, Amytis remains with her benighted husband. The hope for the new order lies in the possibility that the childless Amytis is pregnant by Hannibal and that her son will, as Hannibal says, "duplicate his father's signal triumphs and that he too, will ultimately discover the human equation" (332).

In *Idiot's Delight* (1936), Sherwood depicted the chief dangers to international peace as unthinking national chauvinism and the blind self-interest of capitalism. The play is set in a resort hotel in the Italian Alps, near the frontiers of Switzerland and Austria. It is populated by a cosmopolitan group including a young English couple, a young and passionately idealistic French communist, a German scientist, an international munitions dealer with his apparently Russian mistress, Irene, and the Americans Harry Van and his troupe of dancers, "Les Blondes." In a method typical of his later plays, Sherwood sets this microcosm of characters down in a situation of imminent danger – in this case the beginning of World War II – and lets them react to it.

When war breaks out, the pacifist French communist turns into a wild-eyed patriot and is finally shot for denouncing the Italian regime. The German scientist, who had been on his way to Zurich to work on the cure for a dangerous disease, turns around and heads for Germany to help with germ warfare. The young English couple, who had been quoting Leonardo da Vinci on war as "bestial frenzy," go back to England so that the young man can join up, because "we have to stand by France. We have to make the world a decent place for heroes to live in."[21] Irene confronts the munitions magnate with the reality of the carnage, and he replies with an argument reminiscent of Shaw's Andrew Undershaft:

> Who are the greater criminals – those who sell the instruments of death, or those who buy them, and use them? . . . all of them consider me an arch-villain because I furnish them with what they want, which is the illusion of power. That is what they vote for in their frightened governments – what they cheer for on their national holidays – what they glorify in their anthems, and their monuments, and their waving flags! (117)

Finally, only Irene and Harry are left in the hotel. As the French planes begin bombing, they sit at the piano singing "Onward Christian Soldiers" with ironic bravado. The curtain falls on the rather surrealistic juxtaposition of their singing with the sounds of *"bombs, gas-bombs, airplanes, shrapnel, machine guns"* (135).

But a great deal happened between 1936 and 1939. When Sherwood set *There Shall Be No Night* in Finland during the Finnish resistance, he did so with the clear intention of making a case for America's joining the war. The play is melodramatic in structure, with the heroic Finns fighting for the survival of their country, "small – clean – and exposed."[22] The hero, Kaarlo Valkonen, is a Nobel Prize–winning scientist who, along with his American wife, Miranda, is won over from pacifism to the defense of his country. There are a number of Americans in the play, all enlisted in Finland's cause. Sherwood's changed attitude toward war is evident in the speech of one of the idealistic young American volunteers, a pilot who has just shelled some Nazi staff cars:

> It gave me a thrill. All this time, in fighting the Russians, I've felt just a little bit uncomfortable . . . after my experience with the Loyalists [in Spain]. You know, I couldn't help saying, 'God forgive them – for they know not what they do'. . . . But when I saw those Nazis – those arrogant bastards – and I could even see the looks on their faces – all I could think of was 'God forgive *me* if I miss this glorious opportunity.' I let 'em have it. It was a beautiful sight to see 'em diving into the ditches, mussing their slick grey uniforms in the mud. (275)

The conversion of Robert Sherwood is reflected in the conversion of Kaarlo Valkonen, who articulates the very arguments that Sherwood had found empty when they were used to justify World War I: "I believe it is the long deferred death rattle of the primordial beast. We have within ourselves the power to conquer bestiality, not with our muscles and our swords, but with the power of the light that is in our minds" (292). Kaarlo is killed in action, and Sherwood ends the play with his wife and uncle waiting for the moment when they, too, will be killed, after they burn their house down in "scorched earth" fashion and fight to the end with the discarded ammunition of dead soldiers. But the hope for the future still exists in the Valkonens' unborn grandchild, who will grow up in America, a symbol of their hope that America will join the war.

There Shall Be No Night is a discussion play only in the sense that its characters talk about the war and their reasons for fighting it. The play's purpose is not to inform the audience of the rational arguments for and against joining the war, but to secure its emotional commitment to the cause. Although Sherwood keeps his play within the fourth-wall illusion, his object is persuasion rather than representation. The emotional climaxes of the action as well as the telling points in the discussion all exist to convince the audience that America should go to the aid of brave little democracies like Finland against the Nazi menace. Sherwood's becoming a special assistant to the Secretary of War in 1940 should have come as no surprise to anyone who had been following his plays. They reveal a man who saw no further course but action.

An example of the opposite line of development is S. N. Behrman. In *Rain from Heaven* (1934) he described fascism as "a mania as ravaging as a forest fire that burns down everything before it."[23] In this play a German music critic who has taken refuge in England decides that he must return to Germany to fight the Nazis however he can: "It's a matter of life and death. I see now that goodness is not enough, that kindness is not enough, that liberalism is not enough. I'm sick of evasions. They've done us in. Civilization, charity, progress, tolerance – all the catch-words" (272). Lady Lael, an English liberal, decides to stay in England, maintaining a firm outpost of freedom: "There is a genius for wandering and a genius for remaining behind. There is the shooting star and the fixed. Perhaps when you come back," she tells the German, "you will find that in our own way we have realized your dream" (272).

Behrman continued to defend the position of standing firm to main-tain civilization as far as it has come. In 1939, the same year that Sher-wood wrote *There Shall Be No Night,* Behrman came out with *No Time for Comedy,* a defense of even the least serious writer's role in a world fraught with economic depression, war, fascism, and the various social ills of the thirties. In the play a writer of drawing-room comedies tells his wife and leading lady that his work has become useless in contemporary reality: "What sort of world is this? *Danse Macabre!* And you expect me to sit in my room contriving stage-situations for you to be witty in! Or I go to Hollywood and sit in endless conferences agonizing over novel methods for boy to meet girl. I tell you it's all an irrelevance, an anach-ronism, a callous acquiescence."[24] His wife replies that the besieged Europeans love American films: "What would you have them do? Sit in their shelters and contemplate the eternities? The eternities are a bore. They're inhuman. You can't take them in. We can only laugh at our plight. That's what distinguishes us from the animals and from the sav-ages you're so excited about. They can't laugh" (49). She concludes, "There are two sorts of people, that's all – the brutes and the decent ones – there always have been and as far as I can see there's no hope of exterminating the brutes . . . we've got to have as good a time as we can, be as gay as we can, as delighted as we can – right under their horrid snouts" (50).

Sherwood and Behrman represent two extremes in the realistic writ-ing about social issues during the thirties. Whereas Behrman steadfastly maintained that mimetic art had its rightful place independent of social protest, Sherwood moved to the edge of didactic drama and then all but gave up the theater in favor of direct action. The clash of these two attitudes created what Malcolm Goldstein calls a Hegelian dialectic in the American theater of the thirties.[25] Goldstein considers the split mainly generational. Older writers "believed that their realistic approach to new issues required realistic presentation, not the radical techniques of ex-tremists."[26] According to him, "the gift that the playwrights of this generation made to the theater lay in their ability to discuss all sides of serious issues in dialogue that argued rather than exhorted."[27] Younger writers, such as Clifford Odets, Lillian Hellman, and Irwin Shaw, "did not displace the older writers, but by winning sympathy among audiences for their fierce disquisitions on social justice, they succeeded in sharpening the tone of Broadway drama, so that by the second half of the decade most of the new plays on social themes offered by independent producers were not much less astringent than those presented by the institutional theaters."[28]

There certainly is truth to this statement. The success of plays by the younger writers, such as Odets's *Waiting for Lefty* and Hellman's *Children's Hour,* influenced the general shift to a more polemical tone in the theater. But it would be a mistake to consider the shift away from the mimetic and toward the didactic during the mid-thirties a generational one. Although he could write such realistic plays as *Street Scene* and *Counselor-at-Law,* Elmer Rice had shown himself capable of vehement polemics in his antiwar play *The Iron Cross* (1917) long before he wrote his didactic attack on social ills, *We, the People* (1933), and his antifascist melodrama, *Judgment Day* (1934). It was the change in Sherwood's views that produced his change in technique, not the other way around. Nevertheless, the general tone of serious American social drama during the thirties was polemical. Antiwar didacticism like that of Paul Green's *Johnny Johnson* (1936), Irwin Shaw's *Bury the Dead* and *Siege* (1937), Sidney Howard's *Paths of Glory* (1935), and Sidney Kingsley's *Ten Million Ghosts* (1936) gave way to the antifascism of plays like Oliver Garrett's *Waltz in Goose Step* (1938), Burnet Hershey's *Brown Danube* (1939), Dorothy Thompson and Fritz Kortner's *Another Sun* (1940), Claire Booth's *Margin for Error* (1939), and Lillian Hellman's *Watch on the Rhine* (1941). Compared to plays like the latter, *There Shall Be No Night* was an objective representation.

A playwright who wanted to write realistic drama had a problem during this period. Even if he wanted to stay within the mimetic mode of the discussion play, as Behrman did, he was in danger of breaking the frame by writing reflexive persuasive dialogue to defend this decision. Like those writing between 1910 and 1920, the realistic playwrights of the thirties gave a great deal of attention to structural innovation. Instead of developing new structures to escape the rigidity of convention, however, many of them went back to the most conventional structure of them all, melodrama, and tried to make it accommodate a serious treatment of contemporary social conditions. They succeeded in creating social melodrama. Whether they succeeded in creating realistic melodrama is another question, and, for anyone interested in the evolution of realism, an intriguing one.

STRUCTURE: ACHIEVING THE REALISTIC RHYTHM

The discussion plays of the early twentieth century had demonstrated that American dramatists were capable of embodying serious thought in their plays, and that the American theater public was capable of responding to it. The structural experiments in these plays, and in the realistic one-act plays that emerged from the Provincetown and Washington Square theaters soon after, demonstrate that native realistic drama was vibrant and flexible. The theater was ready for the talented playwrights who worked at realistic drama after World War I, attempting to integrate serious thought about contemporary society into dramatic structures that reflected the patterns of action that human beings perceive in life, rather than imposing the preconceived patterns of conventional drama on human experience. These dramatists gravitated naturally to the discussion play as a realistic structure that left ample room for the development of character and thought. But they also took a newly serious look at comedy and melodrama. In the process, they discovered innovative ways of reworking these conventional patterns to achieve a more believable conception of their contemporary reality, and thus a more fully realistic representation. Finally, a few of them made serious attempts to see the concept of dramatic structure in a completely new light, to create new dramatic structures that expressed rhythms of life that hadn't been accommodated by traditional comedy, tragedy, or melodrama or by the variations on these structures that the discussion format produced. This development constituted the final step of realism's evolution in American drama.

Walter Meserve has suggested that the combination of melodramatic structure with "serious study of contemporary social problems"[29] produced the social melodrama of the twenties that might be seen from our perspective as a short step forward for realism. As in any melodrama, the "social" variety already seen in plays like *The Silver Cord, Craig's Wife,* and *A Square Peg* implies a somewhat simple view of the world as a mass of contending forces that can be labeled either good or bad, worthy of the audience's support or condemnation. Using melodramatic structure, the playwright could resolve a contemporary social issue by identifying one view with the hero and the other with the villain, convincing the audience that characters were good or bad by connecting their ideas with their personalities, and rewarding or punishing them through action rather than elucidating the issue through dialogue.

Craig's Wife is a good example of social melodrama, and a good measure of the extent to which it approached realism. The strength of George Kelly's method is the clarity arising from singleness of purpose. As one of his critics said, "He unsympathetically attacks some personal failing that blights social relations. In *Craig's Wife* the failing which corrupts Harriet Craig is her selfishness, her callous egoism."[30] Kelly's play is effective enough to convince as sharp a critic as Krutch that she is a " 'good housekeeper' who coldly sacrifices her husband's love as well as everything else to her mania for maintaining impeccable order in a house which she mistakes for a home."[31] Kelly's weakness, however, is in the very single-mindedness of his attack. There was, as his biographer reports, a "misogynistic strain in the male-oriented Kelly family,"[32] which restricted the view of reality Kelly was presenting. Flexner has pointed out that, even while Kelly has Mrs. Craig explain that her obsession with her house and her domineering behavior result from her fear of economic dependence and constitute a defense against a husband who is "a lord and master – *my* master,"[33] "Kelly persists in treating Harriet as a *moral* phenomenon. She is dishonest; she is guilty of marrying a man without love and without trust; she is a pitiless nag. For these enormities she is punished. That she has been trapped . . . by forces beyond her control, is also beyond the dramatist's understanding."[34]

The single-minded perception that produced the world of social melodrama made for its powerful emotional effect, but it also made for its limitations as realism. Its narrow perspective on the life it depicts limits its representation of reality. Its predetermined structure makes evocation of the rhythm of life impossible. Its manipulation of the audience's emotions may bring support for the playwright's position but does not lead to the illusion that he is representing reality objectively. All of these limitations suggest that the rejuvenation of this old structure during the late thirties was a step backward in realism's evolution in American drama. Nonetheless, the new social melodrama did not completely revert to the old black-and-white view of reality in nineteenth-century melodrama, but attempted to adapt the old structure to the new demands of realism. The success these playwrights had in producing an illusion of reality depended a great deal on careful use of the previously noted innovations in character and setting and on serious and believable treatment of the social issues arising from the milieu depicted.

The playwrights of the twenties, and especially the thirties, also made innovations in the structure of melodrama that allowed for a much closer approach to realism. For one thing, the writers in the thirties tended to diffuse the evil over a number of characters and social causes in the play rather than present a single personification of motiveless malevolence. Leopold Atlas's *Wednesday's Child* (1934), for example, is as emotionally single-minded a condemnation of divorce as one could find. In focusing on its effect on the child Bobby Phillips, Atlas ensures the audience's sympathy for his figure of embattled innocence. He is careful, however, not to locate the evil in either of Bobby's parents, and thus avoids creating the villainous scapegoat of classical melodrama. Ray, a traveling salesman, tries to be a good husband and father, but he is incapable of showing his feelings and talks to his wife and son in the same "hearty" way in which he greets his customers. Mary, his lonely young wife, loves her son, but she married and had children before she knew what marriage meant, and falls in love with Howard Benton because he is able to show her more affection than her husband does. Even Howard and the young woman Ray eventually marries are presented as attractive, well-meaning people. This is important, for Atlas wants to locate the cause of Bobby's suffering in the institution of divorce, not in any single individual. Bobby's problem arises from the fact that his parents separate, break up his home, and begin to lead new lives with new loyalties. It is divorce that is at fault, Atlas suggests, not the people involved.

Lillian Hellman's melodramas *The Children's Hour* (1934), *The Little Foxes* (1936), and *Watch on the Rhine* (1941) exhibit another strategy. Hellman introduces characters whom the audience can hate with impunity, like the malicious child Mary in *The Children's Hour,* the greedy and sadistic Hubbards in *The Little Foxes,* and the slimy fascist de Brancovis in *Watch on the Rhine.* Hellman's technique is to use her characters as personifications of the forces she wants the audience to condemn. Although she may give her audience an easy figure to hate, she is careful to make a clear connection between the hateful aspects of the individuals and the hateful ideology they espouse, such as fascism or greedy capitalism.

This move from the twenties to the thirties reflected an important development in the drama's representation of social forces. During the twenties, the technique was to set up the end product of imperfect social conditions — the Harriet Craig, for instance, who is so afraid of "feminine dependence and subjection" that she directs her entire life toward controlling the man who could control her — and to attack *her* rather than the conditions. The twenties playwrights produced plots that leave these women alone and lost. Harriet Craig's husband walks out on her; Rena Huckins's husband shoots himself; Mrs. Phelps's son goes off to New York to lead an independent life with his new wife. The thirties playwrights tried to get beyond this simple punishment of individuals in order to suggest the much more complicated social problems that they embodied, thus producing a fuller representation of life.

The writers of social comedy during the twenties and thirties made fundamental changes in conventional comic structure. Self-conscious writers such as Crothers, Barry, and Behrman were fully aware of the statement about society, and particularly marriage, that a writer made simply by using conventional comic structure. As we have seen, this subliminal thematic statement affirms the cycle of the generations while it calls for moderate reform, not destruction, of existing social institutions. As the playwrights began to question some of their society's fundamental assumptions about marriage and the relations between the generations, use of traditional comic structure for their social comedies became increasingly less satisfactory. A number of them were able to restructure traditional comic action to suggest the new attitudes, thus achieving a new thematic statement through a new dramatic structure, or an ironic twist on the old one. Often, by having characters act in accord with a particular position on marriage rather than with the ancient conventions of comedy, playwrights made an effective implicit statement simply through the structure of dramatic action.

One of the earliest of these denatured comedies was Maxwell Anderson's *Saturday's Children* (1927), a play that brings the conventional romantic dream of a happy-ever-after ending up against the postwar reality of inadequate salaries, high prices, and scarce, expensive housing. As in a conventional comedy, Bobby Halevy and Rims O'Neill fall in love, go through the typical courtship, and get married – after some conniving by Bobby's sister Florrie. But this is only Act I. Shortly after they are married, they find that trying to live on Rims's salary in a tiny house has killed their romantic dream. A troubled Bobby gets the plain truth from her father: "Marriage is no love affair, my dear. It's little old last year's love affair. It's a house with bills and dishpans and family quarrels. That's the way the system beats you. They bait the wedding with a romance and they hang a three-hundred-pound landlord around your neck and drown you in grocery bills."[35] Unable to get along under these conditions, the disillusioned couple finally separates, and Bobby goes back to work. They find they still love each other, but are perplexed that they can't stand the prospect of going back to married life, until Bobby comes up with the solution:

> What we wanted was a love affair, wasn't it? Just to be together and let the rest go hang – and what we got was a house and bills and general hell. Do you know what I think a love affair is, Rims? It's when the whole world is trying to keep two people apart – and they insist on being together. And when they get married the whole world pushes them together so they must naturally fly apart. . . . I don't want a house. I don't want a husband. I want a lover. (399)

Bobby and Rims decide to remain lovers without setting up housekeeping together again. By situating his new order not in marriage but in freedom from marriage, Anderson makes a daring social statement without resorting to either the overt arguments of the discussion play or the manipulated action of melodrama. He simply makes his audience believe that his characters act as sensible people would in reality rather than as the conventional characters of comedy are expected to.

The most radical rejection of the traditional comic marriage comes in

Behrman's *Biography* (1932), an acute treatment of that institution from the free woman's perspective. The play is a quixotic comedy, ending with Marion Froude's escape from Orrin Kennicott and Leander Nolan, two conventional middle-aged men who take a conventional interest in possessing her, and from Richard Kurt, the young radical she loves but knows she couldn't live with. At the end of the play, her maid asks if that "crazy Kurt" is going off to California with them. Marion replies in the picaresque spirit of the innumerable male heroes she follows, "No, Minnie – no one – we travel alone."[36] Behrman's statement about his society emerges from Marion's perspective on it as what she calls a "benevolent parasite." A free-lance portrait painter, she is able to maintain her freedom from the male power structure through two strategies – economic independence and abstention from marriage. As an outsider to the system, she can maintain her attitude of tolerant amusement toward the men who are seriously engaged in either trying to succeed within the system or trying to destroy it. The three men in the play represent three positions within the social order. Kurt is the angry radical editor who hates "the brainless muddle of contemporary life, of all the self-seeking second-raters who rise to power and wield power" (250). To Marion his vehemence makes him "a funny boy" (249). Nolan is a middle-aged politician, a "stuffed shirt – flatulent and pompous – [a] perfect legislator" (227). Marion remembers him as "Bunny," a scared and wistful adolescent, and sees him now as "simple and kindly." Kennicott, a wealthy newspaper publisher whom the other men must fear, and whom Kurt hates as "a putrescent old hypocrite" (266), Marion can see as an absurdly narcissistic preener, "the quaintest man I ever met in my life" (266). Because Marion is outside the power structure, her judgments can be based on evaluations of the men as human beings, not as potential enemies or benefactors. The men must take each other's measure in terms of the power they wield, so that the human frailties that make them humorous or touching to Marion become unpredictable characteristics that evoke fear and hatred in other men.

As a reminder of what could happen to Marion should she give up her independence, Behrman introduces Kennicott's young daughter Slade, who is engaged to Nolan. Slade's humorous exchanges with Marion show that she fully appreciates the free woman's view of these men, but because she lacks Marion's economic independence, she has to acknowledge the values that arise from power. She is engaged to Nolan because of his public position, although her private assessment is similar to Marion's. When Marion expresses a momentary wish for "marriage, children – the dear boundaries of routine" (265), Slade counters, "You're independent. You're – yourself. You can be anything you like. . . . I wish we could change places, Marion. You can with me but I can't with you" (265). Slade is aware that marriage will mean exchanging personal liberty for submission to a man in order to have children, social position, and security, but unlike Marion, she has no choice, for this is all she's been trained for. In structuring this play, Behrman made as telling a statement about the economic relations between the sexes and the institution of marriage as any in the discussion plays of Williams, Crothers, or Shaw, and he did so with almost no overt discussion. When the audience applauds Marion's quixotic escape as the wisest course she can take, Behrman has both reversed the social assumptions underlying traditional comic structure and made a telling point about contemporary society.

Barry worked a similar reversal in *The Animal Kingdom* when he began his comedy with a marriage and ended it with Tom Collier's leaving his wife to return to his lover, as did Crothers when she disrupted the expected comic reconciliation in *When Ladies Meet* by suggesting that both Claire and Mary are better off facing their future lives *not* married to Rogers. Such disruptions of comic convention were clearly a step forward in the realistic conception of dramatic structure. Disrupting the predictable chain of events subverted the conventional comic myth and deflated the romantic expectations that arise from it. Freeing the audience from these conventional expectations heightened the illusion that the characters were people who made decisions and took action accordingly, rather than what Howells called the "immemorial puppets of the stage." Thus the experimental view of comedy led to a fuller integration of realistic character and thought with realistic structure.

Although examples are few and far between, there were also realistic playwrights during the period between the wars who discarded conventional dramatic structures altogether and consciously attempted to reflect the rhythms of life around them directly in dramatic action, as Howells had called on them to do. We have seen the beginnings of the notion in isolated scenes like the one that opens *Salvation Nell* and the street-life scenes that punctuate the action of *Sherlock Holmes*. Its full development came in the great realistic plays of Eugene O'Neill, *The Iceman Cometh* (1939) and *Long Day's Journey into Night* (1940). The interest in creating purely realistic action was at its most intense during the twenties, however, and different strategies for developing a realistic structure appear with varying degrees of success in such plays as Davis's *Detour* (1921), Crothers's one-act plays (1920–5), Rice's *Street Scene* (1929) and *Counselor-at-Law* (1931), Ben Hecht and Charles MacArthur's *Front Page* (1929), and, to a lesser extent, plays in which a traditional dramatic structure is surrounded by the action of everyday life to make the mimetic illusion stronger, as in *Porgy* and John Howard Lawson's *Success Story* (1932).

Crothers's one-act plays, vignettes of wealthy women living their daily lives, anticipated Clare Boothe's use of the dress salon and the fashionable restaurant to suggest the Park Avenue milieu in *The Women* (1936). They are similar to the prewar experiments of the Provincetown playwrights in that they represent scenes whose chief action is conversation, and they deflate rather than build audience expectation of a conventional outcome. Because there is no distinct narrative, Crothers manages to suggest that the plays' incidents are typical of the class she depicts. She uses her plays for social satire, and through various means of evoking irony, she exposes the shams, hypocrisies, and social irresponsibility of her chosen subjects.

In *The Detour,* Davis juxtaposes two structures of comedy, the normal plot of marriage between young lovers, and the quixotic plot of escape from the oppressive old order. By emphasizing the action surrounding them, however, he suggests that these traditional rhythms of comedy are merely detours from the fundamental business of everyday life. Helen Hardy is a Long Island farm wife who sees her marriage essentially as slavery: "I get my keep! I haven't had a dress in two years, and then one I made myself. I get my food, but I have to cook it first. Where else would you get a cook who'd work like I work and only get her keep! They ain't but one way to get a girl as cheap as that, and that's to marry her! . . . Alls you paid was one dollar for a weddin' license!"[37] Her dream is to rescue her daughter Kate from a similar future by sending her to New York and turning her into an artist. In the end, however, Kate gives in to her natural mate, Tom, and agrees to marry him, handing over the escape money for a payment on his new garage. Kate's entry into the cycle of life on Long Island nearly does her mother in: "And everything is just the same as it was before? . . . Just the same as it always will be! . . . God – help – me!" (525). But as she starts to cook her husband's supper, it occurs to her that Kate will probably have a baby. Immediately, she latches on to a new dream, and starts saving her "egg and chicken money" for her as yet unconceived grandchild. Davis's point is that the fundamental human need for a mate, the need to escape routine, and the conflicting need for security, account for a good deal more of the action in life than the sensational moments of decision that he, an old master of melodrama, knew so well. Even in *Ethan Frome,* he resists the temptation to focus on the double suicide attempt and instead leaves the audience with the image of the twenty-five years of bitter, boring misery that have followed it, setting the one moment of "heroic" passion in the context of the rhythm of New England life. By emphasizing the cycles of life that encompass the grand moments, Davis made his point that the great moment of decision is not that at all but is one part of the age-old fundamental patterns of human life.

Porgy, The Front Page, Counselor-at-Law, and *Success Story* exhibit a different strategy for creating the illusion of life in the structure of the action. In the simplest of these, *Porgy* and *Success Story,* the structure of the play is provided by a conventional and obvious plot – in *Porgy* the melodramatic love triangle of Porgy, Bess, and Crown, and in *Success Story* the love quadrangle of Sol Ginsberg, Sarah Glassman, Raymond Meritt, and Agnes Carter, which is complicated by Sol's ruthless ambition. The Heywards and Lawson use the detailed action of everyday life in a specific milieu – Catfish Row and a Madison Avenue advertising firm – to lend a greater illusion of reality to their plots. The rhythm of the office routine or of everyday life in the neighborhood softens the sensational melodrama and helps to make the type characters more believable.

The Front Page and *Counselor-at-Law* are more complicated, for in both of them the playwrights create a dynamic tension between the hero's everyday life, depicted in the detail of the pressroom and the law office, and the conventional romantic love plot. In *The Front Page,* the pressroom appears as it does to the protagonist, Hildy Johnson, a world of colorful characters, comradeship, excitement, and possibilities for triumph. Hecht and MacArthur give the audience a good fifteen minutes of this before Hildy appears on the scene, so that its sympathies are with the newspapermen rather than with the bride when his comrades try to talk Hildy out of his plan to get married. The rest of the play is an all-out war for Hildy between Walter Burns, the editor who doesn't want to lose him, and Peggy, his fiancée, with Hildy's own conflicting emotions shifting between excitement about the scoop he stumbles onto and a genuine desire to marry Peggy and settle into a conventional middle-class life. The unavoidable message the playwrights convey is that the pressroom is life, Hildy's life, and it is being weighed in the balance with a fantasy, the romantic dream of the vine-covered cottage. Burns's sending the couple off on their wedding trip with the gift of a gold watch looks at first like a disappointing capitulation, but when he arranges to have Hildy arrested and brought back, the audience enthusiastically applauds his final line, spoken to the police on the telephone: "The son of a bitch stole my watch!"[38] Although this is a "big moment" theatrically, it provides no closure to the action, no satisfying, final resolution of the tension between Hildy's unconventional but real life and his conventional but unreal dream. The implication is that the tension, being genuinely unresolvable, will continue after Burns's momentary victory.

Counselor-at-Law has a similar strategy. But the play that came closest to fulfilling Howells's radical notion of realistic dramatic structure was Rice's panoramic *Street Scene*. Like every other aspect of the play, its structure is consciously realistic, and it is unique in American drama. Alan Downer calls *Street Scene* a "domestic symphony, taking the details

XIV. The opening scene of *The Front Page,* by Ben Hecht and Charles MacArthur, at the Times Square Theatre, 1928. (Photo by Van Damm)

of life, each as accurately rendered as possible, and arranging them within a frame (or perhaps better, against a background) that is itself a familiar commonplace, to yield an interpretation of what this crowded communal life means in terms of the individual and the group."[39] Rice, who acknowledged that the play was "the most experimental I have ever attempted,"[40] described its structure in terms of "concealed architectonics": "No musician, I yet had some grasp of the structure of symphonic music: the statement, restatement and development of themes, the interplay of contrasting instruments. Unconsciously I utilized my slight knowledge of the principles of orchestration."[41]

Rice left a detailed account of the play's construction in the notes on its "Method of Treatment" he submitted with his film scenario in 1933. Here he used the metaphor of the painter to describe the method of its representation: "The accumulation of innumerable small incidents and bits of business and characterization, each in itself unimportant, creates a totality of effect in the same way a painter piles up an effect upon his canvas by the multiplication of brush strokes."[42] The essence of realistic aesthetics emerges from his description of the integration of thought, structure, and milieu in the play:

> The whole point of the play . . . is that life is complex and diversified, that every situation carries with it irrelevant and incongruous elements, that there is no such thing as unmixed joy or unmixed tragedy and that pathos, fun, sordidness, beauty, brutality, tenderness, passion, despair and hope are all inextricably mixed and all form part of one more or less unified whole. To attempt to make these serious elements effective by isolating them is like attempting to bring out the color values of a

painting by separating each pigment and each brush stroke from the others. On the contrary, it is just the blending and contrast of the elements which gives the whole its effect.[43]

Rice's statement is the twentieth-century playwright's practical version of the realistic ideas about dramatic structure that Howells had been enunciating fifty years before. As Rice saw it, the basis for realistic dramatic structure was not discarding all semblance of linear plot, as Howells had suggested, but embedding the "stories" within the seemingly purposeless activity around them, just as they are observed in life. Thus, although most of the action in *Street Scene* involves seemingly unrelated characters, incidents, and dialogue, two linear plots give the play a residual dramatic structure recognizable to the audience. The two plots involve the love triangle of Anna Maurrant, Frank Maurrant, and Steve Sankey, and Rose Maurrant's choice between the innocent love of the naive young student Sam Kaplan and the "easy life" of a Broadway chorus girl offered by her married boss, Harry Easter. The play provides the traditional action of both comedy and melodrama. Sam and Rose have some touching scenes of romantic young love. Frank Maurrant shoots his wife and Sankey, and then is led off to jail after a remorseful scene with Rose.

Rice was aware that he was attempting a tour de force in trying to make a realistic play out of the staples of melodrama and comedy, but his point was precisely that life is made up of melodrama and comedy *as well as* its more commonplace incidents. As an example of the point he was trying to make, he described what would be the most sensational scene in the play if it were treated as melodrama:

> At the end of the second act when the dying Mrs. Maurrant is carried out of the house on a stretcher, a blazé furniture mover follows her, listlessly carrying a bed end and turning the emotion of the audience into sudden laughter. I hesitated for a long time before deciding to risk spoiling the emotional climax of the play, but the introduction of this casual and incongruous incident heightened rather than weakened the effect of the play, for it brought home to the audience that even in the midst of tragedy the commonplaces of life go on, which, of course, was exactly the feeling I wanted to produce.[44]

A similar deflation of intensity occurs at the end of the romantic scene between Rose and Sam in Act I. After they kiss, Rose goes up to her apartment and calls goodnight from the window:

> *She smiles at him. Then she pulls down the shade.* SAM *looks up for a moment, then resumes his seat. A scream from* MRS. BUCHANAN [who is in labor] *makes him shudder. A deep rhythmic snoring emanates from the Fiorentino apartment. A steamboat whistle is heard. The snoring in the Fiorentino apartment continues.*[45]

Setting this moment in the context of the life around it leads the audience to estimate it at its true value, divesting it of the all-consuming importance it would take on in the typical love story.

Rice's most emphatic insistence on realism in the action comes in the play's ending. Rose returns to the apartment to get her clothes after the horror of her mother's death and her father's imprisonment. Now that she is alone, her sole thought is to get her young brother and herself out of the city and start a new life. She refuses Easter's offer of help, and she gently tells Sam that they both need to grow up and "belong to themselves" before they can think of a future together. Rose goes off. Sam goes inside, and presently his father appears saying, "Shoily, vot's de metter again vit Sem? He's crying on de bed" (611). As he sits down to read the newspaper, a shabby, middle-aged couple approaches the house:

The man.   (*Reading the To-Let Sign.*) Here's a place. Six rooms. Want to take a look at it?
(*A group of children, off stage left, begins singing "The Farmer in the Dell." This continues until after the curtain is down.*)
The woman. All right. No harm lookin'. Ring for the janitor. (THE MAN *goes up the stoop and rings the janitor's bell.*) Somebody must o' just died.
The man.   Yeah, maybe that's why they're movin' out. (*Wiping his face with a handkerchief.*) Phoo! Seems to be gettin hotter every minute. (611)

From there, the play winds down to a desultory close, and Rice has made his point that the cycle of life continues, that the real action of life encompasses, overrides, and engulfs the traditional action of the drama. He implies that it is antirealistic to fit the action of life completely into the preconceived patterns of melodrama or comedy, but he also implies that the substance of these patterns has as much of a place in life as the commonplace incidents Howells approved of. In this sense, Rice's realistic structure accommodates the aesthetics of both Howells and James, suggesting that it is possible to represent a "story," or even two or three, and still produce an illusion of life. Rice's aesthetic view accommodates two valid realistic observations – that life is full of interesting stories, and that interesting stories do not completely account for life. His view allows finally for a more fully realistic work of art than could arise from either observation alone.

In calling the method of O'Neill's later plays "dynamic realism,"[46] Timo Tiusanen refers to the dynamics of the psyche, which O'Neill's later realism externalizes. But there is a "dynamic realism" in the structure of the plays as well, and it is the structure that provides the underpinning for the characters. The structure of *The Iceman Cometh* (1939) has received divergent criticism since its opening night in 1946, a good deal of it negative. The first-night reviewers generally called the play long-winded and unstructured. Closer critical study yielded the suggestions that its structure could be compared variously to a wave, a pendulum, or concentric circles.[47] A more useful, though not fully developed, suggestion is that followed by José Quintero in his famous production at the Circle in the Square in 1956: "My approach in directing *The Iceman Cometh* was different from that used in any play I had ever done. It had to be for this was not built as an orthodox play. It resembles a complex musical form, with themes repeating themselves with slight variation, as melodies do in a symphony."[48] Quintero's notion is echoed by Tiusanen in his critical study: "*The Iceman Cometh* is, in its orchestral organization of the material, O'Neill's *The Three Sisters*."[49]

The most developed and most influential view, however, has been Eric Bentley's idea that *Iceman* is an example of Ibsenesque "analytic exposition": "The crucial events having taken place before the curtain rises, [O'Neill] lets them leak out so slowly that we are still discovering them in the last act."[50] The problem with Bentley's approach is that he is so taken with the Ibsenesque method of O'Neill's exposition that he assumes the entire structure of the play must be Ibsenesque as well. Thus he sees it as two intertwined plots: (1) the story of Hickey's murder of Evelyn and subsequent confession and (2) the story of Parritt's betrayal of his mother and subsequent suicide. By his own description, Bentley's production was an attempt to fit the play into his notion of its structure by cutting away vast amounts of material that didn't fit the mold of the typical Ibsenesque one-issue discussion play. Thus, he decided, "one can cut a good many of Larry's speeches since he is forever re-phrasing a pessimism which is by no means hard to understand the first time."[51] Bentley finally condemned O'Neill for not meeting Ibsen's standards for structure in realistic drama: "His sense of theatrical form is frustrated by an eloquence that decays into mere repetitious garrulousness. . . . Within the tyranically, mechanically rigid scenes, there is an excessive amount of freedom. The order of speeches can be juggled without loss, and almost any speech can be cut in half."[52] His attitude is the logical conclusion for one who sees only half of O'Neill's technique in the play.

O'Neill's later plays are supremely important documents in the development of dramatic realism not because, as the cliché goes, they mark his "return to realism" but because they demonstrate his final achievement of inventing a realistic structure in which to represent his dynamic realism of character while maintaining the illusion of reality in all elements of the representation. O'Neill's later plays advance the technique of realism in two major areas, characterization and structure. The more obvious of the two developments occurs in character, for it is the central interest in his later plays as well as the focus of his more daring experiments. From masks, asides, and alteregos, he has finally arrived at the simple device of

alcohol to allow his characters to reveal the truths of their psychological
depths while maintaining the mimetic illusion in the representation.

The structural innovation is more complicated but develops from the
state of the characters. The structure is O'Neill's familiar cycle, suggesting his notion of the recurrent rhythms of life. *Iceman* begins and ends
with the drunks in Harry Hope's saloon trying to forget their pain
through their sustaining illusions and the oblivion of drink. O'Neill uses
the structure to stress the play's realistic worldview *not* by ending it, as
Ibsen would have done, with emphasis on the death of Parritt and the
defeat of Hickey but by easing the dramatic tension off into Harry's
invention of the pathetic new illusion that Hickey was crazy, and the
drunks' celebration of their liberation from his truth telling. By means of
its mixture of pathos and humor, the harmony of the group's celebration
and the cacophony of its singing, O'Neill is careful to avoid any assumption that the play's conclusion is tragic, comic, or melodramatic.

This cyclical realistic structure, with its slow deflation of dramatic
tension, is not new, of course. It is as old for O'Neill as *The Moon of the
Caribees*. What is new in *Iceman* is O'Neill's tight control of the structure
to create and dispel dramatic tension without violating the illusion that
the play's events are those of objective reality. Each of the play's four acts
is a series of conflicts between characters, building with ever greater
duration and intensity toward a peak of tension that ends in one of
Hickey's four disturbing announcements: that he is on the wagon, that
Evelyn is dead, that Evelyn was murdered, and that it was he who killed
her.[53] In Act I, before Hickey arrives, the building tension is pleasurable
– proceeding from the anticipation of Hickey's coming – and the conflicts are mostly mock conflicts, the ritual battles that are part of the
characters' pipe dreams: Harry's complaints about the bartenders, the
taunting of Hugo about The Movement, Harry's complaints about
Willie's singing, Lewis and Wetjoen's refighting of the Boer War, Chuck
and Cora's argument about where to buy a farm. Underlying the mock
conflicts, however, is the building tension that arises from the "mistakes" the characters make by trespassing on each other's pipe dreams,
such as Lewis's comment on Joe's blackness and Pearl's calling Rocky a
pimp.

In Act II, Harry's birthday party, the tension becomes unpleasant, and
begins its slow buildup toward the simultaneous shattering of illusions
and destruction of the sense of community in the saloon. It begins with
the short quarrels between minor characters – Chuck's with Cora over
the flowers, and Rocky's with Pearl and Margie over the cake. The
tension slowly escalates as the characters move in closer and closer on
each other's dreams. Margie and Pearl make fun of Cora's notion of her

wedding; Cora calls them whores; they call Rocky a pimp; Rocky slaps them. Although each of these flare-ups ends in apology and reconciliation, each also leaves a residual tension that gradually increases after the short relief when Hugo and Larry restore harmony to the scene. Joe raises the race issue with a defiance bred of Hickey's reminders; Hickey prods Larry about his "grandstand" attitude. After Willie provides a short interruption in the tension, Parritt makes his hypocritical confession to Larry; Lewis and Wetjoen, and Mosher and McGloin, have short quarrels touching on each other's pipe dreams, then become reconciled. Into this atmosphere of tension bred of conflict, Harry makes his entrance and proceeds to increase the tension by verbally abusing everyone in the room. Hickey's toast provides a temporary respite, until Harry's speech, from which he cannot keep his bitterness, sets it mounting again. And again, in a series of quick reversals, his apology deflates the tension; Hickey's speech inflates it; the iceman joke, in which everyone joins, deflates it; and finally the announcement that Evelyn is dead sends it to a climax as the act closes.

A nearly identical pattern occurs in Act III, when the drunks are setting out on their Hickey-inspired attempts to face tomorrow today; only this time the tension increases in line with what is at stake, as does the physical action. Rocky and Chuck fight physically over Chuck's impending marriage. Joe pulls a knife when they call him a nigger, and Rocky counters with a gun. Lewis and Wetjoen fight openly, as do Mosher and McGloin. Punctuating the building tension are Parritt's sporadic attempts to confess the truth to Larry and the rebuffs of Willie as he attempts to practice law. The tension builds to Hickey's confrontations with Harry and Larry, his own revelation that Evelyn was murdered, and the ominous observation that Harry is not recovering from his disillusionment as Hickey had expected him to.

In Act IV the tension is internalized in Hickey. The other characters sit more or less paralyzed by their disillusionment while he enacts his psychodrama through his famous fifteen-minute modified monologue. The tension here begins within Hickey, then moves out between Hickey and the others – who try to avoid this further confession of disillusionment – and finally erupts in conflict between Parritt and Larry. Hickey's confession of the murder reaches a peak, followed almost immediately by Parritt's confession that he hated his mother and then Hickey's inadvertent confession that he hated Evelyn. Larry's advice to Parritt precipitates Parritt's suicide, a counterturn to the general deflation of tension in the saloon proceeding from Harry's announcement that Hickey was crazy and that their reality was merely his illusion.

O'Neill's balance and manipulation of tension here are as neat as in a Pinero problem-play, a Molière comedy, or a Sophocles tragedy, and understanding his realistic structure is crucial to understanding his realistic aesthetics. Both *The Iceman Cometh* and *Long Day's Journey into Night* depend on subtle manipulation of the internal and external conflict in a series of confrontations to build the tension and provide the necessary exposition in the way that affords firmest support for the modified monologues in which the characters reveal themselves. In these last plays, O'Neill developed a realistic structure to serve his great interest – the portrayal of character. His realistic drama is primarily a drama of characters revealed through conflict, with one another and within themselves.

The Iceman Cometh is a tour de force in one sense of characterization; *Long Day's Journey*, in another. Each of the seventeen major characters in *Iceman* undergoes a recognizable conflict brought about by facing his or her illusion, evinced by fighting with a dear friend and often partner in that illusion, and resolved by disillusionment. Most subsequently reject reality when Harry opens the door to illusion again, but Larry and Parritt accept defeat by a reality that has become inescapable for them. These characters and conflicts mesh into a brilliant representation of reality that stands as the background of Hickey's full-blown reenactment of his individual experience. He speaks for all of them; their experience is universal, yet it is individual as well – a triumph of realistic characterization.

In *Long Day's Journey*, there are only four characters, but each is fully developed, and each has a modified monologue. Whereas the tension in each act of *Iceman* builds from minor conflicts between minor characters to the fundamental questions of life and death, acceptance of failure or living in a pipe dream, *Long Day's Journey* begins with petty quarrels among all the characters and builds up toward the modified monologues that serve both as confessions of failure and defenses against the others' charges. As in *Iceman*, *Long Day's Journey* is imbued with an underlying anxiety that excites tension from the start and explains, within the confines of realistic representation, the constant and escalating confrontations embodying O'Neill's structural method of building tension. Here it is Mary's morphine addiction and Edmund's tuberculosis, both subjects hinted at and avoided by the characters early in Act I, that precipitate their anxiety and, by association, provoke their conflicts. Act I provides exposition and characterization, as well as a developing tension. Its series of small quarrels leads to Edmund's suspicion that his mother has resumed taking morphine. Act II represents a gradual but inexorable building of tension among all four Tyrones. In Scene 1 the subjects of consumption, suspicion, Jamie's failure, Ella's lack of a home, and the boys' drinking are discussed, building to Tyrone's accusation of Mary. In Scene 2 Mary's complaints against Tyrone are followed by the discussion of Dr. Hardy, Jamie's accusation that Tyrone is sending Edmund to the state sanitorium because he is too much of a miser to pay for private care, and Mary's further complaints about her lack of a home, her marriage, and her memories of her baby, ending with Edmund's plea that she stop taking morphine.

O'Neill's structural realism emerges in Acts III and IV, when the tension does not build to the conventional and artificial single climax but is maintained through the long and psychologically wrenching modified monologue of Mary in Act III and the shorter ones of Tyrone, Edmund, and Jamie in Act IV. The monologues are punctuated by enough conflict to maintain the level of dramatic tension and keep the audience aware of the issues: Mary's disillusionment about her marriage, Edmund and Jamie's effectual lack of a mother, Edmund's consumption, Tyrone's miserliness, Jamie's failure.[54] Like that of *The Iceman Cometh,* the play's structure is cyclical. Although the characters reveal their deepest feelings about themselves and one another, and although Edmund achieves some mutual understanding with his father and brother, there is no suggestion that the cycle of their behavior will change, or that the family's dynamics of conflict will undergo any transformation. The very relentlessness of the reality that each of the characters is trying to deny through alcohol or morphine reverberates in Mary's last line: "I fell in love with James Tyrone and was so happy *for a time*"[55] (my emphasis). The play's structure suggests that the rhythm of love for the Tyrones is the rhythm of conflict; that each impulse of affection, generosity, or protectiveness has a corresponding one of resentment, selfishness, or envy; that every strength betrays a corresponding weakness; that every joy evokes a corresponding pain. Mary's final heartrending monologue and the scenic image of James cradling her wedding gown in his arms while she speaks create a moving moment of insight for the audience, but the near oblivion of her three listeners, and indeed, of the speaker herself, undercuts its effect. The rhythm in this play is overwhelming. The "big moment" cannot overcome the cycles of behavior that encompass it, and although the audience may be overcome temporarily by its emotional effect, O'Neill never lets us forget that the characters will go through the same endless cycles the next time they are together, and the next, and the next. There is no release at the end of this play, only exhausted and temporary stasis.

The main focus of *Long Day's Journey into Night* is the revelation of the characters, individually and in relation to one another. The ideas in the play are the ideas of the characters. Mary's fatalism is given equal weight with Jamie's cynicism, Edmund's poetic transcendentalism, and Tyrone's memories of artistic idealism. The sets, like nearly all of O'Neill's sets, are expressions of character as well as aids to mimetic realism. The books in the Tyrones' library, for example, are part of the realistic setting, but they also are a concrete expression of the basic antipathy between James and the boys, particularly Edmund, in their philosophies of life. The bookcase with the Balzac, Zola, Stendhal, Schopenhauer, Nietzsche, Marx, and Engels is clearly Edmund's, while the one with the Dumas, Hugo, Charles Lever, three sets of Shakespeare, and *"The World's Best Literature in fifty large volumes"* (11) is James's. Similarly, the dialogue both maintains the mimetic illusion and signifies more in the characters than the words denote. Tyrone's conscious correctness, Jamie's Broadway slang, laced with quotations from Swinburne and Dowson, Edmund's similar vacillation between slang and poetic diction, Mary's steady lapse into schoolgirl idiom as she drifts farther and farther into the past under the influence of morphine – all, as Jean Chothia has demonstrated, are eloquent expressions of what lies below the surface in the characters' psyches while they also help to maintain the mimetic illusion.[56] In short, in *Long Day's Journey* and in *Iceman,* O'Neill found a way to combine his absorbing interest in psychodrama with his most successful dramatic mode – realism. All of the elements in these plays combine to express the deepest psychological conflicts within the characters at the same time as they produce a fully believable mimetic representation of reality.

In 1922 O'Neill had said in an interview, "Sure I'll write about happiness if I can happen to meet up with that luxury, and find it sufficiently dramatic and in harmony with any deep rhythm in life. . . . I don't love life because it's pretty. Prettiness is only clothes-deep. I am a truer lover than that. I love it naked. There is beauty to me even in its ugliness."[57] He had been searching ever since for the right dramatic expression of those deep rhythms and that nakedness. In these great realistic plays, he finally found a structure to embody the deep rhythms of life and a psychodramatic device for representing the naked souls of his characters within the mode that emphasized their reality.

O'Neill solved the problem of giving dramatic structure to the seemingly unconnected actions of life by adapting unconventional patterns from the dynamics of conflict to the dramatic situation. Elmer Rice took the opposite tack – he acknowledged that conventional patterns do occur in life, but took them out of the limelight and showed them in context. Both solutions resulted in effective realistic drama, and both showed that a fundamentally realistic worldview – that, as Rice said, "there is no such thing as unmixed joy or unmixed tragedy, and that pathos, fun, sordidness, beauty, brutality, tenderness, passion, despair and hope are all inextricably mixed" – could find its expression in dramatic action. It was a considerable achievement. The realistic aesthetics in *The Iceman Cometh, Long Day's Journey into Night,* and *Street Scene* are among the most sophisticated, and the most successfully executed, in any realistic drama.

They are the best evidence there is for the ultimate integration of American literary realism and American drama.

Tremendous progress was made in the development of realism between the world wars. Realistic playwrights developed the notion of setting to the extent that it not only grounded the play in a sense of place, by creating a powerful illusion of a definite milieu, but could also provide a scenic image of the environmental and psychological forces at its center. The new psychological dimension opened up the notion of character from the dramatic or social types to fully realized personalities who reflected the environmental, social, and familial conditions of the play's milieu in their makeup. The new realistic playwrights used the drama to express substantial thought, which often challenged basic assumptions about American society and its institutions, and they changed the way drama conveys thought by changing conventional structures to reflect the society's changing worldview. Finally, in developing new realistic structures for drama, realistic playwrights escaped the artificiality of imposing conventional structures on dramatic action by suggesting the larger rhythms of life in which this action was embedded. With the denial of closure to the play's action, the realistic playwright made the illusion of reality complete. It was a more complicated process than such nineteenth-century realists as Howells and James and Herne had envisioned, but dramatic realism as they conceived of it had finally triumphed in the American theater.

Notes

1. The State of the Art

1 See, for example, "American Novels," *London Quarterly Review* 155 (January 1883): 107–13; "American Literature in England," *Blackwood's Magazine* 133 (January 1883): 136–61; "Howells, James, and Stevenson," *New York Times,* November 29, 1882, 2–7; "Howells's Carved Cherry Stones," *New York Times,* December 1, 1882, p. 6, col. 2.

2 Letter to Howells, March 28, 1883, MS in the Houghton Library, Harvard University, quoted by Everett Carter, *Howells and the Age of Realism* (Philadelphia: Lippincott, 1950), 250.

3 "Henry James, Jr.," *Century* 25 (November 1882): 28.

4 *Atlantic Monthly* 23 (May 1869): 635–44.

5 For an exhaustive account of the season's offerings, see George C. D. Odell, *Annals of the New York Stage* (1879–1882) (New York: Columbia University Press, 1939) 11: 1–217.

6 Barnard Hewitt, *Theatre U.S.A.* (New York: McGraw-Hill, 1959), 187.

7 Arthur Hobson Quinn, ed., *Representative American Plays,* 7th ed. (New York: Appleton-Century-Crofts, 1953), 459. Subsequent page references appear in parentheses in the text.

8 See, for example, Hewitt, *Theatre U.S.A.,* 237; Arthur Hobson Quinn, *A History of the American Drama from the Civil War to the Present Day,* rev. ed., 2 vols. (New York: Appleton-Century-Crofts, 1936), 1: 126; Garff B. Wilson, *Three Hundred Years of American Drama and Theatre* (Englewood Cliffs, N.J.: Prentice-Hall, 1973), 225.

9 Quinn, *A History,* 1: 126.

10 Wilson, *Three Hundred Years,* 226.

11 Ibid., 209–10.

12 "Editor's Study," *Harper's Monthly* 73 (July 1886): 314–19.

13 Edward Harrigan, "American Playwrights on the American Drama," *Harper's Weekly* 33 (February 2, 1889): 98.

14 Richard Moody, *Dramas from the American Theatre 1762–1909* (Cleveland, Ohio: World, 1966), 541.

15 See Richard Moody, *Ned Harrigan: From Corlear's Hook to Herald Square* (Chicago: Nelson-Hall, 1980), 169–70.

16 "Editor's Study," *Harper's Monthly* 73 (July 1886): 318.

17 Moody, *Dramas,* 540–41.

18 Ibid., 564–65. Subsequent page references to *The Mulligan Guard Ball* appear in parentheses in the text.

19 Harrigan, "American Playwrights," 98.

20 See Howells, "Editor's Study," *Harper's Monthly* 79 (July 1889): 314–19, and Harrigan's response quoted in Moody, *Ned Harrigan,* 167.

21 See John Perry, *James A. Herne: The American Ibsen* (Chicago: Nelson-Hall, 1979), 50–65.

22 Quinn, *A History,* 1: 14.

23 In their lengthy note on "The Dramatic Version of the Gilded Age," Henry Nash Smith and William Gibson state that the composition of the play "is still somewhat confusing." Mark Twain bought the adaptation by Gilbert B. Densmore and "made some use of it in preparing the play he copyrighted in July 1874." Mark Twain himself wrote that he had revised Densmore's script three times and that there remained less than "twenty sentences of Mr. Densmore's" in it when it was produced (Henry Nash Smith and William M. Gibson, eds., *Mark Twain–Howells Letters,* 2 vols. [Cambridge, Mass.: Harvard University Press, Belknap Press, 1960], 2: 861–62). Howells wrote, "The structure of the play as John T. Raymond gave it was substantially the work of this unknown dramatist. Clemens never pretended, to me at any rate, that he had the least hand in it" (*My Mark Twain* [New York: Harper, 1910], 22). I have chosen the perhaps perilous course of taking Mark Twain at his word in the text. The reader may make his or her own judgment.

24 Quinn, *A History,* 1: 117.

25 Bartley Campbell, *The White Slave and Other Plays by Bartley Campbell,* ed. Napier Wilt, vol. 19 of *America's Lost Plays* (Princeton, N.J.: Princeton University Press, 1941), 55–6. Subsequent page references to *My Partner* appear in parentheses in the text.

26 *New York Tribune,* January 26, 1894, 7: 1.

27 See Perry, *James A. Herne,* 153–62.

28 Bronson Howard, *Autobiography of a Play* (1886; rpt. New York: Dramatic Museum of Columbia University, 1914), 30.

29 Ibid., 26–30.

30 Bronson Howard, *The Banker's Daughter and Other Plays by Bronson Howard,* ed. Allan Halline (1940; rpt. Bloomington: Indiana University Press, 1963), 123. Subsequent page references appear in parentheses in the text.

31 Howard, *Autobiography of a Play,* 46.

32 Wilson, *Three Hundred Years,* 151.

33 Ibid., 171–2.

34 *New York Herald,* January 23, 1857, 5: 1.

35 "Editor's Study," *Harper's Monthly* 82 (March 1891): 643.

36 Wilson, *Three Hundred Years,* 269.

37 Hewitt, *Theatre U.S.A.,* 237.

38 Wilson, *Three Hundred Years,* 245.

39 Richard Moody, *America Takes the Stage: Romanticism in American Drama and Theatre, 1750–1900* (1955; rpt. New York: Kraus, 1969), 205–34.
40 Ibid., 206.
41 Ibid., 217.
42 Ibid., 207.
43 Quoted in Percy Mackaye, *Epoch: The Life of Steele Mackaye,* 2 vols. (New York: Boni & Liveright, 1927), 2: 300. This is the best account of the Spectatorium (2: 300–437), but brief accounts can be found in Moody, *Dramas,* 228–32, Hewitt, *Theatre U.S.A.,* 265–8, and Wilson, *Three Hundred Years,* 249–50.
44 Hewitt, *Theatre U.S.A.,* 267, reprinted from *Chicago Times,* February 6, 1894.
45 Perry, *James A. Herne,* 51–2.
46 Ibid., 52.
47 David Belasco, *The Theatre Through Its Stage Door* (1919; rpt. New York: Blom, 1969), 173.
48 Ibid., 193.
49 Ibid., 176.
50 Ibid., 182–3.
51 George Jean Nathan, *Mr. George Jean Nathan Presents* (1917; rpt. St. Clair Shores, Mich.: Scholarly Press, 1971), 66.

2. Realistic Dramatic Theory

1 "The Plays of Eugene Brieux," *North American Review* 201 (March 1915): 407.
2 "Editor's Study," *Harper's Monthly* 83 (August 1891): 477.
3 "A New Kind of Play," *Literature,* n.s. 1 (March 31, 1899): 266.
4 "The Play and the Problem," *Harper's Weekly* 39 (March 30, 1895): 294.
5 George Bernard Shaw, "A Dramatic Realist to His Critics," in *Shaw on Theatre,* ed. E. J. West (New York: Hill & Wang, 1958), 20.
6 George Becker, *Realism in Modern Literature* (New York: Ungar, 1980), 64.
7 Edwin H. Cady, *The Light of Common Day: Realism in American Fiction* (Bloomington: Indiana University Press, 1971), 18–22.
8 "Editor's Study," *Harper's Monthly* 83 (August 1891): 478.
9 Henry James, *The Scenic Art: Notes on Acting and the Drama 1872–1901,* ed. Allan Wade (New Brunswick, N.J.: Rutgers University Press, 1948), 34. Subsequent page references appear in parentheses in the text, cited as *SA.*
10 James A. Herne, "Art for Truth's Sake in the Drama," in *American Drama and Its Critics,* ed. Alan S. Downer (Chicago: University of Chicago Press, 1965), 9.
11 Ibid., 2–8.
12 "Editor's Study," *Harper's Monthly* 73 (July 1886): 316.
13 "Henrik Ibsen," *North American Review* 183 (July 1906): 7.
14 "The Art of Fiction," *Longman's Magazine* 4 (September 1884): 510–11.
15 William Dean Howells, *Criticism and Fiction and Other Essays,* ed. Clara M. and Rudolph Kirk (New York: New York University Press, 1959), 15.
16 "Il ne faudrait donc pas simplement affirmer que le théâtre est la représenta-

tion de la vie humaine. Ce serait une définition plus exact de dire: que l'art dramatique est l'ensemble des conventions universelles ou locales, éternelles ou temporaires a l'aide desquelles, en représentant la vie humaine sur un théâtre on donne a un public l'illusion de la vérité." Francisque Sarcey, *Quarante Ans de Théâtre: Feuilletons dramatiques* (Paris: Bibliothèque des Annales, 1900) 1: 132. The translation is that of Harry Levin, in *The Gates of Horn* (New York: Oxford, 1966), 18.

17 H. D. Traill, "About that Skeleton," *The Nineteenth Century* 36 (December 1894): 869.

18 John Gassner, *Form and Idea in Modern Theatre* (New York: Dryden, 1956), 26–7.

19 Northrop Frye, *Anatomy of Criticism* (Princeton, N.J.: Princeton University Press), 34.

20 "Editor's Study," *Harper's Monthly* 73 (July 1886): 315.

21 "Henrik Ibsen," 6.

22 "Editor's Study," *Harper's Monthly* 73 (July 1886): 316.

23 "Life and Letters," *Harper's Weekly* 39 (May 11, 1895): 436.

24 "Privileges of the Theatre," *Harper's Weekly* 48 (January 30, 1904): 162.

25 Augustin Daly et al., "American Playwrights on the American Drama," *Harper's Weekly* 33 (February 2, 1889), Supplement: 98.

26 Ibid., 99.

27 "Life and Letters," *Harper's Weekly* 40 (February 22, 1896): 175.

28 Daly et al., "American Playwrights on the American Drama," 99.

29 "The Recent Dramatic Season," *North American Review* 172 (March 1901): 469.

30 "The New Poetic Drama," *North American Review* 172 (May 1901): 798.

31 "Life and Letters," *Harper's Weekly* 39 (December 28, 1895): 1236.

32 "Life and Letters," *Harper's Weekly* 40 (October 10, 1896): 998.

33 "Life and Letters," *Harper's Weekly* 41 (January 30, 1897): 107.

34 "Some New English Plays," *Harper's Weekly* 48 (January 23, 1904): 124.

35 "Life and Letters," *Harper's Weekly* 39 (December 28, 1895): 1237.

36 "Life and Letters," *Harper's Weekly* 41 (January 30, 1897): 107.

37 H. A. Kennedy, "The Drama of the Moment," *The Nineteenth Century* 30 (August 1891): 263.

38 Aristotle, *Poetics,* trans. S. H. Butcher, ed. Francis Fergusson (New York: Hill & Wang, 1961), 61.

39 Kennedy, "The Drama of the Moment," 263.

40 "Mr. Tennyson's Drama," *Galaxy* 20 (September 1875): 398.

41 "Editor's Study," *Harper's Monthly* 79 (July 1889): 315.

42 "Degeneration," *Harper's Weekly* 39 (April 13, 1895): 342.

43 "Three Differently Interesting Plays," *Harper's Weekly* 50 (November 24, 1906): 1683.

44 "The Play and the Problem," 294.

45 "Some New American Plays," *Harper's Weekly* 48 (January 16, 1904): 88.

46 "The Recent Dramatic Season," 477.

47 "Editor's Study," *Harper's Monthly* 78 (May 1889): 984.

48 "Life and Letters," *Harper's Weekly* 39 (November 9, 1895): 1060.

49 "Editor's Study," *Harper's Monthly* 73 (July 1886): 316.

50 "Life and Letters," *Harper's Weekly* 40 (February 8, 1896): 126.

51 "Life and Letters," *Harper's Weekly* 40 (October 10, 1896): 997.

52 Critics who have noted the influence the French playwrights had on James include Leon Edel, "Henry James: The Dramatic Years," in *The Complete Plays of Henry James* (Philadelphia: Lippincott, 1949), 36; F. W. Dupee, "Henry James and the Play," *The Nation* 171 (July 8, 1950): 41; Henry Popkin, "Pretender to the Drama," *Theatre Arts* 33 (December 1949): 32; Edwin Clark, "Henry James and the Actress," *The Pacific Spectator* 3 (Winter 1949): 90; and August W. Staub, "The Well-Made Failures of Henry James," *Southern Speech Journal* 27 (Winter 1961): 91–101. As C. E. Maguire has pointed out, however ("James and Dumas, fils," *Modern Drama* 10 [May 1967]: 34–42), James's admiration for the Théâtre Français was not without reservation.

53 "Mr. Tennyson's Drama," 398.

54 Quoted in Brander Matthews, *Playwrights on Playmaking* (1923; rpt. Freeport, N.Y.: Books for Libraries, 1967), 194.

55 Ibid., 196.

56 "Editor's Study," *Harper's Monthly* 81 (June 1890): 152–3.

57 "Editor's Study," *Harper's Monthly* 79 (July 1889): 316.

58 Ibid.

59 "Editor's Study," *Harper's Monthly* 79 (July 1889): 315.

60 "Editor's Easy Chair," *Harper's Monthly* 126 (May 1913): 959.

61 "Life and Letters," *Harper's Weekly* 41 (January 30, 1897): 106.

62 "Editor's Easy Chair," *Harper's Monthly* 104 (March 1902): 671.

63 Quoted in "Introduction" to Aristotle, *Poetics,* 8.

64 Gassner, *Form and Idea in Modern Theatre,* 31.

65 Ibid., 35.

66 Levin, *The Gates of Horn,* 6.

67 Paul M. Levitt, *A Structural Approach to the Analysis of Drama* (The Hague: Mouton, 1971), 9.

68 Ibid.

69 Emile Zola, "Naturalism in the Theatre," in George J. Becker, ed., *Documents of Modern Literary Realism* (Princeton, N.J.: Princeton University Press, 1963), 207.

70 Harold Kolb, *The Illusion of Life: American Realism as a Literary Form* (Charlottesville: University Press of Virginia, 1969), 105.

71 Frye, *Anatomy of Criticism,* 286.

72 J. A. Withey, "Form and the Dramatic Text," *Educational Theatre Journal* 12 (October 1960): 205.

73 Brander Matthews, "The Dramatic Outlook in America," *Harper's Monthly* 78 (May 1889): 930.

74 Ibid.

75 Herne, "Art for Truth's Sake," 314.

76 Untitled newspaper clipping in Harrigan's Scrapbook, quoted in Moody, *Ned Harrigan.*

3. The Literary Realists as Playwrights

1 Clemens, Samuel L. *Mark Twain in Eruption,* ed. Bernard De Voto (New York: Harper, 1940), 255.

2 Quoted in Leon Edel, ed., *The Complete Plays of Henry James,* 58.

3 Mildred Howells, *Life in Letters of William Dean Howells,* 2 vols. (Garden City, N.Y.: Doubleday, 1928), 2: 94.

4 Joseph F. Daly, *The Life of Augustin Daly* (New York: Macmillan, 1917), 146.

5 Ibid., 148.

6 Ibid., 171.

7 Ibid., 173–4.

8 Quinn, *A History,* 1: 112.

9 T. Edgar Pemberton, *The Life of Bret Harte* (New York: Dodd, Mead, 1903), 274.

10 See Chapter 1, note 23.

11 Daly, *The Life of Augustin Daly,* 367.

12 Henry Nash Smith and William M. Gibson, eds., *Mark Twain–Howells Letters,* 1: 157.

13 Ibid., 187.

14 Ibid., 246.

15 Walter J. Meserve, ed., *The Complete Plays of W. D. Howells* (New York University Press, 1960), 206. Subsequent page references appear in parentheses in the text.

16 William Dean Howells, *My Mark Twain,* ed. Marilyn Baldwin (New York: Harper, 1910; Baton Rouge: Louisiana State University Press, 1967), 20.

17 Ibid., 21.

18 Clemens, *Mark Twain in Eruption,* 277.

19 Quoted in DeLancey Ferguson, "Mark Twain's Lost Curtain Speeches," *South Atlantic Quarterly* 42 (July 1943): 268–9.

20 Clemens, Samuel L. (Mark Twain) and Bret Harte, *"Ah Sin": A Dramatic Work by Mark Twain and Bret Harte,* ed. Frederick Anderson (San Francisco: The Book Club of California, 1961), v.

21 *The Works of Bret Harte: The Poetical Works* (Boston: Houghton Mifflin, 1882), 370. Subsequent page references appear in parentheses in the text.

22 Clemens and Harte, *"Ah Sin,"* xi.

23 Ibid., 5. Subsequent page references appear in parentheses in the text.

24 See "Henry James: The Dramatic Years," in Edel, ed., *The Complete Plays of Henry James,* 50–2.

25 Following Edna Kenton's lead in "The 'Plays' of Henry James," *Theatre Arts Monthly* 12 (May 1928): 347–52, most critics who have written about James's plays have treated them as a digression from his true path as a fiction writer, as fortunate mistakes that, though failures in themselves, provided the opportunity to improve his sense of form and dramatic technique as he moved into the "major phase" in his fiction. See, for example, Edel, ed., *The Complete Plays,* 62–3; Ronald Peacock, "Henry James and the Drama," in *The Poet in the Theatre* (New York: Harcourt Brace, 1946), 21–38; Jacques Barzun, "James the Melodramatist," *Kenyon Review* 5 (Autumn 1943): 515–18; Henry Popkin, "The Two

Theatres of Henry James," *New England Quarterly* 24 (March 1951): 69–83; René Wellek, "Henry James's Literary Theory and Criticism," *American Literature* 30 (November 1958): 310; Rudolph Kossman, *Henry James: Dramatist* (Groningen, Netherlands: Wolters-Noordhoff, n.v., 1969), 128.

26 Despite the examples of such successful American playwrights as Bronson Howard, Augustin Daly, and Steele Mackaye who adapted European plays and also copied European forms and styles assiduously in writing their own plays, James critics have persisted in ascribing James's failure at commercial success to his early admiration for the criticism of Sarcey and his imitation of Sardou, Dumas *fils*, and Dennery. See, for example, Edel, ed., *Complete Plays*, 35–6; Kossman, *Henry James: Dramatist*, 13; Lionel D. Wyld, "Drama vs. the Theatre in Henry James," *Four Quarters* 7 (May 1957): 21–3; Dupee, "Henry James and the Play," 40–2; Francis Fergusson, "James's Idea of Dramatic Form," *Kenyon Review* 5 (Autumn 1943): 495–507; Popkin, "Pretender to the Drama," 91; and Kimball King, "Theory and Practice in the Plays of Henry James," *Modern Drama* 10 (May 1967): 24–33.

27 *Complete Plays*, Edel, ed., 75. Subsequent page references to James's plays in that volume appear in parentheses in the text.

28 For discussion of *Daisy Miller*'s failure, see King, "Theory and Practice," 25–7, and Michael J. Mendelssohn, " 'Drop a Tear . . . ': Henry James Dramatizes *Daisy Miller*," *Modern Drama* 7 (May 1964): 60–4.

29 *"A Most Unholy Trade"* (Cambridge, Mass.: Scarab Press, 1923), 14–15.

30 James's misunderstanding of his audience has been deplored by a number of critics. See Edel, ed., *The Complete Plays*; Kossmann, *Henry James: Dramatist*, 118; Wyld, "Drama vs. the Theatre," 21; Fergusson, "James's Idea," 495–7; Alfred R. Ferguson, "The Triple Quest of Henry James: Fame, Art, and Fortune," *American Literature* 27 (January 1956): 493; Herbert Edwards, "Henry James and Ibsen," *American Literature* 24 (May 1952): 214; and August W. Staub, "The Well-Made Failures of Henry James," 98–9.

31 Edel, ed., *The Complete Plays*, 179.

32 Ibid., 186.

33 See, for example, Ferguson, "The Triple Quest," 493; King, "Theory and Practice," 27–30; Staub, *The Well-Made Failures*, 91–4; Joe B. Hatcher, "Shaw the Reviewer and James's *Guy Domville*," *Modern Drama* 14 (December 1971): 331–4; Edwin Clark, "Henry James and the Actress," 92–4; David L. Swartz, Jr., "Bernard Shaw and Henry James," *Shaw Review* 10 (May 1967): 52–4; and M. Tomlinson, "The Drama's Laws," *Twentieth Century* (Melbourne) 16 (1962): 292–300.

34 Note to Henry James, *Theatricals: Two Comedies*, in Edel, ed., *The Complete Plays*, 255.

35 Martin Meisel, *Shaw and the Nineteenth-Century Theatre* (Princeton, N.J.: Princeton University Press, 1963), 225.

36 Edel, ed., *The Complete Plays*, 295.

37 Ibid., 349.

38 Ibid.

39 G. B. Shaw, *The Quintessence of Ibsenism* (1891; rpt. New York: Hill & Wang, 1913), 171.

40 Quoted in Edel, ed., *The Complete Plays*, 553.

41 Ibid.

42 Viris Cromer, "James and Ibsen," *Comparative Literature* 25 (Spring 1973): 115.

43 Michael Egan, *Henry James: The Ibsen Years* (New York: Barnes & Noble, 1972), 60. See also Edwards, "Henry James and Ibsen," 208–23, and Clark, "Henry James and the Actress," passim.

44 See the letters to Gosse reprinted in Cromer, "James and Ibsen," 126–7; Elizabeth Robins, *Theatre and Friendship: Some Henry James Letters* (New York: Hill & Wang, 1957); and Edel's Introduction to *The Complete Plays*.

45 Edel, ed., *The Complete Plays*, 678.

46 Ibid., 643. See also Swartz. "Bernard Shaw and Henry James," 54–8.

47 Edel, ed., *The Complete Plays*, 646.

48 Frye, *Anatomy of Criticism*, 185.

49 Ibid.

50 Quinn, *A History* 1: 66.

51 Ibid.

52 Montrose J. Moses and Virginia Gerson, eds., *Clyde Fitch and His Letters* (Boston: Little, Brown, 1924), 257.

53 Augustus Thomas, *The Print of My Remembrance* (New York: Scribner, 1922), 178.

54 Quinn, *A History*, 68.

55 Meserve, ed., *The Complete Plays of W. D. Howells*, xvii.

56 The distinction between form and structure referred to is that made by Paul M. Levitt in *A Structural Approach to the Analysis of Drama*, 9. For a full discussion of this question, see Chapter 2, p. 46.

57 Meserve, ed., *The Complete Plays*, xxii.

58 Ibid.

59 Phyllis Hartnoll, ed., *The Oxford Companion to the Theatre*, 4th ed. (New York: Oxford University Press, 1983), 272.

60 "Recent Italian Comedy," *North American Review* 99 (October 1864): 368.

61 Eric Bentley, "Farce," in *The Life of the Drama* (New York: Atheneum, 1964), 219–57.

62 Ibid., 240.

63 Ibid., 242.

64 See Meserve, ed., *The Complete Plays*, 70.

65 George Monteiro and Brenda Murphy, eds., *John Hay–Howells Letters* (Boston: Twayne, 1980), 24.

66 Archibald Henderson, "George Bernard Shaw Self-Revealed," *Fortnightly Review* 125 (1926): 434–5.

67 On November 4, 1878, R. M. Field rejected the play for the museum because it wasn't "an effective *acting* play . . . further invention and elaboration are required with respect to the plot" (*W. D. Howells Selected Letters* [1873–81], ed. George Arms and Christoph Lohmann [Boston: Twayne, 1979] 206).

68 Perry, *James A. Herne*, 101.

69 Hamlin Garland, "Truth in the Drama," *The Literary World* 20 (September 14, 1889): 308.

70 Herbert J. Edwards and Julie A. Herne, *James A. Herne: The Rise of Realism in the American Drama* (Orono: University of Maine, 1964), 163.

71 Hamlin Garland, *Under the Wheel: A Modern Play in Six Scenes, Arena* 2 (July 1890): 194. Subsequent page references appear in parentheses in the text.

72 Arthur Hobson Quinn, "Ibsen and Herne – Theory and Facts," *American Literature* 19 (1947–8): 173.

73 *Margaret Fleming*, in William Coyle and Harvey G. Damaser, eds., *Six Early American Plays* (Columbus, Ohio: Merrill, 1968), 306. Subsequent page references appear in parentheses in the text.

74 *The Woman's Journal* 22 (May 16, 1891), 1: 1–2.

75 *New York Daily Tribune*, December 10, 1891, 7.

76 *Boston Herald*, May 12, 1891, 7.

77 In a letter to Herne, Howells wrote: "I have no doubt of its success with a fair chance. . . . I predict an epoch-making effect for it." (Quoted in Perry, *James A. Herne*, 153.)

4. The Transition

1 *New York Times*, October 15, 1893, 19: 1.

2 John Gassner, ed., *Best Plays of the Early American Theatre* (New York: Crown, 1967), 660.

3 Moody, *Dramas from the American Theatre*, 852–3.

4 Gassner, ed., *Best Plays*, 558–9.

5 Ibid.

6 Ibid., 319–20.

7 Moody, *Dramas from the American Theatre*, 689.

8 Gassner, ed., *Best Plays*, 512.

9 Ibid., 575.

10 Quinn, ed., *Representative American Plays*, 857. Subsequent page references to *The Boss* appear in parentheses in the text.

11 William Gillette, *Electricity: A Comedy in Three Acts* (New York: Samuel French, 1924), 51–2.

12 Gassner, ed., *Best Plays*.

13 Ibid., 585.

14 Ibid., 561.

15 George Pierce Baker, ed., *Modern American Plays* (New York: Harcourt Brace, 1921), 87.

16 Rachel Crothers, *A Man's World* (Boston: Richard Badger, 1915), 87. Subsequent page references appear in parentheses in the text.

17 Baker, ed., *Modern American Plays*, 66. Subsequent page references to *As a Man Thinks* appear in parentheses in the text.

18 Moody, *Dramas from the American Theatre*, 683.

19 Quinn, *Representative American Plays*, 948. Subsequent page references to *He and She* appear in parentheses in the text.

20 Edward Sheldon, *The Nigger: An American Play in Three Acts* (New York: Macmillan, 1915), 218. Subsequent page references appear in parentheses in the text.

21 Thomas's series of six prefaces to the Samuel French editions of his plays was written "to give some information upon the way of playwriting, in fact, to tell all that the author knows about the art as far as the respective plays call it to mind and make it pertinent" (Preface to *The Earl of Pawtucket* [New York: French, 1917], 3).

22 Bronson Howard, *Kate: A Comedy* (New York: Harper, 1906), 21. Subsequent page references appear in parentheses in the text.

23 Frye, *Anatomy of Criticism,* 163.

24 For a full description of melodramatic form, see David Grimsted, *Melodrama Unveiled: American Theatre and Culture, 1800–1850* (Chicago: University of Chicago Press, 1968).

5. The Cutting Edge

1 For general discussions of O'Neill's literary influences, see the biographies: Arthur and Barbara Gelb, *O'Neill* (New York: Harper & Row, 1962); and Louis Sheaffer, *O'Neill: Son and Playwright* (Boston: Little, Brown, 1968), and *O'Neill: Son and Artist* (Boston: Little, Brown, 1973). See also the general studies by Doris Alexander, *The Tempering of Eugene O'Neill* (New York: Harcourt Brace & World, 1962); Travis Bogard, *Contour in Time* (New York: Oxford University Press, 1972); and John Henry Raleigh, *The Plays of Eugene O'Neill* (Carbondale: Southern Illinois University Press, 1965). For specific studies of Strindberg, Ibsen, and Shaw, see Frederic Fleisher, "Strindberg and O'Neill," *Symposium* 10 (1956): 84–94; M. Hartman, "Strindberg and O'Neill: A Study in Influence," doctoral dissertation New York University, 1960; Sophus K. Winther, "Strindberg and O'Neill: A Study of Influence," *Scandinavian Studies* 31 (August 1959): 103–20; William R. Brashear, "O'Neill and Shaw: The Play as Will and Idea," *Criticism* 8 (Spring 1966): 155–69; and Egil Tornqvist, "Ibsen and O'Neill: A Study in Influence," *Scandinavian Studies* 37 (August 1965): 211–35.

2 For a full account of such references, see Jean Chothia, *Forging a Language: A Study of the Plays of Eugene O'Neill* (Cambridge: Cambridge University Press, 1979), 198–206.

3 Quoted in Chothia, *Forging a Language,* 64.

4 Sheaffer, *O'Neill: Son and Playwright,* 105.

5 Ibid., 205.

6 Personal letter to Barrett H. Clark, quoted by him in *Eugene O'Neill: The Man and His Plays* (1927; rpt. New York: Dover, 1947), 43.

7 Ibid.

8 *The Plays of Eugene O'Neill,* 3 vols. (New York: Random House, 1941), 3: 112. Subsequent page references to each play appear in parentheses in the text.

9 Clark, *Eugene O'Neill,* 51–2.

10 Personal letter to Arthur Hobson Quinn, quoted with facsimile by him in *A History,* 2: 199.

11 Personal letter to Clark, March 13, 1920, quoted in *Eugene O'Neill,* 53.

12 Quoted in Sheaffer, *O'Neill: Son and Playwright,* 419.

13 O'Neill's program notes for Strindberg's *Spook Sonata* (January 3, 1924), quoted in Helen Deutsch and Stella Hanau, *The Provincetown: A Story of the Theatre* (New York: Farrar & Rinehart, 1931), 192.

14 Letter to *New York Times* (December 12, 1921), quoted in Quinn, *A History,* 2: 177.

15 Isaac Goldberg, *The Theatre of George Jean Nathan* (New York: Simon & Schuster, 1926), 154.

16 Ibid.

17 See, for example, Kenneth Macgowan's review "The Centre of the Stage," *Theatre Arts* 5 (April 1921): 102, and Maida Castellun, "'Diff'rent' Is True but Not Good Drama," *New York Call,* January 14, 1921, quoted in Jordan Y. Miller, *Playwright's Progress: O'Neill and the Critics* (Chicago: Scott, Foresman, 1965).

18 Quoted in Sheaffer, *O'Neill: Son and Playwright,* 442.

19 Timo Tiusanen, *O'Neill's Scenic Images* (Princeton, N.J.: Princeton University Press, 1968), 102.

20 Ibid., 107.

21 For discussion of O'Neill's use of expressionism, see Mardi Valgemae, *Accelerated Grimace: Expressionism in the American Drama of the 1920s* (Carbondale: Southern Illinois University Press, 1972), passim; Grace Anshutz, "Expressionistic Drama in the American Theatre," *Drama* 16 (April 1926): 245; and Kenneth Macgowan, "Broadway at the Spring," *Theatre Arts* 6 (July 1922): 182, and "Experiment on Broadway," *Theatre Arts* 7 (July 1923): 175–85.

22 Arthur and Barbara Gelb, *O'Neill,* 520.

23 Tiusanen, *O'Neill's Scenic Images,* 46–7.

24 Tiusanen suggests (Ibid., 74–5) that a distinction be made between realistic setting – "when it is free to reflect different social strata" – and symbolic realistic setting – "when it concretizes an aspect of a more specific theme of the play." He suggests that the latter begins with *Beyond the Horizon,* but I would contend that the notion of symbolic realism as a mode in which to compose an entire dramatic representation did not appear in O'Neill until *Desire Under the Elms.*

25 *New York Evening Post,* February 13, 1926, sec. 5, p. 6, cols. 6–7.

6. Place and Personality

1 Jack Poggi, *Theater in America: The Impact of Economic Forces 1870–1976* (Ithaca, N.Y.: Cornell University Press, 1968), 47.

2 Susan Glaspell, *Plays* (Boston: Small, Maynard, 1920), 3. Subsequent page references to *Trifles* appear in parentheses in the text.

3 See Felix Sper, *From Native Roots: A Panorama of Our Regional Drama* (Caldwell, Idaho: Caxton Printers, 1948), 38, and John Wentz, "American Regional Drama – 1920–40: Frustration and Fulfillment," *Modern Drama* 6 (December 1963): 286.

4 Wentz, "American Regional Drama," 286.

5 Kathryn Coe and William H. Cordell, eds., *The Pulitzer Prize Plays* (New York: Random House, 1935), 233. Subsequent page references to *Hell-bent fer Heaven* appear in parentheses in the text.

6 S. Marion Tucker, ed., *Modern British and American Plays* (New York: Harper, 1931), 679. Subsequent page references to *Sun-up* appear in parentheses in the text.

7 *A History*, 2: 288.

8 Erskine Caldwell, *Tobacco Road* (New York: Viking, 1934), 3. Subsequent page references appear in parentheses in the text.

9 Montrose J. Moses, ed., *Representative American Dramas: National and Local* (Boston: Little, Brown, 1931), 497.

10 Coe and Cordell, eds., *The Pulitzer Prize Plays*, 213. Subsequent page references to *Icebound* appear in parentheses in the text.

11 Coe and Cordell, eds., *The Pulitzer Prize Plays*, 387. Subsequent page references to *In Abraham's Bosom* appear in parentheses in the text.

12 John Gassner, ed., *Twenty-five Best Plays of the Modern American Theatre: Early Series* (New York: Crown, 1949), 403. Subsequent page references to *Porgy* appear in parentheses in the text.

13 John Gassner, ed., *Best American Plays: 1918–1958, supplementary volume* (New York: Crown, 1961), 375. Subsequent page references to *Ethan Frome* appear in parentheses in the text.

14 Zoë Akins, *Déclassé: Daddy's Gone A-Hunting: and Greatness – A Comedy* (New York: Boni & Liveright, 1924), 136. Subsequent page references to *Daddy's Gone A-Hunting* appear in parentheses in the text.

15 Joseph Wood Krutch, *The American Drama Since 1918: An Informal History* (New York: Braziller, 1957), 153.

16 Gassner, ed., *Twenty-five Best Plays*, 568. Subsequent page references to *Street Scene* appear in parentheses in the text.

17 Elmer Rice, *Minority Report: An Autobiography* (New York: Simon & Schuster, 1963), 237.

18 Notes on *Street Scene*, Elmer Rice Papers, University of Texas at Austin.

19 In my discussion of American naturalism, I use the term as Donald Pizer defines it in *Realism and Naturalism in Nineteenth-Century American Literature*, rev. ed. (Carbondale: Southern Illinois University Press, 1984, 10–13). Pizer suggests that the term as it was used in the nineteenth century described an aesthetic vision that encompassed two tensions. The first is the tension between naturalism's focus on the less fortunate members of society and its tendency to depict them in their heroic, adventurous, or passionate moments. The second is the tension between determinism and the humanistic belief in the meaningfulness of human life that informs the naturalist's philosophical viewpoint. American naturalism thus combines some elements of the realistic aesthetic described in Chapter 2 of this book with some elements of romanticism and the pessimistic outlook of philosophical determinism.

20 Bennet Cerf and Van H. Cartnell, eds., *Sixteen Famous American Plays* (New York: Random House, 1941), 453. Subsequent page references to *Dead End* appear in parentheses in the text.

21 See W. David Seivers, *Freud on Broadway* (New York: Hermitage House, 1955), 38.

22 S. N. Behrman, *Three Plays* (New York: Farrar & Rinehart, 1934), 113.

23 "Theme for a Play," Elmer Rice Collection, University of Texas at Austin.

24 Memorandum to Dudley Digges, Elmer Rice Collection, University of Texas at Austin, 1.
25 Ibid., 5–6.
26 Moses, ed., *Representative American Dramas,* 538. Subsequent page references to *Dulcy* appear in parentheses in the text.
27 Coe and Cordell, eds., *The Pulitzer Prize Plays,* 321. Subsequent page references to *Craig's Wife* appear in parentheses in the text.
28 Lewis Beach, *A Square Peg* (Boston: Little, Brown, 1924), 4. Subsequent page references appear in parentheses in the text.
29 Tucker, ed., *Modern British and American Plays,* 671–2. Subsequent page references to *The Silver Cord* appear in parentheses in the text.
30 Brendan Gill, ed., *States of Grace: Eight Plays by Philip Barry* (New York: Harcourt Brace Jovanovich, 1975), 345. Subsequent page references to *The Animal Kingdom* appear in parentheses in the text.
31 Ibid., 523. Subsequent page references to *The Philadelphia Story* appear in parentheses in the text.

7. The Final Integration

1 Letter to Arthur Hobson Quinn, quoted in Arthur Hobson Quinn, ed., *Contemporary American Plays* (New York: Scribner, 1932), 2.
2 Quinn, ed., *Contemporary American Plays,* 62. Subsequent page references to *Why Marry?* appear in parentheses in the text.
3 Alan Downer, *Fifty Years of American Drama, 1900–1950* (Chicago: Regnery, 1951), 112.
4 Donald Koster, "The Theme of Divorce in American Drama 1871–1939," doctoral dissertation, University of Pennsylvania, 1942, 108.
5 *Three Plays by Rachel Crothers* (New York: Brentano, 1923), 286.
6 Rachel Crothers, *Mary the Third: A Comedy in Prologue and Three Acts* (Boston: Baker, 1923), 104. Subsequent page references appear in parentheses in the text.
7 Gassner, ed., *Twenty-five Best Plays,* 265. Subsequent page references to *Paris Bound* appear in parentheses in the text.
8 Sidney Howard, *Half Gods* (New York: Scribner, 1930), 8. Subsequent page references appear in parentheses in the text.
9 Rachel Crothers, *When Ladies Meet: A Comedy* (New York: French, 1932), 133.
10 Eleanor Flexner, *American Playwrights: 1918–1938* (New York: Simon & Schuster, 1938), 84.
11 Malcolm Goldstein, *The Political Stage: American Drama and Theater of the Great Depression* (New York: Oxford, 1974), 128.
12 Maxwell Anderson, *Both Your Houses* (New York: French, 1933), 178–9. Subsequent page references appear in parentheses in the text.
13 Sam Smiley, *The Drama of Attack: Didactic Plays of the American Depression* (Columbia: University of Missouri Press, 1972), 6.
14 Gassner, ed., *Twenty-five Best Plays,* 78. Subsequent page references to *What Price Glory?* appear in parentheses in the text.

15 Joan T. Brittain, *Laurence Stallings* (Boston: Twayne, 1975), 45.

16 Flexner, *American Playwrights,* 80.

17 Ibid., 81.

18 Frank O'Hara, *Today in American Drama* (Chicago: University of Chicago Press, 1939), 264.

19 Krutch, *The American Drama Since 1918,* 38.

20 Gassner, ed., *Twenty-five Best Plays,* 300. Subsequent page references to *The Road to Rome* appear in parentheses in the text.

21 John Gassner, ed., *Twenty Best Plays of the Modern American Theatre* (New York: Crown, 1939), 127. Subsequent page references to *Idiot's Delight* appear in parentheses in the text.

22 Robert E. Sherwood, *There Shall Be No Night,* in John Mason Brown, *The Ordeal of a Playwright: Robert E. Sherwood and the Challenge of War* (New York: Harper & Row, 1970), 285. Subsequent page references appear in parentheses in the text.

23 *4 Plays by S. N. Behrman* (New York: Random House, 1952), 272. Subsequent page references to *Rain from Heaven* appear in parentheses in the text.

24 S. N. Behrman, *No Time for Comedy* (New York: Random House, 1939), 49. Subsequent page references appear in parentheses in the text.

25 Goldstein, *The Political Stage,* 125.

26 Ibid.

27 Ibid., 124.

28 Ibid., 125.

29 Walter Meserve, "Sidney Howard and the Social Drama of the Twenties," *Modern Drama* 6 (December 1963): 257.

30 Arthur Wills, "The Kelly Play," *Modern Drama* 6 (December 1936): 247.

31 Krutch, *The American Drama Since 1918,* 62.

32 Foster Hirsch, *George Kelly* (Boston: Twayne, 1975), 21.

33 Flexner, *American Playwrights: 1918–1938,* 238.

34 Ibid.

35 Gassner, ed., *Twenty-five Best Plays,* 390. Subsequent page references to *Saturday's Children* appear in parentheses in the text.

36 Cerf and Cartnell, eds., *Sixteen Famous American Plays,* 273. Subsequent page references to *Biography* appear in parentheses in the text.

37 Moses, ed., *Representative American Dramas: National and Local,* 516. Subsequent page references to *The Detour* appear in parentheses in the text.

38 Gassner, ed., *Twenty-five Best Plays,* 493.

39 Downer, *Fifty Years of American Drama,* 63–4.

40 Rice, *Minority Report,* 237.

41 Ibid.

42 "Method of Treatment," Elmer Rice Papers, University of Texas at Austin.

43 Ibid.

44 Ibid.

45 Gassner, ed., *Twenty-five Best Plays,* 588. Subsequent page references to *Street Scene* appear in parentheses in the text.

46 See especially Tiusanen, *O'Neill's Scenic Images,* 278–9.

47 See Eugene M. Waith, "An Exercise in Unmasking," *Educational Theatre*

Journal 13 (October 1961): 189; Tiusanen, *O'Neill's Scenic Images,* 272; Tom F. Driver, "On the Last Plays of Eugene O'Neill," *Tulane Drama Review* 3 (1958): 13–14.

48 José Quintero, "Postscript to a Journey," *Theatre Arts* 41 (1956): 88.

49 Tiusanen, *O'Neill's Scenic Images,* 270.

50 Eric Bentley, "The Return of Eugene O'Neill," *The Atlantic Monthly* 178 (November 1946): 65.

51 Eric Bentley, "Trying to Like O'Neill," *The Kenyon Review* 14 (July 1952): 479.

52 Ibid., 483.

53 Michael Manheim, *Eugene O'Neill's New Language of Kinship* (Syracuse, N.Y.: Syracuse University Press, 1982), 8, 150, suggests that what he calls the "rhythm of kinship," "alternating hostility and affection," informs the structures of both *Iceman* and *Long Day's Journey.* Although he has identified and analyzed one of O'Neill's most important means of creating dramatic tension, it will be obvious in my discussion of these two plays that I do not accept his contentions that "the overall effect is unschematized," in *Iceman,* or that the tension is dispelled by each show of affection.

54 For an exhaustive list of the Tyrone family's conflicts, see Manheim, *Eugene O'Neill's New Language of Kinship,* 211–16.

55 Eugene O'Neill, *Long Day's Journey into Night* (New Haven, Conn.: Yale University Press, 1956), 176. Subsequent page references appear in parentheses in the text.

56 For a full analysis of this function of the dialogue, see Chothia, *Forging a Language,* 143–84.

57 From an interview recorded by Malcolm Mollan in the *Philadelphia Public Ledger* (January 22, 1922), quoted in Clark, *Eugene O'Neill,* 86–7.

Selected Bibliography

Note that individual titles are listed only for plays that do not appear in a listed anthology.

Adelman, Irving, and Rita Dworkin. *Modern Drama: A Checklist of Critical Literature on Twentieth Century Plays*. Metuchen, N.J.: Scarecrow, 1967.

Akins, Zoë. *Declasse; Daddy's Gone A-Hunting; and Greatness: A Comedy*. New York: Boni & Liveright, 1924.

    The Old Maid. New York: Appleton-Century, 1935.

    Papa: An Amorality in Three Acts. New York: Kennerly, 1913.

Alexander, Doris. "Eugene O'Neill as Social Critic." *American Quarterly* 6 (Winter 1954): 349–63.

    The Tempering of Eugene O'Neill. New York: Harcourt Brace & World, 1962.

"American Literature in England." *Blackwood's Magazine* 133 (January 1883): 136–61.

"American Novels." *London Quarterly Review* 155 (January 1883): 107–13.

Anderson, Frederick, ed. *"Ah Sin": A Dramatic Work by Mark Twain and Bret Harte*. San Francisco: The Book Club of California, 1961.

Anderson, Maxwell. *Both Your Houses*. New York: Samuel French, 1933.

Anschutz, Grace. "Expressionistic Drama in the American Theatre." *Drama* 16 (April 1926): 245.

Archer, William. "The Development of American Drama." *Harper's Monthly* 142 (1920): 75–86.

Aristotle. *Poetics*. Trans. S. H. Butcher, ed. Francis Fergusson. New York: Hill & Wang, 1961.

Atkinson, Brooks. "Ibsen and O'Neill." *New York Times,* January 31, 1926, 7, 1: 1.

Atkinson, Brooks, and Albert Hirschfeld. *The Lively Years: 1920–1973*. New York: Association Press, 1973.

Atlas, Leopold. *Wednesday's Child and The House We Live In*. New York: Samuel French, 1934.

Auerbach, Erich. *Mimesis*. Trans. Willard R. Trask. Princeton, N.J.: Princeton University Press, 1953.

Baker, George Pierce, ed. *Modern American Plays*. New York: Harcourt Brace, 1921.

Barrett, Laurence. "Young Henry James, Critic." *American Literature* 20 (January 1949): 385–400.

Barry, Philip. *The Animal Kingdom.* New York: Samuel French, 1932.
In a Garden. New York: Doran, 1926.
States of Grace: Eight Plays by Philip Barry. Ed. Brendan Gill. New York: Harcourt Brace Jovanovich, 1975.
You and I. New York: Brentano, 1923.
The Youngest. New York: Samuel French, 1925.

Barzun, Jacques. "James the Melodramatist." *Kenyon Review* 5 (Autumn 1943): 508–21.

Beach, Lewis. *The Goose Hangs High.* New York: Samuel French, 1924.
A Square Peg. Boston: Little, Brown, 1924.

Becker, George J., ed. *Documents of Modern Literary Realism.* Princeton, N.J.: Princeton University Press, 1963.
Realism in Modern Literature. New York: Ungar, 1980.

Beckerman, Bernard, and Howard Siegman. *On Stage: Selected Theatre Reviews from the New York Times, 1920–1970.* New York: Arno, 1973.

Behrman, S. N. *4 Plays by S. N. Behrman.* New York: Random House, 1952.
No Time for Comedy. New York: Random House, 1939.
Three Plays. New York: Farrar & Rinehart, 1934.

Belasco, David. "Dramatizing the Present." *Harper's Weekly* 57 (April 1913): 18.
Six Plays. Boston: Little, Brown, 1928.
The Theatre Through Its Stage Door. 1919; rpt. New York: Blom, 1969.

Bentley, Eric. *The Dramatic Event: An American Chronicle.* New York: Horizon, 1954.
The Life of the Drama. New York: Atheneum, 1964.
The Playwright as Thinker. New York: Reynal & Hitchcock, 1946.
"The Return of Eugene O'Neill." *The Atlantic Monthly* 178 (November 1946): 64–6.
"Trying to Like O'Neill." *The Kenyon Review* 14 (July 1952): 476–92.

Bernheim, Alfred L. *The Business of the Theatre: An Economic History.* 1932; rpt. New York: Blom, 1964.

Berthoff, Warner. *The Ferment of Realism: American Literature, 1884–1919.* New York: Free Press, 1965.

Bogard, Travis. *Contour in Time.* New York: Oxford University Press, 1972.

Boucicault, Dion. "The Future of American Drama." *Arena* 3 (November 1890): 641–52.

Boyer, Robert D. *Realism in European Theatre and Drama, 1870–1920: A Bibliography.* Westport, Conn.: Greenwood, 1979.

Brashear, William R. "O'Neill and Shaw: The Play as Will and Idea." *Criticism* 8 (Spring 1966): 155–69.

Brittain, Joan T. *Laurence Stallings.* Boston: Twayne, 1975.

Brooks, Peter. "The Melodramatic Imagination." *Partisan Review* 39 (1972): 195–212.

Brown, John Mason. *The Ordeal of a Playwright: Robert E. Sherwood and the Challenge of War.* New York: Harper & Row, 1970.

The Worlds of Robert E. Sherwood: Mirror to His Times. New York: Harper & Row, 1965.

Brown, Marshall. "The Logic of Realism: A Hegelian Approach." *PMLA* 96 (March 1981): 224–42.

Bucks, Dorothy S., and Arthur H. Nethercot. "Ibsen and Herne's Margaret Fleming: A Study of the Early Ibsen Movement in America." *American Literature* 17 (January 1946): 311–33.

Burnett, Frances Hodgson, and William Gillette. *Esmeralda.* New York: Madison Square Theatre, 1881.

Burton, Richard. "William Gillette." *The Drama* 12 (November 1913): 5–11.

Cady, Edwin H. *The Light of Common Day: Realism in American Fiction.* Bloomington: Indiana University Press, 1971.

Caldwell, Erskine. *Tobacco Road.* New York: Viking, 1934.

Campbell, Bartley. *The White Slave and Other Plays.* Vol. 19 of Napier Wilt, ed., *America's Lost Plays.* Princeton, N.J.: Princeton University Press, 1941.

Campbell, Oscar. "Robert Sherwood and His Times." *College English* 4 (February 1943): 275–80.

Cargill, Oscar, N. Bryllion Fagin, and William J. Fisher. *O'Neill and His Plays: Four Decades of Criticism.* New York: New York University Press, 1961.

Carpenter, Frederick I. *Eugene O'Neill.* Rev. ed. Boston: Twayne, 1979.

Carter, Everett. *Howells and the Age of Realism.* Philadelphia: Lippincott, 1950.

Cerf, Bennett, and Van H. Cartmell, eds. *Sixteen Famous American Plays.* New York: Random House, 1941.

Cerf, Walter. "Psychoanalysis and the Realistic Drama." *Journal of Aesthetics and Art Criticism* 16 (March 1958): 328–36.

Chothia, Jean. *Forging a Language: A Study of the Plays of Eugene O'Neill.* Cambridge: Cambridge University Press, 1979.

Clapp, John Bouve, and Edwin Francis Edgett. *Plays of the Present.* 1902; rpt. New York: Blom, 1969.

Clark, Barrett H. *Eugene O'Neill: The Man and His Plays.* New York: Dover, 1947.

Clark, Barrett H., and Kenyon Nicholson. *The American Scene.* New York: Appleton, 1930.

Clark, Edwin. "Henry James and the Actress." *The Pacific Spectator* 3 (Winter 1949): 84–99.

Clemens, Samuel L. (Mark Twain). "About Play-Acting." *The Complete Essays of Mark Twain,* ed. Charles Neider. Garden City, N.Y.: Doubleday, 1963, 200–8.

Mark Twain in Eruption. ed. Bernard DeVoto. New York: Harper, 1940.

Clemens, Samuel L. (Mark Twain), and Bret Harte. *"Ah Sin": A Dramatic Work by Mark Twain and Bret Harte,* ed. Frederick Anderson. San Francisco: The Book Club of California, 1961.

Coe, Catherine, and William H. Cordell, eds. *The Pulitzer Prize Plays.* 2nd ed. New York: Random House, 1935.

Coleman, Arthur, and Gary R. Tyler. *Drama Criticism: A Checklist of Interpreta-*

tion Since 1940 of English and American Plays. 2 vols. Denver: Alan Swallow, 1966.

Corbin, John. "Drama." *Harper's Weekly* 43 (February 11 and March 4, 1899): 139, 213.

Coyle, William, and Harvey G. Damaser. *Six Early American Plays*. Columbus, Ohio: Merrill, 1968.

Cromer, Viris. "James and Ibsen." *Comparative Literature* 25 (Spring 1973): 114–27.

Crothers, Rachel. *As Husbands Go*. New York: Samuel French, 1931.

   Criss Cross. New York: Dick & Fitzgerald, 1904.

   Expressing Willie, Nice People, 39 East. New York: Brentano, 1924.

   "The Future of the American Stage." *New York Times Magazine,* December 3, 1916, 13.

   The Heart of Paddy Whack. New York: Samuel French, 1925.

   Let Us Be Gay. New York: Samuel French, 1929.

   A Man's World. Boston: Richard Badger, 1915.

   Mary the Third: A Comedy in Prologue and Three Acts. Boston: Baker, 1923.

   "The Producing Playwright." *Theatre Magazine* 27 (January 1918): 34.

   The Rector: A Play in One Act. New York: Samuel French, 1905.

   Six One-Act Plays by Rachel Crothers. Boston: Baker, 1925.

   Susan and God. New York: Random House, 1938.

   The Three of Us. New York: Samuel French, 1916.

   Three Plays by Rachel Crothers. New York: Brentano, 1923.

   "Troubles of a Playwright." *Harper's Bazaar* 45 (January 1911): 14, 46.

   The Valiant One. Minneapolis: Northwestern Press, 1937.

   When Ladies Meet: A Comedy. New York: Samuel French, 1932.

Daly, Augustin. "The American Dramatist." *North American Review* 142 (May 1886): 485–92.

   Under the Gaslight; a Totally Original and Picturesque Drama of Life and Love in These Times, in Five Acts. New York: Samuel French, 1895.

Daly, Augustin, William Gillette, Edward Harrigan, James A. Herne, Bronson Howard, John Grosvenor, Steele Mackaye. "American Playwrights on the American Drama." *Harper's Weekly* 33 (February 2, 1889), Supplement, 98–100.

Daly, Joseph F. *The Life of Augustin Daly*. New York: Macmillan, 1917.

Davis, Owen. *The Detour: A Play*. Boston: Little, Brown, 1922.

Deutsch, Helen, and Stella Hanau. *The Provincetown: A Story of the Theatre*. New York: Farrar & Rinehart, 1931.

Dickinson, Thomas H. *Playwrights of the New American Theatre*. New York: Macmillan, 1925.

   Wisconsin Plays, 2nd. series. New York: Huebsch, 1918.

Downer, Alan S. *American Drama and Its Critics*. Chicago: University of Chicago Press, 1965.

   The American Theatre Today. New York: Basic, 1967.

   Fifty Years of American Drama – 1900–1950. Chicago: Regnery, 1951.

Doyle, Arthur Conan, and William Gillette. *Sherlock Holmes: A Comedy in Two Acts*. New York: Samuel French, 1922.

Dreiser, Theodore. *Plays of the Natural and Supernatural*. New York: Lane, 1916.

Driver, Tom F. "On the Last Plays of Eugene O'Neill." *Tulane Drama Review* 3 (1958): 8–21.

Duckett, Margaret. *Mark Twain and Bret Harte*. Norman: University of Oklahoma Press, 1964.

Dukore, Bernard F. "Off-Broadway and the New Realism." In *Modern American Drama*, ed. William E. Taylor. Deland, Fla.: Everett/Edwards, 1968.

Dupee, F. W. "Henry James and the Play," *The Nation* 171 (July 8, 1950): 40–2.

Durham, F. H. "Henry James's Dramatizations of His Novels." *Bulletin of the Citadel* 6 (November 1942): 51–64.

Durham, Frank. *Elmer Rice*. New York: Twayne, 1970.

Edel, Leon. *Henry James: The Middle Years*. Philadelphia: Lippincott, 1962.

Edel, Leon, ed. *The Complete Plays of Henry James*. Philadelphia: Lippincott, 1949.

  Henry James Letters. Vol. 3: 1883–1895. Cambridge, Mass.: Harvard University Press, Belknap Press, 1980.

Edwards, Herbert J. "The Dramatization of the Rise of Silas Lapham." *New England Quarterly* 30 (June 1957): 235–43.

  "Henry James and Ibsen." *American Literature* 24 (May 1952): 208–23.

Edwards, Herbert J., and Julie A. Herne. *James A. Herne – The Rise of Realism in the American Drama*. Orono: University of Maine, 1964.

Edwards, Thomas R. "The Evolution of Play Publishing." *The Drama* 15 (March 1925): 121–2.

Egan, Michael. "Henry James and Ibsen." In *Henrik Ibsen: The Critical Heritage*. London: Routledge & Kegan Paul, 1972, 16–18.

  Henry James: The Ibsen Years. New York: Barnes & Noble, 1972.

Ellison, Jerome. *God on Broadway*. Richmond, Va.: John Knox Press, 1971.

Fagin, N. Bryllion. "'Freud' on the American Stage." *Educational Theatre Journal* 2 (December 1950): 296–305.

Ferguson. Alfred R. "The Triple Quest of Henry James: Fame, Art, and Fortune." *American Literature* 27 (January 1956): 476–98.

Ferguson, Delancey. "Mark Twain's Lost Curtain Speeches." *South Atlantic Quarterly* 42 (July 1943): 262–9.

Fergusson, Francis. "James's Idea of Dramatic Form." *Kenyon Review* 5 (1943): 495–507.

Fine, Lewis. "Two Unpublished Plays by Stephen Crane." *Resources for American Literary Study* 1 (1971): 200–16.

Fitch, Clyde. *Barbara Frietchie: The Frederick Girl*. Boston: Little, Brown, 1900.

  The Climbers. Boston: Little, Brown, 1915.

  Clyde Fitch and His Letters, ed. Montrose J. Moses and Virginia Gerson. Boston: Little, Brown, 1924.

  The Cowboy and the Lady. New York: Alice Kauser, 1908.

  The Frisky Mrs. Johnson. New York: Alice Kauser, 1908.

  The Moth and the Flame. New York: Alice Kauser, 1908.

  Plays, ed. Montrose J. Moses and Virginia Gerson. 4 vols. Boston: Little, 1915.

Fleisher, Frederic. "Strindberg and O'Neill." *Symposium* 10 (1956): 84–94.

Flexner, Eleanor. *American Playwrights: 1918–1938*. New York: Simon & Schuster, 1939.

Flower, Benjamin O. "Masks or Mirror." *Arena* 8 (August 1893): 304–13.

Frazer, Winifred. *Love as Death in The Iceman Cometh*. Gainsville: University of Florida Monographs (Humanities No. 27), 1967.

Freedman, Morris. *American Drama in Social Context*. Carbondale: Southern Illinois University Press, 1971.

Frohman, Daniel. *Encore*. New York: Lee Furman, 1937.

Frye, Northrop. *Anatomy of Criticism*. Princeton, N.J.: Princeton University Press, 1957.

Gagey, Edmond M. *Revolution in American Drama*. New York: Columbia University Press, 1947.

Gale, Zona. *The Clouds*. New York: Samuel French, 1932.

Evening Clothes. Boston: Baker, 1932.

Miss Lulu Bett: An American Comedy of Manners. New York: Appleton, 1921.

Mister Pitt. New York: Appleton, 1925.

"Period Realism." *Yale Review* 23 (Autumn 1933): 111–24.

Garland, Hamlin. "The Greek Play." *Boston Evening Transcript,* May 1, 1889, 2.

"Herne's Sincerity as a Playwright." *Arena* 25 (September 1901): 282–4.

"I. Zangwill." *Conservative Review* 2 (November 1899): 402–12.

"Ibsen as a Dramatist." *Arena* 2 (June 1890): 72–82.

"Mr. and Mrs. Herne." *Arena* 4 (October 1891): 543–60.

"On the Road with James A. Herne." *Century* 88 (August 1914): 574–81.

"Starring the Play." *The Nation* 92 (July 20, 1911): 54.

"Truth in the Drama." *The Literary World* 20 (September 14, 1889): 307–8.

Under the Wheel: A Modern Play in Six Scenes. *Arena* 2 (July 1890): 182–228.

Garland, Hamlin, J. J. Enneking, and B. O. Flower. "James A. Herne: Actor, Dramatist, and Man." *Arena* 2 (September 1901): 282.

Gassner, John. *Form and Idea in Modern Theatre*. New York: Dryden, 1956.

Ideas in the Drama. New York: Columbia University Press, 1964.

Theatre at the Crossroads. New York: Holt, Rinehart & Winston, 1960.

Gassner, John, ed. *Best American Plays: 1918–1958*. Supplementary volume. New York: Crown, 1961.

Best Plays of the Early American Theatre. New York: Crown, 1967.

Best Plays of the Modern American Theatre. New York: Crown, 1947.

O'Neill: A Collection of Critical Essays. Englewood Cliffs, N.J.: Prentice-Hall, 1964.

Twenty Best Plays of the Modern American Theatre. New York: Crown, 1939.

Twenty-five Best Plays of the Modern American Theatre: Early Series. New York: Crown, 1949.

Gelb, Albert, and Barbara Gelb. *O"Neill*. 2nd ed. New York: Harper & Row, 1962.

Gild, David C. "Psychodrama on Broadway: Three Plays of Psychodrama by Philip Barry." *Markham Review* 2 (October 1970): 65–74.

Gill, Brendan, ed.   *States of Grace: Eight Plays by Philip Barry*. New York: Harcourt Brace Jovanovich, 1975.

Gillette, William.   *All the Comforts of Home*. New York: Samuel French, 1924.
Electricity: A Comedy in Three Acts. New York: Samuel French, 1924.
Held by the Enemy: The Five-Act War Drama. New York: Samuel French, 1898.
"On the Illusion of the First Time in Acting." New York: Dramatic Museum of Columbia University, Ser. 2, vol. 1, 1915.
The Painful Predicament of Sherlock Holmes: A Fantasy in One Act. Chicago: Abramson, 1955.
Too Much Johnson. New York: Samuel French, 1912.

Glaspell, Susan.   *Plays*. Boston: Small, Maynard, 1920.
Three Plays. London: Benn, 1924.
Trifles and Six Other Short Plays. London: Benn, 1926.

Goldberg, Isaac.   *The Theatre of George Jean Nathan*. New York: Simon & Schuster, 1926.

Goldstein, Malcolm. *George S. Kaufman: His Life, His Theatre*. New York: Oxford University Press, 1979.
The Political Stage: American Drama and Theater of the Great Depression. New York: Oxford University Press, 1974.

Gorelik, Mordecai.   *New Theatres for Old*. New York: Samuel French, 1940.

Gottlieb, Lois.   *Rachel Crothers*. Boston: Twayne, 1979.

Gould, Jean.   *Modern American Playwrights*. New York: Dodd, Mead, 1966.

Granger, Bruce Ingram.   "Illusion and Reality in Eugene O'Neill." *Modern Language Notes* 73 (1958): 179–86.

Grimm, Clyde L.   "The American Claimant: Reclamation of a Farce." *American Quarterly* 19 (Spring 1967): 86–103.

Grimsted, David.   *Melodrama Unveiled: American Theatre and Culture, 1800–1850*. Chicago: University of Chicago Press, 1968.

Halfmann, Ulrich.   *"Unreal Realism": O'Neills Dramatisches Werk Im Spiegel Seiner Szenische Kunst*. Bern: Francke Verlag, 1969.

Halline, Allan Gates.   *American Plays*. New York: American Book, 1935.

Hapgood, Norman.   *The Stage in America, 1897–1900*. New York: Macmillan, 1901.

Harte, Bret.   *Two Men of Sandy Bar*. In *The Works of Bret Harte: The Poetical Works*. Boston: Houghton Mifflin, 1882.

Harte, Bret, and T. Edgar Pemberton.   *Sue: A Play in Three Acts Adapted from Bret Harte's Story the Judgment of Bolinas Plain*. London: Greening, 1902.

Hartman, M.   "Strindberg and O'Neill: A Study in Influence." Doctoral dissertation, New York University, 1960.

Hartnoll, Phyllis, ed.   *The Oxford Companion to the Theatre*. 4th ed. New York: Oxford University Press, 1983.

Haskell, Daniel Carl.   *List of American Drama in the New York Public Library*. New York: New York Public Library, 1916.

Hatcher, Joe B.   "Shaw the Reviewer and James's *Guy Domville*." *Modern Drama* 14 (December 1971): 331–4.

Haugen, Einar.   "Ibsen in America." *Norwegian-American Studies and Records* 20 (1959): 1–23.

Henderson, Archibald. "George Bernard Shaw Self-revealed." *Fortnightly Review* 125 (1926): 434–5.

Herne, James A. "Art for Truth's Sake in the Drama." *Arena* 17 (1897): 361–70; rpt. in *American Drama and Its Critics,* ed. Alan S. Downer. Chicago: University of Chicago Press, 1965, 1–9.

"Old Stock Days in the Theatre." *Arena* 6 (September 1892): 401–16.

Shore Acres and Other Plays. New York: Samuel French, 1928.

Herron, Ima Honaker. *The Small Town in American Drama.* Dallas: Southern Methodist University Press, 1969.

Hewitt, Barnard. *Theatre U.S.A.* New York: McGraw-Hill, 1959.

Heyward, DuBose, and Dorothy. *Brass Ankle.* New York: Farrar, 1931.

Hirsch, David H. *Reality and Idea in the Early American Novel.* The Hague: Mouton, 1971.

Hirsch, Foster. *George Kelly.* Boston: Twayne, 1975.

Howard, Bronson. *Autobiography of a Play.* 1886; rpt. New York: Dramatic Museum of Columbia University, 1914.

The Banker's Daughter and Other Plays by Bronson Howard, ed. Alan Halline. 1940; rpt. Bloomington: Indiana University Press, 1963.

Kate: A Comedy. New York: Harper, 1906.

Saratoga. New York: Samuel French, 1870?.

Howard, Sidney. *Alien Corn.* New York: Scribner, 1931.

Half Gods. New York: Scribner, 1930.

Ned McCobb's Daughter. New York: Scribner, 1926.

"Howells, James, and Stevenson." *New York Times,* November 29, 1882, 2: 7.

Howells, Mildred. *Life in Letters of William Dean Howells.* 2 vols. Garden City, N.Y.: Doubleday, 1928.

Howells, William Dean. *The Complete Plays of William Dean Howells,* ed. Walter J. Meserve. New York: New York University Press, 1960.

Criticism and Fiction and Other Essays, ed. Clara M. and Rudolph Kirk. New York: New York University Press, 1959.

"Henry James, Jr." *Century* 25 (November 1882): 28.

My Mark Twain, ed. Marilyn Baldwin. New York: Harper, 1910; Baton Rouge: Louisiana State University Press, 1967.

W. D. Howells Selected Letters. Vol. 2: 1873–1881, ed. George Arms and Christoph Lohmann. Boston: Twayne, 1979.

Howells's Drama Criticism (Arranged Chronologically)

"Recent Italian Comedy." *North American Review* 99 (October 1864): 364–401.

"The New Play at Wallacks." *The Nation* 1 (November 2, 1865): 570–1.

"The New Taste in Theatricals." *Atlantic Monthly* 23 (May 1869): 635–44.

"Niccolini's Anti-Papal Tragedy." *North American Review* 115 (October 1872): 333–66.

"Drama." *Atlantic Monthly* 35 (June 1875): 749–50.

"Recent Literature." *Atlantic Monthly* 36 (August 1875): 240–1.

"Recent Literature." *Atlantic Monthly* 39 (February 1877): 242–3.

"Carlo Goldoni." *Atlantic Monthly* 40 (November 1877): 601–13.

"Editor's Study." *Harper's Monthly* 73 (July 1886): 314–19.

"Editor's Study." *Harper's Monthly* 78 (February 1889): 490.

"Editor's Study." *Harper's Monthly* 78 (May 1889): 984–5.

"Editor's Study." *Harper's Monthly* 79 (July 1889): 314–19.

"Editor's Study." *Harper's Monthly* 81 (June 1890): 152–7.

"Editor's Study." *Harper's Monthly* 82 (March 1891): 643–4.

"Editor's Study." *Harper's Monthly* 83 (August 1891): 477–9.

"Editor's Study." *Harper's Monthly* 84 (January 1892); 320.

"The Play and the Problem." *Harper's Weekly* 39 (March 30, 1895): 294.

"Degeneration." *Harper's Weekly* 39 (April 13, 1895): 342.

"The Ibsen Influence." *Harper's Weekly* 39 (April 27, 1895): 390.

"Life and Letters." *Harper's Weekly* 39 (May 11, 1895): 436.

"Life and Letters." *Harper's Weekly* 39 (August 3, 1895): 725.

"Life and Letters." *Harper's Weekly* 39 (September 14, 1895): 868–9.

"Life and Letters." *Harper's Weekly* 39 (September 21, 1895).

"Life and Letters." *Harper's Weekly* 39 (November 9, 1895): 1060.

"Life and Letters." *Harper's Weekly* 39 (November 16, 1895): 1084–5.

"Life and Letters." *Harper's Weekly* 39 (December 28, 1895): 1236–7.

"Life and Letters." *Harper's Weekly* 40 (January 11, 1896): 30–31.

"Life and Letters." *Harper's Weekly* 40 (February 8, 1896): 126.

"Life and Letters." *Harper's Weekly* 40 (February 22, 1896): 175.

"Life and Letters." *Harper's Weekly* 40 (February 29, 1896): 199.

"Life and Letters." *Harper's Weekly* 40 (March 7, 1896): 246.

"Life and Letters." *Harper's Weekly* 40 (April 4, 1896): 318–19.

"Life and Letters." *Harper's Weekly* 40 (October 10, 1896): 997–8.

"Life and Letters." *Harper's Weekly* 41 (January 30, 1897): 106–7.

"Life and Letters." *Harper's Weekly* 41 (March 20, 1897): 291.

"Life and Letters." *Harper's Weekly* 41 (December 4, 1897): 1194.

"Life and Letters." *Harper's Weekly* 42 (February 26, 1898): 202.

"Suggestions of a Patriotic Play." *Literature* (New York), n.s. 1 (February 24, 1899): 145–6.

"A New Kind of Play." *Literature* (New York) n.s. 1 (March 31, 1899): 256–66.

"A Subscription Theatre." *Literature* (New York) n.s. 1 (April 14, 1899): 313.

"A Question of Propriety." *Literature* (New York), n.s. 1 (July 7, 1899): 609.

"The Recent Dramatic Season." *North American Review* 172 (March 1901): 468–80.

"The New Poetic Drama." *North American Review* 172 (May 1901): 794–800.

"Editor's Easy Chair." *Harper's Monthly* 104 (March 1902): 670–4.

"Woman's Limitations in Burlesque." *Harper's Weekly* 46 (October 11, 1902): 1465.

"Diversions of the Higher Journalist: The Apotheosis of M. Rostand." *Harper's Weekly* 47 (July 4, 1903): 1112.

"Some New American Plays." *Harper's Weekly* 48 (January 16, 1904): 88, 90.

"Some New English Plays." *Harper's Weekly* 48 (January 23, 1904): 124, 126.

"Privileges of the Theatre." *Harper's Weekly* 48 (January 30, 1904): 160, 162.

"Editor's Easy Chair." *Harper's Monthly* 111 (September 1905): 633–5.
"Mr. Barrie's Benefactions to Humanity on the Stage." *Harper's Weekly* 50 (February 24, 1906): 272, 281.
"Editor's Easy Chair." *Harper's Monthly* 112 (May 1906): 958–9, 961.
"Henrik Ibsen." *North American Review* 183 (July 1906): 1–14.
"Editor's Easy Chair." *Harper's Monthly* 113 (October 1906): 795–8.
"Three Differently Interesting Plays." *Harper's Weekly* 50 (November 24, 1906): 1682–3.
"On Reading the Plays of Mr. Henry Arthur Jones." *North American Review* 185 (October 1907): 205–12.
"Editor's Easy Chair." *Harper's Monthly* 117 (August 1908): 473–5.
"Editor's Easy Chair." *Harper's Monthly* 126 (May 1913): 958–61.
"Editor's Easy Chair." *Harper's Monthly* 128 (March 1914): 634–7.
"The Plays of Eugene Brieux." *North American Review* 201 (March 1915): 402–11.
"Editor's Easy Chair." *Harper's Monthly* 133 (March 1916): 634–7.
"Editor's Easy Chair." *Harper's Monthly* 133 (June 1916): 146–9.
"An Appreciation." *New York Times,* October 21, 1917, 4: 405, 415.
"Editor's Easy Chair." *Harper's Monthly* 139 (October 1919): 765–8.
"Howells's Carved Cherry Stones." *New York Times,* December 1, 1882, 6: 2.
Hughes, Glenn R. *A History of the American Theatre, 1700–1950.* New York: Samuel French, 1951.
Irvine, William. "Shaw and America." *Modern Drama* 2 (September 1959): 160–1.
James, Henry. "The Art of Fiction." *Longman's Magazine* (September 1884): 502–21.
The Complete Plays of Henry James, ed. Leon Edel. Philadelphia: Lippincott, 1949.
Introduction to *Art and the Actor by Constant Coquelin.* New York: Dramatic Museum of Columbia University, 1915, 1–36.
"A Most Unholy Trade." Cambridge, Mass.: Scarab Press, 1923.
"Mr. Tennyson's Drama." *Galaxy* 20 (September 1975): 393–402.
The Scenic Art: Notes on Acting and the Drama 1872–1901, ed. Allan Wade. New Brunswick, N.J.: Rutgers University Press, 1948.
Views and Reviews. Boston: Ball, 1908.
Kaplan, Charles. "S. N. Behrman: The Quandary of the Comic Spirit." *College English* (March 1950): 317–23.
Kaufman, George S., and Marc Connelly. *Dulcy: A Comedy in Three Acts.* New York: Putnam, 1921.
Kaufman, George S., and Moss Hart. *Six Plays by Kaufman and Hart.* New York: Modern Library, 1942.
Kaufman, R. J. "On the Suppression of the Modern Classic Style." *Modern Drama* 2 (February 1960): 358–69.
Kelly, George. *Behold the Bridegroom.* Boston: Little, Brown, 1928.
Daisy Mayme: A Comedy. Boston: Little Brown, 1927.
The Torch-Bearers: A Satirical Comedy in Three Acts. New York: Samuel French, 1924.

Kennedy, H. A. "The Drama of the Moment." *The Nineteenth Century* 30 (August 1891): 258–74.

Kenton, Edna. "The 'Plays' of Henry James." *Theatre Arts Monthly* 12 (May 1928): 347–52.

Keough, Lawrence C. "Shaw's Introduction to New York: The Mansfield Production." *Shavian* 4 (1969): 6–10.

King, Kimball. "Theory and Practice in the Plays of Henry James." *Modern Drama* 10 (May 1967): 24–33.

Kirby, David K. "Henry James's *The Other House*: From Novel to Play." *Markham Review* 3 (May 1972): 49–53.

Kirby, Michael. "Structural Analysis/Structural Theory." *Drama Review* 20 (December 1976): 51–68.

Kirland, Jack. *Tobacco Road*. New York: Viking, 1934.

Kolb, Harold H. *The Illusion of Life: American Realism as a Literary Form*. Charlottesville: University Press of Virginia, 1969.

"In Search of a Definition: American Literary Realism and the Clichés." *American Literary Realism* 2 (1969): 165–73.

Kossman, Rudolph. *Henry James: Dramatist*. Groningen, Netherlands: Wolters-Noordhoff, n.v., 1969.

Koster, Donald N. "The Theme of Divorce in American Drama, 1871–1939." Dissertation, University of Pennsylvania, 1942.

Krutch, Joseph Wood. *The American Drama Since 1918: An Informal History*. New York: Braziller, 1957.

Larson, Judy. "The Drama Criticism of Henry James." *Yale/Theatre* 4 (1973): 103–9.

Levin, Harry. *The Gates of Horn: A Study of Five French Realists*. 1963; rpt. New York: Galaxy, 1966.

"What Is Realism?" In *Contexts of Criticism*. Cambridge, Mass.: Harvard University Press, 1957, 67–79.

Levitt, Paul M. *A Structural Approach to the Analysis of Drama*. The Hague: Mouton, 1971.

Levy, B. M. " 'The High Bid' and the Forbes-Robertsons." *College English* 8 (March 1947): 284–92.

Lewisohn, Ludwig. *The Drama and the Stage*. New York: Harcourt Brace, 1922.

The Modern Drama. New York: Huebsch, 1916.

Lukács, George. *Realism in Our Time: Literature and the Class Struggle*. New York: Harper & Row, 1962.

McCarthy, Mary. *Mary McCarthy's Theatre Chronicles 1937–1962*. New York: Noonday Press, 1963.

McCullough, Joseph B. *Hamlin Garland*. Boston: Twayne, 1978.

Macgowan, Kenneth. "Broadway at Spring." *Theatre Arts* 6 (July 1922): 182.

"Experiment on Broadway." *Theatre Arts* 7 (July 1923): 175–85.

Mackaye, Percy. *Epoch: The Life of Steele Mackaye*. 2 vols. New York: Boni & Liveright, 1927.

Magnus, Julian. "A Plea for Reality in Plays." *Century* 31 (November 1885): 155–6.

Maguire, C. E.   "James and Dumas, fils." *Modern Drama* 10 (May 1967): 34–42.

Manheim, Michael.   *Eugene O'Neill's New Language of Kinship*. Syracuse, N.Y.: Syracuse University Press, 1982.

Marker, Lise-Lone.   *David Belasco: Naturalism in the American Theatre*. Princeton, N.J.: Princeton University Press, 1975.

Matthews, Brander.   "The American on the Stage." *Scribner's Monthly* 18 (July 1879): 321–33.

The Decision of the Court: A Comedy. New York: Harper, 1893.

"The Dramatic Outlook in America." *Harper's Monthly* 78 (May 1889): 924–30.

"Henry James and the Theatre." *Bookman* (New York) 51 (June 1920): 389–95.

Playwrights on Playmaking. 1923; rpt. Freeport, N.Y.: Books for Libraries, 1967.

Meisel, Martin.   *Shaw and the Nineteenth-Century Theatre*. Princeton, N.J.: Princeton University Press, 1963.

Meister, Charles W.   "Comparative Drama: Chekhov, Shaw, Odets." *Poet Lore* 15 (1950): 249–57.

Mendelssohn, Michael J.   " 'Drop a Tear . . .': Henry James Dramatizes Daisy Miller." *Modern Drama* 7 (May 1964): 60–4.

Mersand, Joseph.   *A Decade of Biographical Plays, 1928–1938*. New York: Modern Drama Chapbooks, 1939.

Meserve, Walter J.   "Colonel Sellers as a Scientist: A Play by S. L. Clemens and William Dean Howells." *Modern Drama* 1 (September 1958): 151–6.

Discussions of American Drama. Boston: D. C. Heath, 1965.

"Philip Barry: A Dramatist's Search." *Modern Drama* 13 (1970): 93–9.

Robert E. Sherwood: Reluctant Moralist. New York: Bobbs-Merrill, 1970.

"Sidney Howard and the Social Drama of the Twenties." *Modern Drama* 6 (December 1963): 256–66.

Meserve, Walter J., ed.   *The Complete Plays of William Dean Howells*. New York: New York University Press, 1960.

Miller, Jordan Y.   *Playwright's Progress: O'Neill and the Critics*. Chicago: Scott, Foresman, 1965.

Miller, Tice L.   *Bohemians and Critics: American Theatre Criticism in the Nineteenth Century*. Metuchen, N.J.: Scarecrow, 1981.

Mitchell, Langdon.   *The Kreutzer Sonata, Adapted from the Yiddish of Jacob Gordin*. New York: Harrison Grey Fiske, 1907.

Monteiro, George, and Brenda Murphy, eds.   *John Hay–Howells Letters*. Boston: Twayne, 1980.

M[ontgomery], G. E.   "Edward Harrigan." *The Theatre* 1 (1886): 397–8.

Moody, Richard.   *America Takes the Stage: Romanticism in American Drama and Theatre, 1750–1900*. 1955; rpt. New York: Kraus, 1969.

Dramas from the American Theatre 1762–1909. Cleveland: World, 1966.

Ned Harrigan: From Corlear's Hook to Herald Square. Chicago: Nelson-Hall, 1980.

Mordden, Ethan.   *The American Theatre*. London: Oxford University Press, 1981.

Morrow, Patrick D.   *Bret Harte: Literary Critic.* Bowling Green, Ky.: Bowling Green State University Popular Press, 1979.

Moses, Montrose.   *The American Dramatist.* 1925; rpt. New York: Blom. 1964.
"Belasco: Stage Realist." *The Independent* 29 (May 1916): 336.

Moses, Montrose J., ed.   *Representative American Dramas: National and Local.* Boston: Little, Brown, 1931.

Moses, Montrose J., and John Mason Brown.   *The American Theatre as Seen by Its Critics.* New York: Norton, 1934.

Moses, Montrose J., and Virginia Gerson, eds.   *Clyde Fitch and His Letters.* Boston: Little, Brown, 1924.

Nathan, George Jean.   *Mr. George Jean Nathan Presents.* 1917; rpt. St. Clair Shores, Mich.: Scholarly Press, 1971.

The Theatre in the Fifties. New York: Knopf, 1953.

Noe, Marcia.   "Region as Metaphor in the Plays of Susan Glaspell." *Western Illinois Regional Studies* 4 (Spring 1981): 77–86.

Nolan, Paul T.   *Provincial Drama in American: 1870–1916 – A Casebook of Primary Materials.* Metuchen, N.J.: Scarecrow, 1967.

Nye, Russell.   *The Unembarrassed Muse: The Popular Arts in America.* New York: Dial, 1970.

Odell, George C. D.   *Annals of the New York Stage.* 15 vols. New York: Columbia University Press, 1927–49.

Odets, Clifford.   *Six Plays of Clifford Odets.* New York: Modern Library, 1939.

O'Hara, Frank.   *Today in American Drama.* Chicago: University of Chicago Press, 1939.

Olauson, Judith.   *The American Woman Playwright: A View of Criticism and Characterization.* Troy, N.Y.: Whitston, 1981.

O'Neill, Eugene.   *Hughie.* New Haven, Conn.: Yale University Press, 1959.
The Iceman Cometh. New York: Random House, 1946.
Long Day's Journey into Night. New Haven, Conn.: Yale University Press, 1956.
Lost Plays of Eugene O'Neill. New York: Citadel, 1963.
A Moon for the Misbegotten. New York: Random House, 1959.
More Stately Mansions. New Haven, Conn.: Yale University Press, 1964.
The Plays of Eugene O'Neill. 3 vols. New York: Random House, 1941.
A Touch of the Poet. New Haven, Conn.: Yale University Press, 1957.

Palmer, A. M., J. M. Buckley, J. Gilbert, and William Winter.   "The Moral Influence of the Drama." *North American Review* 136 (June 1883): 581–606.

Parrington, Vernon L.   *The Beginnings of Critical Realism in America: 1860–1920.* New York: Harcourt Brace & World, 1930.

Peacock, Ronald.   "Henry James and the Drama." In *The Poet in the Theatre.* New York: Harcourt Brace, 1946: 26–47.

Pemberton, Thomas Edgar.   *The Life of Bret Harte.* New York: Dodd, Mead, 1903.

Perry, John.   *James A. Herne: The American Ibsen.* Chicago: Nelson-Hall, 1979.

Phelps, William Lyon.   *Essays on Modern Dramatists.* New York: Macmillan, 1921.

Pizer, Donald. *Realism and Naturalism in Nineteenth-Century American Literature.* Rev. ed. Carbondale: Southern Illinois University Press, 1984.

Poggi, Jack. *Theater in America: The Impact of Economic Forces 1870–1976.* Ithaca, N.Y.: Cornell University Press, 1968.

Popkin, Henry. "Pretender to the Drama." *Theatre Arts* 33 (December 1949): 32–5.

"The Two Theatres of Henry James." *New England Quarterly* 24 (March 1951): 69–83.

Quinn, Arthur Hobson. *A History of the American Drama from the Civil War to the Present Day.* Rev. ed. 2 vols. New York: Appleton-Century-Crofts, 1936.

"Ibsen and Herne – Theory and Facts." *American Literature* 19 (1947–8): 171–7.

Representative American Plays. 7th ed. New York: Appleton-Century-Crofts, 1953.

"The Significance of Recent American Drama." *Scribner's Monthly* 72 (July 1922): 97–108.

Quinn, Arthur Hobson, ed. *Contemporary American Plays.* New York: Scribner, 1932.

Quintero, José. "Postscript to a Journey." *Theatre Arts* 41 (April 1957): 27–9.

Rabkin, Gerald. *Drama and Commitment: Politics in the American Theatre of the Thirties.* Bloomington: Indiana University Press, 1964.

Raleigh, John Henry. *The Plays of Eugene O'Neill.* Carbondale: Southern Illinois University Press, 1965.

Reed, Kenneth T. *S. N. Behrman.* Boston: Twayne, 1975.

Rice, Elmer. "Method of Treatment." TS. University of Texas at Austin.

Minority Report: An Autobiography. New York: Simon & Schuster, 1963.

"Notes on Characters." TS. University of Texas at Austin.

"Notes on Street Scene." TS. University of Texas at Austin.

Seven Plays by Elmer Rice. New York: Viking, 1950.

"Theme for a Play." TS. University of Texas at Austin.

Robins, Elizabeth. *Theatre and Friendship: Some Henry James Letters.* New York: Hill & Wang, 1957.

Roppolo, Joseph Patrick. *Philip Barry.* New York: Twayne, 1965.

Rowell, George. *Victorian Dramatic Criticism.* London: Methuen, 1971.

Roy, Emil. "*The Iceman Cometh* as Myth and Realism." *Journal of Popular Culture* 2 (Fall, 1968): 302.

Salem, James M. *A Guide to Critical Reviews. Part I: American Drama, 1909–1969.* Metuchen, N.J.: Scarecrow, 1973.

"Philip Barry and the Spirituality of Love." *Renascence* 19 (Winter 1967): 101–9.

Sarcey, Francisque. *Quarante Ans de Théâtre.* Vol. I. Paris: Bibliotheque des Annales politique et litteraire, 1900.

Seivers, W. David. *Freud on Broadway.* New York: Hermitage House, 1955.

Shafer, Yvonne B. "The Liberated Woman in American Plays of the Past." *Players* 49 (April–May 1974): 95–100.

Shaw, George Bernard.   *Dramatic Opinions and Essays*. Vol. 1. New York: Brentano, 1916.

The Quintessence of Ibsenism. 1891; rpt. New York: Hill & Wang, 1913.

Shaw on Theatre, ed. E. J. West. New York: Hill & Wang, 1958.

Sheaffer, Louis,   *O'Neill: Son and Artist*. Boston: Little, Brown, 1973.

O'Neill: Son and Playwright. Boston: Little, Brown, 1968.

Sheldon, Edward.   *The Garden of Paradise*. New York: Macmillan, 1915.

The Nigger: An American Play in Three Acts. New York: Macmillan, 1915.

Sherwood, Robert E.   *This Is New York*. New York: Scribner, 1931.

Shuman, R. Baird.   "The Shifting Pacifism of Robert Sherwood." *The South Atlantic Quarterly* 65 (Summer 1966): 382–9.

Simonson, Harold P.   *Zona Gale*. New York: Twayne, 1962.

Skinner, R. Dana.   *Our Changing Theatre*. New York: Dial, 1931.

Smiley, Sam.   *The Drama of Attack: Didactic Plays of the American Depression*. Columbia: University of Missouri Press, 1972.

Smith, Henry Nash, and William W. Gibson, eds.   *Mark Twain–Howells Letters*. 2 vols. Cambridge, Mass.: Harvard University Press, Belknap Press, 1960.

Sper, Felix.   *From Native Roots: A Panorama of Our Regional Drama*. Caldwell, Idaho: Caxton Printers, 1948.

Stafford, William T.   *James's 'Daisy Miller': The Story, the Play, the Critics*. New York: Scribner Research Anthologies, 1963.

Stamm, Rudolph.   " 'Faithful Realism': Eugene O'Neill and the Problem of Style." *English Studies* 40 (August 1959): 242–50.

Staub, August W.   "The Well-Made Failures of Henry James." *Southern Speech Journal* 27 (Winter 1961): 91–101.

Stern, J. P.   *On Realism*. London: Routledge & Kegan Paul, 1973.

Stone, William B.   "Towards a Definition of Literary Realism." *Centrum* 1 (1973): 47–60.

Styan, J. L.   *Modern Drama in Theory and Practice*. Vol. I: *Realism and Naturalism*. Cambridge: Cambridge University Press, 1981.

Swartz, David L., Jr.   "Bernard Shaw and Henry James." *Shaw Review* 10 (May 1967): 50–9.

Taylor, William E.   *Modern American Drama: Essays in Criticism*. Dehand, Fla.: Everett/Edwards, 1968.

Thomas, Augustus.   *Alabama*. Chicago: Dramatic Publishing, 1898.

Arizona. New York: Russell, 1899.

The Burglar. New York: Samuel French, 1932.

A Constitutional Point. New York: Samuel French, 1932.

The Copperhead. New York: Samuel French, 1922.

The Earl of Pawtucket. New York: Samuel French, 1917.

The Harvest Moon. New York: Samuel French, 1922.

In Mizzoura. New York: Samuel French, 1909.

The Man Upstairs. Washington: Commission on Training Camp Activities Among the Soldiers, 1918.

Mrs. Leffingwell's Boots. New York: Samuel French, 1916.

Oliver Goldsmith. New York: Samuel French, 1916.

The Other Girl. New York: Samuel French, 1917.

The Print of My Remembrance. New York: Scribner, 1922.

A Proper Impropriety. New York: Samuel French, 1932.

Still Waters. New York: Samuel French, 1926.

The Witching Hour. New York: Samuel French, 1916.

Tiempo, Marco. "James A. Herne in Griffith Davenport." *Arena* 22 (September 1899): 375–82.

Tiusanen, Timo. *O'Neill's Scenic Images*. Princeton, N.J.: Princeton University Press, 1968.

Tomlinson, M. "The Drama's Laws." *Twentieth Century* (Melbourne) 16 (1962): 292–300.

Tornquist, Egil. *A Drama of Souls: Studies in O'Neill's Super-naturalistic Technique*. New Haven, Conn.: Yale University Press, 1969.

"Ibsen and O'Neill: A Study in Influence." *Scandinavian Studies* 37 (August 1965): 211–35.

Towse, John R. *Sixty Years of the Theatre*. New York: Funk & Wagnalls, 1916.

Traill, H. D. "About that Skeleton." *The Nineteenth Century* 36 (December 1894): 864–74.

Tucker, S. Marion, ed. *Modern American and British Plays*. New York: Harper, 1931.

Twain, Mark. (See Clemens, Samuel L.)

Valency, Maurice. *The Flower and the Castle: An Introduction to Modern Drama*. New York: Octagon, 1975.

Valgemae, Mardi. *Accelerated Grimace: Expressionism in the American Drama of the 1920s*. Carbondale: Southern Illinois University Press, 1972.

Van Druten, John. "The Sex Play." *Theatre Arts* 11 (January 1927): 23–7.

Vielleux, Jere. "Shavian Drama: A Dialectical Convention for the Modern Theatre." *Twentieth Century Literature* 3 (January 1958): 170–6.

Waggoner, Hyatt H. "The Growth of a Realist: James A. Herne." *New England Quarterly* 15 (March 1942): 62–73.

Waith, Eugene M. "An Exercise in Unmasking." *Educational Theatre Journal* 13 (October 1961): 182–91.

Waldau, Roy S. *Vintage Years of the Theatre Guild: 1928–1939*. Cleveland: Case Western Reserve University Press, 1972.

Waterman, Arthur. *Susan Glaspell*. New York: Twayne, 1966.

Weales, Gerald. *American Drama Since World War II*. New York: Harcourt Brace & World, 1962.

Wellek, René. "The Concept of Realism in Literary Scholarship." In *Concepts of Criticism,* ed. Stephen G. Nichols (New Haven, Conn.: Yale University Press, 1963), 222–56.

"Henry James's Literary Theory and Criticism." *American Literature* 30 (November 1958): 293–321.

Wentz, John C. "American Regional Drama – 1920–40: Frustration and Fulfillment." *Modern Drama* 6 (December 1963): 286–93.

White, Sidney Howard. *Sidney Howard*. Boston: Twayne, 1977.

Williams, Jesse Lynch. *Why Marry?* New York: Scribner, 1918.

Why Not? Boston: Baker, 1924.

Williams, Jesse Lynch, Langdon Mitchell, Lord Dunsany, Gilbert Emery, and Rachel Crothers. *The Art of Playwriting*. Philadelphia: University of Pennsylvania, 1928.

Williams, Raymond. *Drama From Ibsen to Brecht*. New York: Oxford University Press, 1969.

Williams, Tennessee. *The Glass Menagerie*. New York: Random House, 1945.

Wills, Arthur. "The Kelly Play." *Modern Drama* 6 (December 1963): 245–55.

Wilson, Garff B. *A History of American Acting*. Bloomington: Indiana University Press, 1966.

    Three Hundred Years of American Drama and Theatre. Englewood Cliffs, N.J.: Prentice-Hall, 1973.

Winther, Sophus K. "Strindberg and O'Neill: A Study of Influence." *Scandinavian Studies* 31 (August 1959): 103–20.

Witham, Barry. "Owen Davis, America's Forgotten Playwright." *Players* 46 (October–November 1970): 30–35.

Withey, J. A. "Form and the Dramatic Text." *Educational Theatre Journal* 12 (October 1960): 205–11.

Wyld, Lionel, D. "Drama vs. the Theatre in Henry James." *Four Quarters* 7 (May 1957): 17–23.

Young, William C. *American Theatrical Arts: A Guide to Manuscripts*. Chicago: American Library Association, 1971.

Index

227